SCOTT NEARING: APOSTLE OF AMERICAN RADICALISM

Scott Nearing

SCOTT NEARING:
APOSTLE OF
AMERICAN RADICALISM

STEPHEN J. WHITFIELD

COLUMBIA UNIVERSITY PRESS
New York and London   1974

The Andrew W. Mellon Foundation, through a special grant, has assisted the Press in publishing this volume.

Library of Congress Cataloging in Publication Data

Whitfield, Stephen J   1942–
  Scott Nearing: Apostle of American radicalism.

  Bibliography: p.
  1. Nearing, Scott, 1883–   I. Title.
HX84.N4W5   335.'0092'4   74-10641
ISBN 0-231-03816-X

for
BERT and JOAN
WHITFIELD

ACKNOWLEDGMENTS

"**H**AVE YOU EVER HEARD OF SCOTT NEARING?"
I had barely arrived at Brandeis University when the
chairman of its graduate history program posed that question. My reply was vague enough to induce research, which
resulted in a dissertation and finally this biography. The
reader should note, however, that although the subject of
this study has written over fifty books and pamphlets, this is
not an intellectual portrait of Scott Nearing. I suspect that
his thought cannot bear the weight of intensive scrutiny,
that its exposition would be tedious, and that in any event
its influence has not been prepossessing. I have therefore
chosen to forego a thorough analysis of Nearing's ideas,
especially as they are examined in dissertations recently
written by Alan Cywar at the University of Rochester and
Gerald Coles at the State University of New York at Buf-
falo. This book focuses instead upon the intersection of his
career with the travail of dissent in this century.

The earlier version of this work has had the benefit of al-
ternate sponsors: Professor Leonard W. Levy, now of Clare-
mont Graduate School, who asked the initial question; and
Professor John P. Roche, now of Tufts University, who
directed me toward less tentative answers. Because of the
sanity of their counsel, the peppery persistence of their in-

terest, the generosity of their encouragement, and the pleasure of their friendship, their influence has been—in the best and precise sense of the word—instructive, although this book is scant tribute to such splendid teachers. Two of their colleagues, Professors Morton Keller and Marvin Meyers, not only offered incisive commentary upon my work but more generally exuded intellection and erudition with a grace that I can envy if not emulate. Despite their reputation for scholarly probity, the responsibility for errors of fact and judgment is, of course, mine.

Scott and Helen Nearing kindly yielded to importunities for interviews; and their cooperation, especially as greater popular interest in their life subverted their privacy, is deeply appreciated. The most seductive flaws of oral history are that the narrator may have done much more than he remembers and may remember much more than he has done. But in tracking down Nearing's associates and relatives before the trail gets cold, I believe that this biography has been enhanced. Except for those who preferred anonymity, they are cited in appropriate footnotes and in the bibliography; and I wish to thank them again for sharing their memories.

My appreciation is further extended to Gerald Coles, Frederic Cornell, Professor Arthur Edelstein of Brandeis University, Estelle Freedman, Professor Arthur A. Goren of the Hebrew University in Jerusalem, Lin Horwitz, and Richard Tedlow. Because they too had heard of Scott Nearing, progress on this work was accelerated. Two economists of long acquaintance, Professor Phillip M. Weitzman of Lehman College and Professor Ronald M. Whitfield of Bucknell University, have been exceptionally patient with one who sympathizes with the youthful decision of the eminent physicist Max Planck to abandon economics because of its inordinate difficulty.

Librarians were uniformly pervious to my supplications,

but for their special thoughtfulness I wish to praise Alline Dixon of the University of Pennsylvania Archives, Bernice Nichols of the Swarthmore College Peace Collection, Judy Goldberg and Dorothy Swanson of the Tamiment Institute Library of New York University, and Victor A. Berch and Daniel Lourie of Brandeis University. For providing bibliographies of Nearing's writings, I wish to acknowledge the aid of Herbert Aptheker, director of the American Institute for Marxist Studies, and his assistant Carl Griffler; and Jessica Smith, the editor of *New World Review.*

Of inestimable help was an Irving and Rose Crown Fellowship, which permitted concentration on a life struggle other than my own.

And, finally, I am most grateful to my parents, to whom this book is dedicated. They supplied me, as a kid, with a collection of Landmark Books and perhaps did not suspect it would come to this.

S.W.

CONTENTS

Photographs of Scott Nearing: frontispiece and pages 71
and 215

SCOTT NEARING:
APOSTLE OF
AMERICAN RADICALISM

CHAPTER ONE

THE MAKING OF A PROGRESSIVE

Nestled between the rock above and the hard clay below lay the coal, dull black in color, blocky in texture, sometimes in slivers a few inches thick, sometimes as slabs several yards wide. Ferns cradled it from the coarse grit, the quartz pebbles, and the gray and red sandstone; while above rolled the gentle hills and streams of Tioga County, Pennsylvania. There "in the forest far from any habitation," Sir Charles Lyell recorded in his journal in 1841, "I was struck with the perfect silence of the surrounding woods. We heard no call or note of any bird." The eminent author of *Principles of Geology* thought of Darwin alighting from the *Beagle* onto the shores of the Galapagos and, in the absence of human predecessors, felt awe and wonder.[1]

Yet elsewhere in the state lived 1.7 million people, enough to make it second only to New York in population. The tranquillity inspiring Voltaire's claim that a golden age "had probably never existed anywhere except in Pennsylvania" was no longer credible enough to absorb a jest. Within two generations of Lyell's visit to the county, lumber companies were felling trees and coal companies were opening wounds in the soil; and in the new cities and company towns of the state lived men driven by the lure of success and families haunted by the fear of starvation. The existence of injustice is an independent variable in any historical equation, and suffering could neither be attributed solely to industrial capitalism nor confined to one state, but the new wealth that concentrated in Pennsylvania, as the machine invaded the garden by the late nineteenth century, caused apprehension and outrage.

Pittsburgh so horrified Herbert Spencer, whose philosophy helped vindicate the power of the wealthy, that he told Andrew Carnegie a six-months' residence there would justify suicide. Carnegie's lieutenant, Henry Clay Frick, unleashed hundreds of Pinkerton detectives to crush one of the bloodiest strikes in American history, at Homestead in 1892, just as the Molly Maguires had been beaten over a decade earlier. Charles Yerkes made a fortune in Philadelphia and then left town in a hurry; as a Chicagoan he later became the prototype for Theodore Dreiser's *The Titan*. Writing the magazine articles that became *The Shame of the Cities*, Lincoln Steffens postponed a visit to Philadelphia because the discovery of its corruption would pose no challenge for him. The Standard Oil Company did everything to the Pennsylvania General Assembly "except refine it," Henry Demarest Lloyd complained.[2] The state legislature was also one of three which in the nineteenth century legalized company police and facilitated the deputizing of officers; in 1905 it established the nation's first state police after employers doubted the reliability of the National Guard. Exploiting both natural resources and workers with the connivance of one of the best legislatures money could buy, the entrepreneurs shaped out of blood and iron and coal the county and state where Scott Nearing was born and came to maturity.

FOUNDED UPON A TRIBUTARY OF THE TIOGA RIVER, MORRIS
Run claimed a population of almost 3,000 when Nearing
was born there on August 6, 1883. Tioga County's annual
production of a million tons of semibituminous coal enabled
its largest town to erect five churches, a school, a public hall,
a general store, a grocery·store, and even a hotel. A third of
its inhabitants were Welsh, a fifth were Irish; and nearly everyone else had been born in England, Sweden, Scotland,
the United States, Germany, France, or what had once been
Poland. But whatever his national origin or station in life, a
resident of Morris Run was economically dependent upon
the Morris Run Coal Company and its superintendent,
Winfield Scott Nearing.[3]

Scott Nearing's grandfather had arrived in Tioga County
at the height of a successful career as an engineer and sur-
veyor for railroads and canals. Exercising undivided authority over the drift bosses, saw mill foremen, and workers,
Winfield Scott Nearing quickly mastered the financial and
technical affairs of the Morris Run Coal Company. He was
also imperious and remorseless toward his employees.
When miners demanded the right to form a union in 1873,
he considered such an organization superfluous, since the
Odd Fellows, the Masons, the Knights of Pythias, and
various church societies already flourished in Morris Run.
Nevertheless the workers went out on strike. Since the company owned every house in the town, the superintendent
served every family with an eviction notice, giving the
strikers ten days to disappear. Those remaining after the
expiration date were pitched into the street immediately
ahead of their belongings, forced into flatcars, driven out of
town, and then ejected onto a snowbank, where a child was
born whom Winfield Scott Nearing's eldest grandson later
met. But the evicted miners were sheltered by neighboring

farmers and villagers; and the severity of the depression of 1873 forced the company to end its lockout after three months and to recognize the union, which disappeared shortly thereafter.[4]

Like unions, lawyers were considered something of a frill in Morris Run. Almost every afternoon the superintendent sat on the side porch of his house to adjudicate disputes. Fines usually ranged from $5 to $25, and these deductions from paychecks were divided among the churches in order to operate Sunday schools. Even if the miners had lived in amity, however, the clergy was assured of a solid income; for Nearing fined citizens for the effrontery of speaking to him on the street and of inviting him in for drinks. Groceries and beverages could be purchased only at the company store, which the superintendent's son operated. If a paycheck revealed too small a deduction for purchases at Louis Nearing's store, its recipient was advised to become a better customer; and whatever was purchased outside of town had to be imported after dark, past the gauntlet of company spies. No wonder that, as the wiry, agile little autocrat stalked through the town, clutching his hickory walking stick, or charging past behind one of the three teams of horses kept ready for him, or permitting imploring women to kiss his hand, a nickname clung to him like an odor: the "Tsar of Morris Run." [5]

His notoriety spead when the longest strike in the history of American bituminous mining left Morris Run a deserted village. Deep in the drifts, organizers for the United Mine Workers had gained the allegiance of enough workers to make Nearing recognize the challenge to his authority. He thereupon sliced the miners' wages by 14 percent, demanded adherence to the yellow-dog contract, and thus provoked a strike in 1903. Even when chief stockholders preferred conciliation, Nearing was adamant, although the

Morris Run Coal Company eventually lost over a million dollars' worth of orders.[6]

Tsar Nearing imported both scabs and policemen, waited till the temperature hovered at zero, and then slapped the suspected leaders of the strike with eviction notices. But the rest of the miners refused to yield, despite the loss of a half-million dollars in wages. Eviction notices cascaded, until by 1905 about 400 striking families had been expelled; the families of the two dozen miners willing to work were spared. A New York reporter observed that Nearing "treads the deserted streets of his little domain today as proudly and as firmly as when those streets swarmed with people who trembled or frowned at his approach. He is indomitable." [7]

Winfield Scott Nearing was an intense, driven man, "always active, tremendously interested in all kinds of things." He studied nature, enjoyed science, carpentry, and gardening, and regularly received crates of books from New York to amass a large private library.[8] He combined the ice of personality with the fire of curiosity, traits shared by an eldest grandson whose own life would demonstrate forceful independence, self-assurance, and dedication.

Far less influential was Scott's father, Louis Nearing, whose laconic exterior apparently did not conceal deeper processes of thought but disguised further layers of dullness. In 1882 he had married Minnie Zabriskie, whose ancestors had landed in America in the seventeenth century and whose father was a contractor and banker. Minnie Nearing was a vibrant, energetic, and dynamic woman who easily dominated her husband and deeply touched the lives of the children who arrived after Scott: Mary Frances, born in 1886; Dorothy, born in 1888; Guy, born in 1890; Beatrice, born in 1892; and Max, born in 1895. Lacking a formal education, she provided intellectual inspiration by reading to her children in the afternoons and evenings. Besides a part-time tutor, she employed two Polish servants to clean the gleaming white house and even to scrub the trees in the surrounding grove. There, atop a hill overlooking the town, Scott Nearing was raised.[9]

Bright, handsome, stable, the aptest pupil of his grandfather, the darling of his mother, Scott Nearing grew up accustomed not only to love but to respect. The citizens of Morris Run, his brother recalled, "treated him the way they would treat the heir to the nobleman. . . . They all treated him with awe." Discouraged from playing with the children who lived in shacks pieced together with logs or blackened hemlock boards, he was sent to Philadelphia's Manual Training High School. He returned to Tioga County in the summers, serving as a saw mill foreman and working in the mines and on the railroad; and guests of the proper social level came to visit from Philadelphia.[10]

Yet the adolescent Scott Nearing also developed a social conscience, a burr under his skin that none of his relatives acquired and that no interpretation satisfactorily explains. True, he knew the Bible, as did millions of other Christians who managed to live with the social conditions that Nearing wanted to rearrange. He cherished other books as well: John Ruskin's *Unto This Last,* which, Gandhi wrote, "made me transform my life"; Henry George's *Progress and Poverty,* which pulled George Bernard Shaw toward economics; and Edward Bellamy's *Looking Backward,* which had the same effect upon Thorstein Veblen, and led his wife to call it "the turning-point in our lives." And though Nearing never made the pilgrimage to Yasnaya Polyana, he found inspiration in the philosophy and example of Tolstoy, who had renounced privilege in order to reverence life.[11] Here, too, the intellectual and moral forces that suffused Nearing's sensibility hardly made him unique. It was nevertheless evident by late adolescence that he could not ignore human suffering.

After his graduation from high school in 1901, Nearing's parents wanted him to attend West Point. But when an ice snowball hit him and destroyed the central vision of his right eye, he became eligible only for civilian pursuits. His mother advised him to enroll in the University of Pennsylvania Law School, where corporate bias so violated his idealism that after one year he quit.[12] While studying oratory at Temple University, he also enrolled in the Wharton School of the University of Pennsylvania, which was to be his home base during the next dozen years.

THE FIFTH-LARGEST AMERICAN UNIVERSITY AT THE DAWN of the century had not quite kept the cosmopolitan faith of its founder, Benjamin Franklin. Many of its 5,000 students exhibited contempt for the poor and the foreign-born, for Jews and for women; as for blacks, one student acknowledged that they "generally get run out sooner or later." Automobiles could be observed shuttling the sartorially resplendent from their fraternity houses to the classroom, but a visitor to the campus might also notice a diversity rare among prestigious colleges, such as non-Republicans and "pale-faced, stoop-shouldered young men who snatch ravenously at a scrap of learning and hurry away with it to unknown parts of the city." After a Pierkaski brought All-American honors to Penn in 1904, others with distinctly Polish names were offered the opportunity to forsake the coal fields for the football fields. A national craze that confirmed the belief in upward social mobility, diminished the likelihood of student rebellions, and toughened the various fibers, sinews, and backbones of American manhood swept up the otherwise staid University of Pennsylvania too.[13]

Whenever their team left for an out-of-town engagement, students disrupted classes to form a mob and march across a bridge over the Schuylkill River. During one such exercise, one of the screaming undergraduates, Rex Tugwell, saw a gaunt gentleman "with badly fitted, badly kept clothes, and heavy clodlike shoes" approaching from the other side. Other students recognized the lonely figure, a cheer erupted, and Tugwell heard someone identify him with admiration: "Old Si Patten . . . founded the Wharton School." [14]

No one, apart from his grandfather and his mother, affected Scott Nearing more than Simon Nelson Patten. Often regarded as a diffident teacher and an inchoate thinker, Patten nevertheless became a founding father of the American Economic Association, helped construct the intellectual foundations of both the discipline of social work and the dimensions of post-scarcity economics, and constantly felt "the tension within him between the prophet and the professional." He had conceived of a "College of Practical Affairs" to develop operational ideas in economics, politics, and statistics. Joseph Wharton, a Quaker devoted to the practice of an austere father, who spent another part of his time in the manufacture of guns, implemented Patten's idea with a $100,000 donation in 1881 and another half a million dollars later. That Patten shared Joseph Wharton's protectionism, even though few other eminent economists did, did not embarrass relations between the benefactor and the school that bore his name. [15]

Nearing almost never missed an opportunity to listen to Patten, who had a way of insinuating the most alert and curious students into his own thought processes, daring them to emulate the imaginative thrusts of his own mind. Nearing, who raced through his undergraduate program in three years while simultaneously engaging in campus politics and championship debating, was deeply impressed with the factual knowledge at Patten's command and with the ease of his manner.[16] From his favorite teacher he undoubtedly acquired his disdain for conventional scholarship, his desire for synthesis fused with moral earnestness, his deployment of exaggeration as a pedagogical technique. Patten, in turn, considered Nearing "his fair-haired boy, at least for a while" and "had great hopes for him," according to a mutual friend.[17]

Nearing nevertheless repudiated specific intellectual debts to Patten, a Republican who perceived advantages to empire and did not object to war. Even his prophetic formulation of the implications of abundance—the need to raise aggregate demand and to devise new forms of restraint and channels of energy—flowed from his pride in American nationality and his articulation of a manifest destiny to which his star pupil was indifferent. Although Patten guided Samuel McCune Lindsay, Edward T. Devine, Frances Perkins, and other students into significant positions in what he was first to call social work, his mind was primarily speculative. Nearing's was instrumental, and his temperament activist and optimistic. A humanitarian glow suffused his belief in science and rationality; the Progressive atmosphere he breathed sharpened his criticism of privilege and his sympathy for the excluded. As Patten engaged in serpentine criticism of pecuniary values, Nearing took him seriously, like "a vigorously innocent Billy Budd." [18]

NEARING'S COMMITMENT TO SOCIAL UPLIFT WAS QUITE distinguishable from the "Pennsylvania idea," which was Boies Penrose's contribution to political science. Rather than depend upon petty boodling, Penrose insisted upon direct corporate donations in exchange for sympathetic legislation. The "Pennsylvania idea" thus deodorized the air of scandal, permitting those who served the "employers of the people" to announce that they did not stoop to graft. It was an idea whose time had come, though Penrose's own rise to eminence was more providential. In 1895, as a candidate for mayor of Philadelphia, he had been photographed emerging from a brothel. The reaction of its employees to the visit of the 300-pound "Old Grizzly" had gone unrecorded, but the moral outrage of the citizenry had been so predictable that he was dropped from the ticket. Two years later Penrose was given a consolation prize: a seat in the Senate of the United States. From that position he was able to succeed Matthew Quay as boss of the Keystone State in 1904.[19]

No art lover, Penrose once gave $1,500 to a political cartoonist who had drawn and quartered his allies, to sit out an election in Atlantic City. He cared little for amassing personal wealth, having already inherited it. He cared little for reform, although he permitted its legionnaires the consolation of a few victories. By including educational and charitable institutions among the beneficiaries of state appropriation bills, the Penrose machine inculcated a spirit of gratitude and obligation among the prominent citizens who served on their governing boards. Among them was Russell Conwell, whose "Acres of Diamonds," a speech he delivered more than 5,000 times, advocated the laying up of treasure upon earth in order to serve humanity. As an adolescent, Nearing regularly attended Conwell's Grace Baptist Temple, joined the Christian Endeavor Society, taught in Sunday School, and so admired its popular preacher that he considered becoming a minister himself.[20]

In the mayoralty campaign of 1905 Conwell joined other ministers in favoring "a clean Philadelphia," which meant the election of the reform candidate, Rudolph Blankenburg. But from the pulpit one Sunday, Reverend Conwell suddenly announced that he no longer opposed the Republican machine. Disputing the first half of Steffens' description of the city as "corrupt and contented," he asserted that "Philadelphia is one of the best governed cities of its size in the country." Dazed, Nearing stalked out of the church and never returned. Nurtured on the social gospel of Walter Rauschenbush, as well as on the New Testament, he attempted to avoid organized Christianity without forsaking his conception of the ethics of the Gospels. He resolved to become a teacher, entering the graduate program of the Wharton School in 1905.[21] At the same time he served as volunteer secretary of the Pennsylvania Child Labor Committee.

At the turn of the century 1.7 American children between the ages of ten and fifteen were working, an increase of over a million from 1870. The proponents of child labor—and there were many—claimed that it diminished the dangers of juvenile crime and promiscuity, that it was simply the bottom rung on the ladder of success, that it built character. Others disagreed, arguing that accidents were three times more likely to strike child laborers than adults and that education should be the foundation of a free society and of personal achievement. Demonstrating that child labor was both the cause and effect of poverty, Socialists like Robert Hunter and John Spargo were among the most effective publicists in the struggle against it. But when the National Child Labor Committee was formed in 1904, its molders mixed searing humanitarian rhetoric with strikingly cautious tactics. Its first chairman, Felix Adler, recommended that the Committee advocate only "the absolute minimum which the enlightened public sentiment of the community demands." Although a student of the period has called the committee one of the three voluntary associations most typical of Progressivism, the distinction between contemporary reformers and conservatives blurs hopelessly if some of its trustees and members are listed: ex-President

Grover Cleveland and "Pitchfork" Ben Tillman, the banker Isaac Seligman and the Socialist Robert Hunter, with James Cardinal Gibbons and the president of the Pennsylvania Railroad thrown in for good measure. Major contributors to the Committee included John D. Rockefeller, J. P. Morgan, Andrew Carnegie, and Henry Clay Frick.[22]

The agency nevertheless bore the particular impress of social workers like Florence Kelley, Jane Addams, and Lillian Wald; and Samuel McCune Lindsay, Nearing's sociology instructor, served as its first general secretary. Intending to abolish child labor through state and national legislation, the Committee tried to arouse middle-class Americans whose children were in schools rather than in factories. So, in order to dramatize the plight of working children, the Committee massed its forces against the state that employed more children than any other: Pennsylvania.[23]

When Nearing enlisted in the fight, almost 50,000 children worked in factories and 24,000 worked in the mines—and these figures had been rising. But statistics offer inadequate testimony. A trade unionist summoned to organize the silk workers of Scranton entered the meeting hall, looked at the audience, and wept: the workers were little girls. "I did not come here to organize children," he exclaimed. "For God's sake, go home!" [24] Another labor organizer, Mary Jones, described the boys who separated slate from 15,000 tons of coal a day, sitting in "the gloom of the breakers, the dust from the coal swirling continuously up their faces. To see the slate they must bend over their task. Their shoulders were round. Their chests narrow. A breaker boss . . . had a long stick to strike the knuckles of any lad seen neglecting his work." Their fingers "bled onto the coal," and they could scarcely be expected to know—or fear—that their spines contained lime deposits. "They looked like little old men," another mine organizer observed.[25]

Although no anthracite miners were supposed to be under sixteen years of age, or breaker boys under fourteen, the law was casually enforced. After one accident in 1907, a foreman described the victim as "kind of a small boy, but I thought he might be older than he looked." The work certificate listed him as fourteen, although he had been nine years old when he died. But even when children survived by growing into gnomes three miles from daylight, they could find little surcease from pain. Children as young as four were found rolling "Pittsburgh stogies" in that city's sweatshops. The children in the glass factories constantly cut and burned themselves and, because of the intense glare and heat, suffered from pneumonia, rheumatism, heat prostration, headaches, tracheal defects, tuberculosis, and other diseases.[26]

Lindsay spearheaded a frenetic lobbying campaign in Harrisburg that produced a slightly more humane child labor law in May 1905; the next year the state's supreme court declared it unconstitutional. For two years Nearing spoke widely throughout the state, conducted investigations of factory conditions, and supervised the operations of the state organization virtually without the intercession of the parent body in Washington. His most imaginative venture was an industrial exhibition in which actual working conditions were portrayed. While he, Kelley, Lindsay, Spargo, and others excoriated child labor in the Philadelphia exhibition hall in December 1906, workers occupied booths to stimulate their conditions of employment. A mother and her two sons, fourteen and six years old, stripped rags in a 6'-by-12' room, where they also cooked, ate, and slept. Others showed how they pasted paper bags fourteen hours per day at an average of fifty cents per day, or pressed trousers thirteen hours a day, for which the average weekly earnings were $3.63.[27]

Under Nearing's direction a new child labor bill was

drafted, and again a fight was waged in Harrisburg. But this time the legislature rejected the proposal even before the judiciary got an opportunity to invalidate it. Owen Lovejoy, who replaced Lindsay as national secretary, blamed the influence of manufacturers and the sabotage of the factory inspection department, but acknowledged the failure of the national and state committees "to pursue the campaign with . . . persistence and ability. . . . If the National Child Labor Committee had been able to maintain skilled workers at the Harrisburg Legislature during the last two months of the legislative session, not less than 10,000 children would be in school who are today in the mines and factories of that state." Lovejoy's confidential report doubted whether, under voluntary part-time generalship such as Nearing's, a "state committee sufficiently strong to wage a successful campaign" could emerge.[28]

But the graduate student getting his first taste of social reform could plead extenuating circumstances. In the first decade of the century, the state's industrial growth declined in relation to similar states, so that businessmen not only created the Pennsylvania Manufacturers' Association in 1909 but were especially anxious to reduce the costs of labor. Philadelphia's Central Labor Union was comfortably nestled inside the Penrose machine; and as for the high accident rates in the mines, the state commissioner of labor recommended simply that careless children be fired. Almost as disconcerting was Nearing's discovery that a member of the Pennsylvania committee was himself an employer of children. Nor could Nearing's minions buck a national trend: the 1910 census showed that the number of working children had increased to two million, or almost one out of every five Americans between the ages of ten and fifteen.[29]

Given such obstacles, Nearing's failure is not surprising; but given the evils of child labor, his moderation is. The immediate objectives of the state committee were to raise the

minimum age in factories from thirteen to fourteen for day
work and to sixteen for night work. More stringently enforced certification of age was also advocated, plus the extension to bituminous mines of a minimum age of sixteen.
With the exception of some industries, the state legislature
agreed with these goals in 1909, two years after Nearing
had resigned his position. Yet even in his 1911 book on the
subject of child labor, Nearing was surprisingly restrained
in his criticism of exploitation, and unsystematic in his description of the political economy that fostered it.[30]

A YEAR AFTER NEARING LEFT THE COMMITTEE, THE SOCIETY
pages announced his marriage to Nellie Seeds, the daughter
of a Germantown realtor whom Nearing had known since
high school. She had also fought against child labor after
her graduation from Bryn Mawr, and Nearing later described her as "serious and studious." The Nearings were to
have two sons: John, born in 1912; and Robert, an adopted
child, born two years later.[31]

Together with the pursuit of graduate studies, the struggle for social reform, and the establishment of a family,
Nearing managed to participate in an unusual communitarian experiment. Nineteen miles from Philadelphia, in
Arden, Delaware, disciples of Henry George had purchased
two hundred acres of land and then divided it into lots for
rent, but not for sale. The colony also attracted those who
sought a rural setting close enough to New York, like
Upton Sinclair; those who wanted "a good place to take the
children," like Ella Reeve Bloor, a Socialist militant in the
child labor campaign; those who wanted intellectual stimu-
lation, like Guy Nearing; and those who desired "to live in
the country, to build your own house, and have your own
garden," like Scott Nearing, who arrived in 1906.[32]

A poet also came with a couple of suitcases of manu-
scripts, and left with Sinclair's wife. Taking the loss in
stride, Sinclair helped Nearing build a one-room cabin
upon the half-acre that the graduate student rented for $13
per year. The novelist set up a couple of tents for himself
next to the Nearings' lot and in 1911 rented their house
during the winter. But the acclaimed author of *The Jungle*
was not permitted to borrow the tools because they "might
be mislaid." [33]

Life in Arden was highly politicized, an intensified version of the rambunctious local democracy that had so be-
witched Tocqueville. Sixty to eighty families made the colony their summer home; and all residents, including
children, were eligible to vote during the frequent town
meetings. Here the single-taxers' policy of hospitality and
low rents boomeranged, for disputatious Socialists and liberals nearly outnumbered the apostles of Henry George.
Once a week the leading single-taxer even had to race six
miles to Wilmington to secure a desirable street corner
ahead of Ella Reeve Bloor, who wanted to remind Delaware
citizens that merely a tax on land would not achieve the cooperative commonwealth.[34] For single-taxers criticized only
one kind of economic exploitation: the rent accruing to
those whose only apparent function in the community was
their ownership of desirable real estate. The only remedy
which *Progress and Poverty* offered was a tax on land so huge
that rent would be abolished and all other taxes would be
unnecessary. This particularized attack on privilege influenced some liberals, but Socialists dismissed the single-taxers' analysis as grievously inadequate. In the interest of justice and efficiency, Socialists insisted that not merely land
but all socially necessary means of production should be
publicly and collectively owned. Not land, but the corporation and the factory had become the dominant economic institutions of modern civilization. Two sorts of proof for this
contention were to emerge during the Great Depression,

when total income from rent was only about 6 percent of the national income; and when "Landlord," the Arden colonists' game designed to show the iniquity of capitalist realty, was adapted and very successfully marketed by Parker Brothers under the name of "Monopoly." [35]

In the ebullient atmosphere of Arden, Nearing lived every summer and many more weekends until 1916, relishing the proximity to nature, playing in the amateur theatricals, joining in the political controversies. A conspicuous gap in Nearing's formal education was partially rectified when he heard, for the first time, the name of Karl Marx. Another first was the opportunity to read regularly the New York *Call,* a Socialist daily whose future editor, Charles Ervin, also lived in Arden. One of Bloor's sons, Carl Reeve, who was also destined for the vocation of radical journalism, tried to foist socialism on Nearing, who demurred, but later acknowledged that *"The Jungle* certainly had an influence on my thinking." [36] That novel had been aimed at the reader's heart, but its author was hardly indifferent to the stomach. Sinclair veered erratically from the consumption of only fruits and vegetables to the consumption of only lean meat, to the consumption of no food whatsoever, to the consumption of sand. Nearing enthusiastically imitated the first of those phases and later became prominent in international vegetarian circles. Otherwise he scarcely felt the pull of Sinclair's mind, which was too kinky even for Ezra Pound, who called him a "polomaniac [*sic*]." Nearing's education on the other hand inclined him toward rational and statistical procedures, so that Sinclair was not too inaccurate in dismissing his neighbor at Arden as "a mild liberal." [37]

AFTER RECEIVING HIS DOCTORATE IN ECONOMICS IN 1909, he became an instructor in the Wharton School at a salary of $800 per year. Though only twenty-six years old, Nearing had already taught sociology to theological students at Temple College (1903–1905), served as an assistant instructor at the Wharton School since 1906, and offered courses in economics at Swarthmore College (1908–1912).[38]

As a teacher Nearing was not only experienced but, by all accounts, excellent. Because Patten objected to the textbook assigned in the introductory course, Nearing helped write another volume while still a graduate student. When he became an instructor, the introductory course was rearranged from small groups to a required lecture series and quiz classes; and his lectures usually attracted about 500 students, the largest enrollment in the university. Nearing thus occupied "a very key position in the whole academic pattern in the Wharton School." Patten called his "ability to understand, befriend, and help the newly arrived freshmen almost amount[ing] to genius"; and Rex Tugwell recalled that Nearing's "economics was pragmatic with no more than a bow to orthodox categories. . . . He was an utterly free mind and spirit. And he managed to pass along . . . some of his courage and dedication." [39] Nearing also persuaded Tugwell, who had lavished much of his freshman and sophomore experience upon extracurricular exploits, to concentrate upon economics, with the dubious consequence of the following versification: ". . . I am sick of a nation's stenches,/I am sick of propertied czars. . . ./My plans are fashioned and practical;/I shall roll up my sleeves—make America over!" [40]

But the gift of pedagogy did not assure professional advancement. Even in the meetings of the Athletic Research Society, coaches solemnly read monographs to their colleagues; and at the University of Pennsylvania, teachers who evaded research and publication were not esteemed. Nearing was quite prolific, however: from 1911 to 1916 he wrote two books per year, harnessing the methods of statistical analysis to the demands of Reform Darwinism.

Nearing was one of the first economists to examine wage and income distribution in America. But his survey of wages from 1908 to 1910, for example, was tenuously supported by data from the only three major industrial states, Ohio, Massachusetts, and New Jersey, that made possible realistic appraisal of wage scales. And besides Kansas and Oklahoma, no other state published reliable information, or classified its data by occupation, or even published payroll figures at all. The federal government provided no information on wages since 1907. Nearing therefore studied payrolls of a few companies like the Bell System and railways to infer admittedly unsupported yet "far-reaching conclusions." [41]

The thrust of Nearing's generalizations was to puncture complacency, to emphasize the pervasive poverty gnawing at the working class. Even extant wage statistics were misleading, he announced, because of unemployment, "a constant factor in industry . . . [which] in the lean years . . . is a spectre of appalling magnitude to the average workingman." Nor could computation of average wages show how numerous were the unskilled workers and how little they earned. He therefore devised a weighted average to reveal the vacancy of "room at the top," for "not more than 10 percent of the adult male wage earners receive annually . . . more than $1,000." Half the adult male workers earned under $600, while women averaged $350 per year in industries that employed them in large numbers.[42]

Wages in the United States focused upon a period immediately following a recession. Nearing did not study the course of wages over time, or compute real wages; nor could he be expected to know that real wages had not risen between 1890 and 1914, a unique phenomenon in American economic history. He did conclude, however, that because many were earning so little, others were getting too much. Socialists found his books useful, even though the author went no further than "industrial democracy," which meant a more equitable distribution of wealth and the public control of large utilities.[43]

A more extensive critique of American society suffused books like *Social Adjustment* and *Social Sanity*, which predicted the abolition of human misery, if reform were wedded to technological advance. Nearing conceded the restrictions of heredity and indeed championed eugenics, praising "long lines of able men and women, exemplified in the Hohenzollern family" and urging the citizenry to "crush out with an iron hand every tendency which makes against virility, in order that the child may be well born." Marriages should be based upon "ability and civic worth, as well as beauty and dower." Dismissing prevalent fears of "race suicide," he opposed large families because of their susceptibility to poverty. Small families would also make women more free, useful, and productive.[44]

Yet Nearing blamed social and cultural influences more often than genes for the perpetuation of suffering. Women, for example, were "apparently inferior" only because men forced them into an "inferior position." A complex of values established male dominance, so that man endows woman with "only the virtues which he does not desire for himself and limits her to the immoralities of which he does not greatly disapprove." With the denigration of the cult of the home, women might adopt the cooperative ideals which Nearing urged his fellow social scientists to inculcate.[45] Experts should utilize the press and lecturn, organizations and legislative commissions, to "explain that welfare must be put before wealth; that the iron law of wages may be shattered by a minimum wage law; [and] that . . . economic maladjustments will disappear before an educated, legislating public opinion." Nearing concluded with the hope that "combination and cooperation may be employed to silence forever the savage demands of unrestricted competition." [46]

Nearing welcomed philanthropy as "a growth in the feeling of social responsibility" and exalted social work, which not only offered immediate assistance to the victims of a wasteful economy, but also provoked the professionals to serious reflection and further social action. Denouncing the congestion in American cities, he advocated immigration restriction because the low standards and expectations of foreigners kept wages down and squalor rampant. Like countless American reformers, Nearing believed in salvation by education: "Children should be taught that normal men and women are good, and that badness is merely [sic] an indication of abnormality. . . . It is antisocial to pay low wages, and the school children should know it." Teachers and social engineers would together reduce the friction of unsavory living conditions and outmoded values, to achieve healthy work, fulfilling leisure, and efficiency—a key to Progressive thought that one of its historians characterized as "turning . . . toward discipline and away from sympathy," invoking "social harmony and the leadership of the competent." [47]

But despite Nearing's success in diffusing his ideas in the classroom and in print, eight years passed—three years more than was customary—before he was promoted from the rank of instructor. During that period his salary never rose above $1500, which helps to account for his interest in income disparity in the United States. And even when he became an assistant professor, the appointment was provisional, for one year only. [48]

These were, nevertheless, buoyant and promising years for Scott Nearing, for he felt himself a genuine part of a movement of national and civic regeneration. With seven other young teachers in the Wharton School, he adhered to the ideal of service that Charles Van Hise, the president of the University of Wisconsin, enunciated: "Members of the faculty should ascertain the truth through research, should impart the results of their research to their students, and should attempt to build it into the life of the community." Tinged with the self-righteousness that often accompanies moral zeal, each member of the group concentrated upon an aspect of the economy—public utilities, the Pennsylvania Railroad, taxation, child labor. Extending the Wisconsin Idea off-campus, the eight teachers still "worked with the administration in our academic duties, faithfully and loyally," the specialist in child labor later maintained. "We never attempted to sabotage the university. But, on the other hand, in our spare time we were our own masters." [49]

Each of them also defied the familiar injunction against fighting City Hall; and when a feud between Penrose and his allies in Philadelphia could not be mended, Rudolph Blankenburg happily promised that "neither booze, boodle, nor fraud can beat us next fall." With the aid of the Democrats, the Philadelphia *North American,* and a thousand volunteer poll-watchers, the reformers' Keystone Party finally installed the "Old Dutch Cleanser" in the mayor's office in 1911. "The election of Blankenburg," Senator Robert La-Follette beamed, "has not been unlike the fight we made in Wisconsin." [50]

Penn professors suddenly found their expertise challenged and rewarded; and although Nearing did not devote himself to municipal administration and reform, his activism persisted. He lectured before women's clubs, labor unions, civic associations, literary and scientific societies, and church groups. He spoke weekends and during holidays and summer vacations, as far away as Chicago and St. Louis. He taught at the Chautauqua Summer School, the Philadelphia School for Social Work, and the New York School for Social Work. He even wrote four articles on education for the *Ladies Home Journal,* for which he received $500 more than his annual salary.[51]

Those who had hired the fluent young instructor were

not inattentive to his extracurricular engagements. In 1911 the Dean of the Wharton School suggested that Nearing speak less frequently and less passionately about the exploitation of children. Nearing reported this advice to the other members of the Progressive group, which agreed that, with a new child labor bill under legislative consideration, no quarter be given. In the next two weeks, he delivered ten speeches and distributed excerpts to the press.[52]

Later the Provost of the University, Edgar F. Smith, also urged Nearing "to try to give no ground for sensational and exaggerated misconceptions of his views" and hoped that Patten would help domesticate him. On the other hand, one trustee of the University did not propose moderation. Effingham B. Morris, the President of the Girard Trust Company, once invited Nearing into his office and warned him: "We will give you young fellows plenty of rope, and you will hang yourselves." [53]

The candidates for professional suicide continued to agitate and to advise, and genuine reforms were instituted. "Honest specifications, open bidding, and the fearless assessment of fines when companies tried to cheat the city" were among the achievements of the Blankenburg regime, according to its most scrupulous student. "The administration improved the city's water system, municipal dock area, roadways, police and fire protection, and park facilities. . . . By forcing contractors to pare once-exhorbitant profits, Blankenburg saved over $5 million for the city." But by demanding a special tax to balance the municipal budget, the mayor lost the indispensable support of the *North American*. The Republican machine stymied reform programs in the bicameral city council. City employees were hired on merit rather than on loyalty to the Keystone Party; thus the mayor repudiated those who had helped elect him.[54]

Even though the Progressives hired 400 detectives to

guard the polls, the Republicans triumphed in municipal by-elections in 1913. The next year Senator Penrose ran for the first time in a popular election and won a plurality of the votes; Philadelphians preferred him by a two-to-one margin. The Republican gubernatorial candidate, Martin Brumbaugh, coasted to victory and soon thereafter appeased reformers with a stroke of the pen. He signed a law limiting factory work for children between fourteen and sixteen to nine hours per day or fifty-two hours per week, with one day of school allowed. Newsboys, shoeshine boys, and others plying "street trades" henceforth had to be at least twelve years old.[55]

Although the sovereignty of the people was apparently compatible with boss rule, Nearing's reform philosophy remained Manichean in its espousal of popular will against entrenched privilege. Defining the professor as a public servant, he extolled the Wharton School's "splendid little nucleus . . . which is up and alive and full of the very old devil when they [sic] go into a scrap. It is a good place to be. They have not yet promoted us." [56]

CHAPTER TWO

REPORT FROM THE ACADEMY

EARLY IN THE MORNING OF JUNE 16, 1915, Nearing's secretary telephoned him in Arden to report that a letter from the Provost had arrived:

June 15, 1915

My dear Mr. Nearing:

As the term of your appointment as assistant professor of economics for 1914–1915 is about to expire, I am directed by the trustees of the University of Pennsylvania to inform you that it will not be renewed. With best wishes, I am

Yours sincerely,
Edgar F. Smith

As an undergraduate Nearing had known and liked Smith, but he was offered no justification and no apologies for his dismissal.[1] What he got instead was a niche in the history of the free pursuit of truth.

Although expulsion caught him by surprise and his martyrdom was inadvertent, Nearing's capacity for rubbing conservatives the wrong way was bound to cause serious friction; and by 1915 the relationships between trustees, politicians, and academics had become combustible.

The upper ranks of America's third largest city needed no qualifications like "old" or "proper" to identify themselves as "Philadelphians." Uttering "middle class" as a derogatory term, taking pride in their traditions and treated with deference, the Philadelphians admired business acumen somewhat less than New York's elite, and intellectual eminence less than proper Bostonians. Only rarely, in the nineteenth century, did they hold national or even civic office, for the Quaker legacy stressed private duty rather than public responsibility. So the city teemed with private charitable and cultural institutions, whose boards of directors were coated with the polish and prestige of the Philadelphians. Among the most prestigious was that of the University of Pennsylvania.[2] Indeed, the Philadelphians sometimes seemed to believe that "the only legitimate purpose of the University is to provide an excuse for the existence of such a Board."[3]

Such a board! In 1915 its luminaries included the banker Effingham Morris; corporation lawyers George Wharton Pepper and J. Levering Jones; E. T. Stotesbury, a partner of J. P. Morgan and Company of New York; and Randal Morgan, the vice-president of the United Gas Improvement Company. Elected to the board by each other, the trustees rarely shared the intellectual interests of the teachers they appointed, nor did their social planes often intersect. An exception to this rule of isolation occurred in late 1915 when Stotesbury's stepson walked out of an economics class because the instructor had remarked that "the transit company has Philadelphia by the throat and is strangling it." After consultation with his stepfather, the young scholar told the *Times:* "I have decided to give up permanently that part of my education. I knew nothing about economics before I started the course, but if that lecture is a sample of what is to follow, I'm mighty glad I dropped it."[4]

But normally the Philadelphians were not subjected to

such insults when they made contact with academicians; even Smith's immediate predecessors as provost, William Pepper and Charles Harrison, had been members of the aristocracy. They also had the knack of keeping an expanding institution solvent. "The University of Pennsylvania presents the same puzzle to me as the earth did to the ancients," one journalist wrote. "I cannot see what supports it. . . . I have been told that the real financial foundation of the university is a little memorandum book which Provost Harrison carries in his vest pocket when he makes his calls, and that if this fails him, he puts his hand into another of his pockets and supplies the deficit." Then came the inevitable question: "What would become of the university if something should happen to that memorandum book?"[5]

Soon the biggest entry in the book was provided from Harrisburg. The legislature had haphazardly made donations since the early nineteenth century; but only when Judge Samuel Pennypacker, a trustee, was elected governor in 1903 did grants to the University flow regularly. After the inauguration of Smith, an affable chemistry professor, in 1910, private sources could not be tapped so easily and the state legislature became even more generous. In one year its grant doubled; by 1913 it exceeded $1 million. The board of trustees became less exclusive, welcoming into its ranks John C. Bell, formerly the state's attorney-general, and one Richard Penrose, who was the Senator's brother.[6]

While the trustees became more intimate with politicians, the politicians remained sensitive to the interests of businessmen. Among them was Joseph Grundy, a Bristol woolen manufacturer whose father had once accompanied Blankenburg to Russia to supervise famine relief and to visit Tolstoy. Although the scion of a wealthy family, Joseph Grundy was so committed to the work ethic that he once proclaimed: "Let us train our children to work. . . . The state could get along without a lawyer, or an author, or an artist if it had to, but it must be the strong-armed, strong-backed toilers who keep the wheels of industry turning." This physical fitness program for youth nevertheless faced a threat from "do-gooders"; and partially to combat their zealotry, Grundy raised funds for the Republican party and helped found the Pennsylvania Manufacturers' Association.[7]

He had the courage of his convictions, and a high proportion of women and children adorned his payroll. The Pennsylvania Child Labor Committee had criticized Grundy's employment practices as early as 1905; and when its proposed bill to reduce child labor was sent to a special committee of the state senate in 1913, Grundy's forces deflected this appeal to the legislators' hearts by twisting their arms instead. An official of the Pennsylvania Manufacturers' Association denounced the initial proponents of the bill as "longhaired men and short-haired women." After the bill was crushed, the Philadelphia *North American*'s cartoonist depicted the "conquerors," with Penrose front and center and Grundy immediately to his right. In the following year the textile magnate held a cordial meeting with Nearing after a Bristol congregation heard an address that a local newspaper shrieked was "at war with the entire order of civilization."[8]

In 1915 Clarence Buckman of Grundy's own Bucks County became chairman of the senate's appropriations committee, which determined the size of the University's annual grant. "Grundy . . . had repeatedly said that something should be done about my connection with the University," Nearing was told. "Mr. Grundy notified the trustees that unless I was eliminated from the University staff the appropriation would not come through." A drunken legislator is supposed to have revealed the arrangement that summer in a Harrisburg hotel;[9] but since his name is unknown and his story cannot be verified, this aspect of the case may be relegated to the category of apocrypha.

Joseph Wharton's son-in-law, Harrison S. Morris, claimed that Nearing was expelled "because he dared to advocate industrial and municipal reforms inimical to the private interests of millionaire members of the board of trustees." Nearing himself was convinced that his "utterances on economic problems" made him undesirable, yet he was not in any obvious way more radical than other members of the Wharton School's "splendid little nucleus." William Draper Lewis was an even more active Progressive than Nearing, yet he remained dean of the law school despite alumni pressure. As befitted a teacher in the veterinary school, Horace Hoskins denounced the University as "the fatted calf of special privilege" and yet kept his position. Nor did any specific act of misconduct provoke Nearing's dismissal. Even the influential trustee George Wharton Pepper considered him "a most exemplary young professor." [10]

But Pepper also voiced the most common complaint: Nearing kept "the community in a continual ferment on every subject from the high cost of living to the resuscitation of the apparently drowned." The attorney was not exaggerating. When a couple of boys unable to stay afloat on the Schuylkill were brought ashore and to the attention of policemen, Nearing happened by and and joined in the attempt to revive the youngsters. But rescue efforts were abandoned too quickly, Nearing told the press, which thereupon printed a "scorching interview" and a headline blaring, "Nearing Raps Police." [11]

Or take the time the young instructor, like many other citizens, was called for jury duty. But few other jurors chose to describe their experiences as Nearing did in the Philadelphia *Evening Bulletin:* "I entered the panel with a measure of faith in the courts and the law. I left the panel with my faith utterly destroyed. . . . Property is a god in criminal jurisprudence." [12]

Or take the time Nearing tried to explain to Swarthmore students not to live beyond their means and not to dress extravagantly. He was reported telling "young women . . . [to] attend evening functions in night dresses rather than spend immense amount for Paris creations." Young men were advised to "go attired in pajamas," and the headline predictably summarized Nearing's speech on prudent expenditure: "Lauds Nighties as Evening Dress." [13]

Or take the time Nearing tried to dramatize the condition by which "the average man everywhere . . . must either cut down on his food, change his dietary or enforce the payment of higher wages." But his serious intentions boomeranged when the Philadelphia *Evening Times* inflated one aspect of his speech: "How would you like to be made to eat prison fare just because you are a student at college? . . . Professor Scott Nearing . . . wants the university to adopt the dietary of the federal prison at Atlanta, Georgia. . . ." [14]

When he was not making headlines himself, he was firing off letters to the editor. In Altoona, church elders barred an adolescent girl who had been found in a hotel room with their minister, who had been driven out of town. Nearing injected himself into the scandal: "Today throughout the land Christ is being nailed to crosses of bigotry and ignorance and hate and greed, and the Church of Christ wields the hammer that drives in the nails. . . . Oh, the pity of it—the pity and the shame!" [15]

Reverberations followed even when Nearing, in the office of Dean Roswell McCrea, asked a student to explain his deficient grades. Told where the student had received his preparatory education, the apostate instructor exclaimed, "If I had a son, I would rather see him in hell than have him go to the Episcopal Academy." The daughter of a

Wharton professor recalled that "nobody mentioned the Episcopal Academy for years without quoting what Scott Nearing had said," and a trustee gave as the only example of Nearing's intemperate remarks this choice of religiously affiliated institutions.[16]

But none of these incidents compared in importance to the arrival of Billy Sunday, who inaugurated a major revival campaign in the city early in 1915. A wooden tabernacle was erected, and the flamboyant evangelist spent eleven spectacular weeks there seeking conversions for Christ. "Billy Sunday makes people look to the salvation of their own souls," a businessman explained, "and when a man is looking after his own soul's good he forgets his selfish desire to become rich. Instead of agitating for a raise in wages, he turns and helps some poorer brother who's down and out."

Others were less enthusiastic. Rabbi Stephen S. Wise called Billy Sunday "the greatest theological strike breaker in history," and Scott Nearing unleashed an open letter in the *North American*. The evangelist was told to apply the Gospel to the conditions of industrial capitalism, to wrestle with "the railroad interests . . . the traction company . . . the manufacturers, intrenched in Harrisburg . . . the vested interests." The Wharton School economist observed that, amidst excruciating misery, "those whose ease and luxury are built upon this poverty, child labor and exploitation, sit in your congregation." [17]

This open letter may well have hastened Nearing's dismissal; for the University could not countenance unlimited freedom of speech "on fundamentals of religion or morality," announced William A. Redding, the President of the General Alumni Society and a former partner of J. Levering Jones. For what it is worth, Sinclair also believed that the provost's letter of dismissal was the trustees' way of replying to the apostrophe to Billy Sunday. Certainly the revival was on their minds; one trustee called Nearing "the Billy Sunday of the university world" and another argued that both tub-thumpers were essentially free-lancers who did not belong in institutions.[18]

One recent definition of the celebrity—"a person who is known for his well-knownness" [19]—may be turned inside-out: Nearing's notoriety can be partially attributed to his reputation for notoriousness. A judge reported that, in quizzing his son in class, Nearing had responded to one answer rather sarcastically: "Well, that is the kind of ignorance I would expect in judicial circles." In fact, Nearing never questioned the student and had never even met him until he heard the rumor, after which he rushed to secure from the lad a signed statement testifying to its inaccuracy. But perhaps because of the perversity of humanity, the tale may well have influenced a few of the trustees to question Nearing's academic suitability. Already, in 1911, the trustees expressed shock that Nearing had reportedly lectured at Arden in his bare feet; the rumor was barefaced, however, for Nearing was able to prove that he had been in Europe at the time. Given what Pepper termed his "genius for publicity," Nearing was unusually vulnerable to distortion and false rumors.[20]

Nearing was willing to take such a risk; he made good copy and knew it. In E. A. Van Valkenburg, the editor of the *North American,* he had a valuable friend and ally under no obligation to the board of trustees. In 1914, 183,000 persons bought the newspaper, even though "any decent person . . . caught reading it," Governor Pennypacker had noted, "excused himself by saying he picked it up on the cars." Nearing's academic career was one of the causes it promoted, wondering throughout the 1915 academic year "why, if this man is incompetent, don't they fire him; and if he is competent, why don't they promote him. . . . The *North American* kept needling, needling. . . ." Nearing also took Charles Ervin's advice to deliver many speeches on the Sabbath, "as Sunday night was . . . 'hell night' for news. He would be sure to get publicity for his ideas on that night." [21]

But with the University suffering from financial anemia, the trustees were naturally disturbed. Speaking as a solicitor of funds, trustee J. William White called it "positively harmful to be handicapped by statements . . . put forth by Dr. Nearing and, of course, offering a convenient handle to that large class of givers . . . who are not averse to being supplied with a good ready-made excuse for a declination or postponement." Although the board made no attempt to separate fact from fancy, it justified his dismissal on the basis that Nearing's "efforts . . . were constantly and continuously misunderstood by the public and by many parents of students." Nearing's reputation for agitation and propaganda was not formed within the walls of the Wharton School, and no evidence to the contrary was ever presented from parents or anyone else.[22] Nearing had simply become a lightning rod for controversy, so the trustees—contrary to celebrated educational theory—decided to spare the rod.

Trustees further insisted that Nearing's manner rather than his subject matter gave offense, that he displayed the rude aggressiveness of the incendiary rather than the mature detachment of an educator. Talleyrand, who quite literally kept his head while those around him were losing theirs, had also warned his diplomats against showing too much zeal, just as Smith and McCrea had advised Nearing on how to save a career. But the active campaign that the alumni waged to remove Nearing indicated than many Philadelphians objected to what the assistant professor said, not merely how he said it.

For example, the *Alumni Register* complained early in 1915 that "the bizarre and radical theories often advanced by enthusiastic young instructors are likely to have a poor effect upon Freshmen." The alumni committee of the

Wharton School offered more constructive criticism, recommending "a slight rearrangement of the curriculum and the assignment of work of this character to the more mature and better seasoned instructors." [23] So much for Nearing's distinctive talent for teaching freshmen, which so impressed Patten, and for his innovative methods, which so captivated Tugwell.

Two months before the ouster, the Wharton School alumni committee stated its case less obliquely. Chaired by Thomas S. Gates, president of the Philadelphia Trust, Safe Deposit and Insurance Company and a future president of the University, the advisory group resented "the tendency on the part of a certain element in the teaching staff to seek publicity . . . likely to arouse class prejudice and fallacious conclusions, based on a biased attitude of mind." The Gates committee concluded that teachers who "use . . . the fair name of the University as a point of vantage for utterances foreign to the scheme of its . . . ideals . . . should be dispensed with." [24]

The Wharton School alumni report received the unanimous approval of the directors of the General Alumni Society on April 9, 1915, and was then presented to the trustees. One of them was Joseph Rosengarten, who had graduated from college over six decades earlier and who fired off a letter to the *Alumni Register*. Rosengarten deplored professorial irreverence toward "the conservative opinions of men of affairs" and the emergence of "class prejudice" and "fallacious conclusions"—the phraseology of the Gates committee.[25] The alumni had made an impression where it counted.

On June 8 the Committee on the Wharton School met in order to evaluate the academic program. Its members consisted of Provost Smith; Dean McCrea; and two trustees— Wharton Barker, an investment banker, and Louis Madeira, a director of mining and insurance companies. One item on the agenda was Nearing, whose promotion to the rank of assistant professor a year earlier brought a presumption of reappointment. Although Patten had described Nearing as "an efficient, energetic teacher, a man of rare personal magnetism," McCrea was asked if the assistant professor had "professorial 'gumption.' " McCrea conceded that "Nearing is impulsive and has not been so tactful as he might be," and yet "inspiring" as a teacher and a person. And though the dean of the Wharton School recommended reappointment, he acknowledged that he already had a substitute "if . . . anything should happen to Nearing." [26]

Madeira later claimed that he learned more about "Dr. Nearing's peculiarities from the remarks of Dean McCrea than from any other source." McCrea nevertheless upheld Nearing's fitness to teach; and although Provost Smith, by nature unobtrusive, was only lukewarm, the Wharton School committee recommended reappointment. On June 14 the board of trustees resoundingly spurned the explicit recommendations of its own committee and of the provost, dean, and department chairman. The minutes of the meeting do not indicate the reasons for dismissal, only the lopsided 11–2 margin, J. Bertram Lippincott and Wharton Barker dissenting. Lippincott had graduated from the Episcopal Academy but dropped out of the University, only to bounce back from adversity by becoming the vice-president of his father's publishing company. Barker had served as a lieutenant in a Negro regiment in the Civil War, edited a weekly, secured the first concession the Chinese government ever granted to a foreigner, engaged in investment banking, and campaigned as the splinter Populist candidate for President in 1900. The issue in the Nearing case, he wrote, was "whether the People or the Oligarchy of Capitalists are to dominate" America. [27]

To the surprise of the trustees, that was how many other citizens chose to interpret one teacher's dismissal.

NEARING'S ABRUPT EXPULSION FROM THE ACADEMY RICO-
cheted through Philadelphia and beyond. His colleagues
responded immediately, firmly, and generously. McCrea
and Patten first learned of the dismissal when Nearing
showed them Smith's letter, and they each issued statements
condemning a decision "as unexpected as it is unwelcome,"
giving Nearing's "exceptional value to the University." [28]
The Progressive members of the Wharton School nucleus
quickly mimeographed a summary of the facts of the case
and sent it to 1500 newspapers, journals, and academicians.
The chairman of the political science department urged the
alumni and the general public to wage a protest campaign.
Edward Mead, who taught finance, organized a faculty
drive that guaranteed Nearing's salary for the coming year.
A geographer praised Nearing in the most glowing terms a
racist nation could conceive, describing him as "one of the
. . . whitest fellows I know." Edward P. Cheyney, an historian whose recent speech before the graduate school alumni
had been censored in the official University journal, wrote
that freedom was "endangered" and proposed great faculty
control over appointments.[29]

Even conservatives were aroused because, as one Wharton School professor observed, "the moment Nearing went,
any conservative statement became but the spoken word of
a 'kept' professor." The chairman of the English department exclaimed, "Gentlemen do not do such things"; and
Lightner Witmer, a clinical psychologist who had regularly
argued politics with Nearing in the faculty club, was so
shocked that he attacked the dismissal in a series of newspaper articles later included in his anthology on *The Nearing
Case*. Even the Wharton School Association, an alumni
group, protested the scuttling of the school's distinguished
graduate; although thirty-three other Penn alumni ran

truer to form in charging that Nearing's "intemperate . . . expression of untested theories . . . passed the most generous bounds of freedom of speech allowed by any institution." [30]

Nearing's most resolute and articulate champion turned out to be a Philadelphian, Harrison S. Morris. A former editor of *Lippincott's* magazine, a former managing director of the Pennsylvania Academy of Fine Arts, Morris was also the executor of the estate of his father-in-law, Joseph Wharton. He lavished praise upon Nearing for his personal and intellectual contributions to a University lamentably "supported by great sums of money appropriated by our corrupt legislatures." Under his direction hundreds of letters and telegrams unsuccessfully urged Governor Brumbaugh to veto the $1 million appropriation to the University. But Morris did not propose to undertake a private substitute for a corrupt legislature: the Wharton estate had considered a $1 million donation to the building fund of the business school, "but it would hardly be given under the present management." [31] The class discipline of the Philadelphians was imperfect.

More circumspect in protesting the expulsion was Lindsay, who was then teaching at Columbia University. When Patten wrote him that a fight was difficult because "the enemy are [*sic*] away in their summer homes out of reach," the sociologist stoutly replied: "We must put the Provost on record. If he supports the action of the trustees we must demand and secure his resignation, or if he fights with us we ought to make a direct and persistent attack on Randal Morgan and . . . other trustees upon whom we fix the most direct responsibility." With proper pressure from alumni, Lindsay confidently predicted, "we can drive two or three of those trustees off the board and get some men in their places who will be of some use to the University." And to another of Nearing's mentors he called the dismissal "the best rallying point that we shall probably have in a generation." [32]

Lindsay, Witmer, and Clyde L. King of the Wharton School planned a mass meeting of alumni to follow the University's opening exercises on September 24. Without specifically endorsing Nearing's behavior, they intended to repudiate the Gates committee report and the editorials in the *Alumni Register*. Although the meeting was aborted, undergraduates campaigned for Nearing's reinstatement when classes resumed. Placards blossomed, and in one day 876 students signed a petition, despite a low-keyed approach "in order to prevent any distraction from class work and in order to avoid the disadvantageous publicity which might come to the University." The senior who spearheaded the campaign promised to raise the ante of signatures at any time; and eventually about 1500 students, including the captain of the 1914 football team, cauterized the "reactionary attitude of our board of trustees." [33]

Some of this pressure annoyed George Wharton Pepper, who wanted to read the mail of Nearing's students to other trustees: "The letters of protest that are coming to me . . . throw a good deal of light upon the character of the instruction that they have been receiving." He suspected that "by unconscious imitation they have acquired a controversial method that is as discreditable as it is ineffective." The textbook that Nearing co-authored nevertheless continued to be assigned at the Wharton School, and the librarian reported that student demand for Nearing's other writings was more brisk than ever.[34]

England's *New Statesman* detected "a remarkable rally to the side of the dismissed professor" and called the expulsion "the principal topic of discussion among academic circles all over America." Fifteen Columbia graduate students, including Paul H. Douglas, released an open letter asking the trustees for a public explanation of the dismissal. But academic opinion was not unanimous. Syracuse Chancellor James R. Day, who had fired the labor economist John R. Commons in 1899, regretted that Nearing did not leave with a whimper: "It is a serious reflection upon the honesty and manliness of any man to kick up a rumpus and to appeal to the sympathy of the public." [35]

The city's Central Labor Union called the board's action "un-American"; and Philadelphia's Director of Public Works, Morris L. Cooke, a stalwart Progressive, attributed the dismissal to such brave acts as "his discussion of working men's budgets, given . . . before the industrial relations commission. . . . To display such facts in a convincing manner makes one the mortal enemy of those who are still living in the dark night where working men's compensation, child labor, and minimum wage legislation are still opposed." The chairman of the commission, Frank P. Walsh, and the A.F. of L.'s Samuel Gompers, who was twice prohibited from speaking on the Penn campus, joined the protest.[36]

Gompers also served as first vice-president of the National Civic Federation, an organization of business and labor leaders seeking to resolve industrial conflict. On one issue at least, its secretary, Ralph M. Easley, disagreed with Gompers, and asserted that Nearing "should have been kicked out of the University long before this." The economist's piece in the March issue of the *International Socialist Review* was the coup de grâce: "There will be no trouble to prove that Scott Nearing is a socialist and a man whose utterances . . . make him unworthy of being connected with . . . the University." Trustee John C. Bell agreed with Easley and called the ex-assistant professor "undesirable, not to say intolerable." [37]

The *International Socialist Review* caught "the fine hand of the propertied interests" throttling Nearing, because "college youths, university professors, trade unionists and rebels of every hue alike widened their horizon by reading his works." The *People,* the official organ of the Socialist Labor party, also praised Nearing for his "many books which have furnished the Socialists with ammunition against capitalist control of industry. While not a Socialist, he is distinctly 'radical.' " Upton Sinclair professed to see a blessing in disguise. "You do not belong in a university," he wrote Nearing in an open letter. "You belong with us Socialists and free lances. . . . Instead of addressing small audiences of college boys, you will be able to address large audiences of men." [38] The *Masses,* which the masses did not read, printed a masque in which Nearing and various trustees, professors, coeds, freshmen, and sprites demonstrated the inanity of the higher learning in America. One pedagogue describes his campus as "but a seat of learning,/And no place for message burning;/Flame and ardor, inspiration,/Here give way to Education." [39] The editors of the *New Republic,* whom Penn's *Alumni Register* deprecated as "a few ardent young men in New York," called the case "an issue between interested policy and accurate, technical fact . . . a case of old tradition against new science, the prejudiced guesses of corporation officials against the data of a scientific" economist.[40]

The New York *Evening Sun* directly contradicted the new liberal journal and defended the expulsion: "The University of Pennsylvania . . . still prefers cold truth to impassioned guesswork." And, like Chancellor Day, the newspaper called Nearing's "insistence upon preaching heresy in the home of orthodoxy . . . neither honorable nor manly." The Philadelphia *Evening Bulletin* also approved the trustees' decision, while the *North American* praised Nearing for "having earned the bitter enmity of the grundies and their allies by his scientific exposure of the exploitation of the young." Although Van Valkenburg's newspaper found the economist "singularly independent in thought" and "a tireless worker," the New York *Times* registered its disdain for Nearing by comparing him to "some young crank [trying] . . . to rewrite the constitution of the universe. Pretending to work against social injustice, these cub professors are too often engaged in preaching the doctrine of laziness." The editorial writer obviously had not read Nearing's strictures against the leisure class. The *Times* urged dissatisfied teachers of "raw and false doctrines" not to work for reform from within but to establish new universities and "then make a requisition on the padded cells of bedlam for their teaching staff." [41]

No wonder that *Survey* magazine yielded to hyperbole in describing Nearing as "the Dred Scott of the teaching profession. . . . The trustees received in the press and elsewhere a condemnation perhaps never before equalled in amount or geographic extent." The *Times* found itself heavily outnumbered in claiming that Nearing's transformation into "a martyr of 'academic freedom' is grotesque," a doctrine that denoted "freedom to cheapen the reputation of the university and repel students. Academic freedom!" The principle that freedom of speech is as applicable to teachers as to other citizens constituted the vantage point of many of Nearing's defenders, but by 1915 the idea had scarcely been developed, its ramifications explored, or its limits clarified. Scott Nearing's sudden expulsion helped to establish and to extend what one trustee privately termed "unwholesome doctrine." [42]

IN GERMANY, IN THE NINETEENTH CENTURY, ACADEMIC FREE-dom meant both *Lernfreiheit,* the right of fairly unrestricted study, and *Lehrfreiheit,* the freedom of teachers to pursue and proclaim the truth. In America, once the elective system was commonly adopted, the former generally ceased to generate controversy, at least until its revival as "student power" in the 1960's. *Lehrfreiheit* became identified with the canonization of the scientific method and with the professionalization of academic disciplines. Teachers were expected to be disinterested in their quest for truth and in the promulgation of their findings; and immunity from ecclesiastical, political, or economic authority would help achieve the neutrality necessary to elicit appropriate facts and values. Conditional upon the intellectual standards within a discipline and applicable to only one class of citizens, *Lehrfreiheit* has been defined as "a special, not a general or universal right; it is a right that must be earned." [43]

It was also a right that, early in the twentieth century, was barely recognized. Except for fraud, bad faith, or statutes to the contrary, trustees and regents could dismiss professors for any reason whatsoever. In *Ward* v. *Regents of Kansas State Agricultural College* (1905), a United States Court of Appeals denied both a contractual defense and positive features of common law to professors, who were thrown upon the mercy of nonprofessional governing boards. The consequences were often melancholy, as when the president of Brown University was fired in 1897 after advocating the remonetization of silver. Because the widow of the founder of the university disliked his economic views, Edward A. Ross was forced to leave Stanford in 1900. Because he concluded that secession from the Union was wrong, an historian was fired from the University of Florida in 1911. Because he suggested wider latitude in Sabbath observance and church attendance, an economist was expelled in 1913 from Wesleyan, where he had taught for twenty years.[44]

Though these cases were merely a sample, near misses also indicated the fragility of *Lehrfreiheit*. Because of his defense of strikes and boycotts, Ross's teacher Richard T. Ely was nearly fired from the University of Wisconsin in 1894. Because of his criticism of lynching and his categorization of Booker T. Washington as the greatest Southerner —except for Lee—in a century, an historian barely escaped dismissal from Trinity College in North Carolina. Some teachers were able to publish without perishing, such as Veblen, who camouflaged his heresies in polysyllabic obfuscation. And dismissal for heterodoxy in one college often meant appointment as a defender of the faith elsewhere; here the West provided a safety valve for some reformers. When Marietta College in Ohio sacked a supporter of William Jennings Bryan in 1896, a vacancy materialized at the University of Missouri, whose president wanted to dismiss a "gold bug" professor. When Populists and Democrats won political victories in Kansas that year, they purged the state agricultural college of their foes; but in 1899 a Republican triumph eliminated Populists from the presidency and from chairs of economics and political science.[45] Generally silence was as advisable in the academic world as its equivalent of *omerta* would become in the underworld; professorial prudence undoubtedly kept the list of dismissals from growing inordinately.

What one historian called "the most famous breach of academic freedom" during this period helped establish its theoretical foundations, for the Nearing controversy spurred the attempt to define the proper role and rights of the teacher. When Pepper announced that the trustees were no more obligated to justify Nearing's removal than in firing his own secretary, professors expressed preference for a judicial analogy.[46] Appointed judges are supposed to be independent and secure in their tenure, given good behavior, and not required to mirror the opinions of the executives who have appointed them. Liberals claimed that, unlike editorial writers or military officers, professors are not institutional representatives and must be free to act according to their own intellectual lights.[47]

Nearing's defenders could not praise his neutrality while

keeping a straight face; for although he did not propagandize within the echo chamber of his classroom, he scarcely upheld a cloistered ideal of scholarship. Because printer's ink had been spilled so often upon the white smock of the researcher, his champions concentrated instead upon the method of removal: the vagueness of the charges against him, the uncertainty of the evidence, the absence of a hearing, the secrecy of the proceedings, the repudiation of the faculty recommendation, the curt dismissal which short-circuited opportunities to find a position elsewhere. Quondam colleagues like Cheyney could deplore Nearing's rudeness and radicalism and still insist upon fair play, and others cared less about what Nearing said than about how the board stopped him from saying it.[48] The ways in which the fight for academic freedom intertwined with formulations of appointment, dismissal, and tenure help substantiate the generalization of the legal historian Henry Maine that "substantive law has at first the look of being gradually secreted in the interstices of procedures."

The agency that plucked genuine standards from the interstices of procedure was the American Association of University Professors, which a couple of philosophers instigated half a year before Nearing's expulsion. In institutional terms then, John Dewey and Arthur O. Lovejoy invented academic freedom; although the shambling Columbia professor endangered his credentials as a prophet by asserting that violations of *Lehrfreiheit* were "too rare to even suggest the formation of an association." In his presidential address a year later, Dewey hoped that the AAUP would manage to assume projects other than investigating violations of academic freedom.[49]

Not all of the distraction was due to the University of Pennsylvania, for eleven cases were reported in the first year of the AAUP and twenty in the second. The task of examining charges of infringement fell to Committee A, the

Committee on Academic Freedom and Tenure, which spent most of its time evaluating the causes of friction between a teacher and his dean or president. Its chairman in 1915 was E. R. A. Seligman, an economist from Columbia University. A peculiarity of American intellectual history is that Seligman was the first economist to expound a materialist theory of development that emphasized economic causation, not because he was a Marxian socialist, but because he was "the shrewdest defender of capitalism" Nearing ever encountered. They had debated economic questions since 1913, long after Seligman had helped the American Economic Association investigate Ross's removal from Stanford. The suave conservative did not object to a radical teacher, "provided he had the true scientific spirit and expressed himself with moderation"; Seligman looked merely for "the line between the University teacher and the agitator." [50]

Much more discriminating was Arthur O. Lovejoy, who once was asked on an examination whether he believed in God; after rattling off thirty-three different definitions, he inquired which Supreme Being was meant. After Ross's dismissal Lovejoy had resigned from Stanford in protest and later headed a joint committee of the American Philosophical Association and the American Psychological Association to investigate another violation of academic freedom at Lafayette College in 1913.

Dewey did not involve himself in the Nearing case except to acknowledge drily that he had "read some articles in Philadelphia papers which indicated that his views and methods were not liked by all connected with the University." But the secretary of the organization actively participated in the investigation of Nearing's dismissal. "If the Pennsylvania trustees wish to state their reasons for dropping Nearing," Lovejoy wrote Richard Ely, "they can present a fairly effective case. It seems clear that he has been singularly destitute of courtesy, tact, and ordinary common sense in the manner and occasion of his utterances, on other questions as well as upon economic and sociological matters." [51]

The Johns Hopkins philosopher was perhaps too much of a rationalist, however, for the question was not whether the trustees might easily have provided a plausible justification for their decision but whether they had in fact acted upon those reasons. Clyde King of the Wharton School nucleus had asked a trustee why the members of the board "could not make some statement to the effect that Nearing was reckless in his statements, in other words, unscientific. . . . He replied very tersely that they could not do so unless they wanted to stand in the eyes of each other as liars . . . [because] such an argument played no part in the arguments of those who were in favor of his dismissal." [52] Given the reliability of King's informant, the reticence of the board becomes comprehensible, for the trustees could not expose their fear of retribution from Joseph Grundy. Supplied with a million dollars from the taxpayers, the board insisted upon the fiction of privacy because it dreaded the public reaction to the truth.

Therefore the University found it prudent to delay and evade the thrust of the AAUP investigation. When Seligman asked Provost Smith in June for an explanation of the decision, he did nothing but promise that the trustees would consider the letter in October. When Lovejoy became chairman of a subcommittee of Committee A, Penn officials obviously did not rank the group very highly on their own great chain of being. After the board cryptically divulged that the public had "misunderstood" the forthright, highly articulate assistant professor, the Lovejoy subcommittee pertinaciously asked Smith and the trustees to clarify their decision and to explain their general procedures. The provost declined comment on Nearing; the board declined comment, period. [53]

Individual trustees were nevertheless free to answer fourteen questions which the subcommittee submitted, but only
three board members chose to respond in any way to the
AAUP. One was Pepper, who could "not recall any instance
in which . . . [Nearing] had gone beyond the limit of fair
comment—except, perhaps, a statement that anybody living
on the income of invested wealth is necessarily a social menace. Whether he actually said this I do not know." Hastily
disclaiming "authority to speak for the board," Pepper presented Lovejoy with a fading and out-of-focus snapshot as a
substitute for an official portrait of the board.[54]

After the trustees met again in December, they informed
the investigative subcommittee that further clarification of
the case would be superfluous. In May, almost a year after
Nearing was dismissed, the AAUP issued a report over the
signatures of Lovejoy, Davis R. Dewey of MIT, Henry
Farnam of Yale, Franklin H. Giddings of Columbia, and
Roscoe Pound of the Harvard Law School. A dissident
academic had failed to beat the system; now some distinguished professors sought to change it. Their fifty-seven-
page report attempted to answer three questions:

1. Was the character of Dr. Nearing's social or economic teachings the cause, or a contributory cause, of the discontinuance of
his appointment?
2. Was the procedure followed . . . such as to afford him an opportunity to present evidence concerning the correctness of any
charges or complaints made against him; and, in general, was it
such as to provide a judicial hearing, before the board of trustees
or any other body?
3. Were the grounds of the action taken . . . approved by, or
submitted for report to, his professional colleagues or the faculty,
especially those in his own and cognate departments?[55]

The AAUP subcommittee recognized the force of the
alumni drive to remove Nearing and concluded that his
teachings had deterred his promotion and prevented the

renewal of his contract. The committee rebuked the board of trustees for its indifference to due process. Its strongest criticism, however, was reserved for the board's repudiation of the acclaim of Nearing's colleagues. In an era in which university boards of trustees had become almost identical with corporate boards of directors, the Lovejoy subcommittee came close to questioning the legitimacy of trustees who "are neither teachers nor economists by profession, and . . . being busy men of large affairs, are not intimately acquainted with the daily work of the University or the man concerned." Only in exceptional cases, and upon presentation of cogent justification, could "lay intervention in what is essentially a professional question" be defended.[56]

While claiming that it had contemplated reform even before accumulating a volume of adverse newspaper clippings, the board announced a few new procedures in late December 1915. Nearing's legacy to the University included three-year, instead of annual, appointments to the rank of assistant professor and notices of dismissal at least one year in advance instead of on-the-spot. A more formal procedure of faculty recommendation was also promulgated and greater faculty involvement in making the final decision promised.[57]

The *Outlook* praised the trustees' new policy and predicted that other colleges would follow suit. The *Nation* agreed: having "frankly admitted its fault in the Nearing case," the board then affirmed "the principle that the teaching force has a right to be heard in case of the dismissal of one of its members." Lovejoy called the reforms "a notable step in the right direction" and credited not only the efforts of Penn professors but also "the weapon of publicity." [58] The subcommittee that he directed was more criticial, in part because dismissal procedures were not required to be "judicial in spirit and method," more so because final determination of professional competence was still to be shared with nonacademics. The AAUP suggested that only "the representatives of the science in which the teacher affected is a specialist" could ascertain qualifications for promotion or retention.[59] Even after the December reforms, the trustees possessed the instruments with which to scuttle Nearing; as Lovejoy realized when he first investigated the case, the trustees need only have acted more prudently.

Charles Beard had scored the AAUP as "a futile enterprise," but the Nearing controversy helped it to formulate principles and procedures by which alleged violations of academic freedom could be judged. By 1922 even the Association of American Colleges, whose members were trustees and administrators, accepted the definition of academic freedom that the AAUP enunciated in 1916.[60]

But belated consensus was no immediate consolation to Nearing himself. The AAUP's concern for procedural safeguards in walking the plank was a slow way to rescue anyone who had been summarily thrown overboard; and on this occasion, at least, no one could charge that resuscitation efforts had been prematurely abandoned. The organization defined itself as a vanguard representing and enlightening academics but constricted its tactical flexibility for the sake of respectability. Although Lovejoy acknowledged the advantages of publicity in the Nearing case, the group did not disseminate a blacklist of errant institutions until 1938; and its 1940 revision of principles advised against the introduction of controversial material, even when related to the subject of the course.[61]

Nor was the association inclined to confront the apparent anomaly of upper-class control of private universities, or to examine whether its own requirement of professional decorum trammeled inquiry or masked authentic violations of rights. When the lights went out in America as well as in Sir Edward Grey's Europe, Dewey, Lovejoy, and other professors agreed to sell a war that Scott Nearing could not buy;

and the ideals of objectivity and neutrality were shamelessly jettisoned. Then dissenters like Nearing would find the AAUP no help at all.

ABOVE THE MELEE OF THE SUMMER AND FALL OF 1915 WAS Scott Nearing himself. Rather than conspicuously rebelling against his fate, he exuded the quietude of a storm-center. While the *Literary Digest* was calculating the progress of "the biggest fight for academic freedom yet launched in an American university," the magazine noted in passing that "Dr. Nearing is still silent." [62]

Privately he was not listless, urging the Socialist Rose Pastor Stokes to help publicize the case, emphasizing the conflict "between plutocracy and democracy in university control." [63] But publicly he was as mute as a trustee, because "until the University alleged something, there was nothing I could answer." Nor did he cite Grundy's power play in Harrisburg because the rumor, however plausible, "wasn't documented." Yet he never asked the board for an explanation of its decision, nor did he himself summon the assistance of the American Association of University Professors. He doubted whether it would ever "be good taste for me to discuss the University of Pennsylvania." [64]

That summer he disappeared into the forests of Arden, surfacing to lecture on economics before the Chautauqua Society and to collaborate on a civics textbook for rural schoolchildren with a YWCA field secretary. But his isolation from the academic freedom capaign could not resolve his dilemma: remaining in Philadelphia jeopardized his chances for a teaching position elsewhere, but taking another job undermined the struggle to renew his contract.[65]

By the end of the summer Nearing recognized the futility of reversing a decision that, however unjust, was perfectly legal. Lindsay was "particularly anxious that he receive a flattering call for service elsewhere that may serve as a recognition of his excellent teaching ability as well as a rebuke to those who have been so anxious to cast him aside." An attractive position would absorb the shock of exile and would end the affair with some grace; a worse position than the Wharton School provided would confirm the trustees' devaluation. Nearing preferred "one of the smaller colleges, away from the big centres. It would give me breathing space." Morris L. Cooke and Louis D. Brandeis reportedly tried to place him at Amherst, but without success; and when the board's October meeting amplified its June decision, Nearing accepted an offer from Toledo University.[66]

The months immediately following the provost's note were filled with hesitancy, as he stood poised between two visions of the society he sought to create. After Morris Run, Nearing had sufficiently sensed the power and privileges of the wealthy that he advocated the gradual establishment of "industrial democracy." After the University of Pennsylvania he never underestimated the tentacles of the "plutocracy," and he felt the magnetic force of socialism. Until he accidentally achieved prominence at the age of thirty-one, Nearing had fused curiosity with moral passion and identified himself with the most idealistic energies of Progressivism. As the reform movement waned, however, he preserved his idealism; but it was encrusted with scar tissue, the consequence of expulsion from an institution that he had loyally served.

Nearing left Philadelphia during a winter of local elections. Mayor Blankenburg, feeling intimations of mortality, had declined renomination; and his chosen substitute lost all but six wards to a cog in the Penrose machine. The jaded editor of the *North American* then pronounced a brief valedictory for his erstwhile ally and, perhaps, for Nearing's Progressivism as well: "While no one ever questioned the integrity, the sincerity, and the lofty patriotism of Mayor Blankenburg . . . his lamentable lack of political common sense and his utter incapacity to compel cooperation . . . from hostile councils . . .—these were the things that broke him down." [67]

CHAPTER THREE

THE MAKING OF A RADICAL

"**S**OME DAMNED FOOLISH THING IN THE Balkans" was Bismarck's prediction of the genesis of a major European war. A revolution can be ignited on a tennis court or in a beer hall or with a "tea party." A war can begin when an archduke's driver takes a wrong turn in the steaming city of Sarajevo and stops in front of a would-be assassin who is about to go home. Without grandeur the trivial can explode into the consequential.

One American with a prognostic gift was Benjamin Huebsch, who told Nearing in 1913 that a major European war was imminent and that America would reverberate with its effects. Nearing and his liberal friends took the publisher's "counsel very seriously. I mean none of us could go scot-free if we continued the things that we were doing. . . . It was a calculated risk." [1] The next year the reports of the slaughter in Europe deepened his revulsion at the horror and brutality of war, and he began to denounce the conflict and then to propose the systematic alternative of socialism.

Every seat was taken in the autumn of 1915 when Nearing debated in favor of socialism at the Brooklyn Academy of Music. He "was most carefully scrutinized," the New York *Sun* observed. "Nearing was a well set up young man, of quick and nervous gestures . . . blond of complexion, with thin, very light brown hair, light blue eyes that sometimes brooded, sometimes gleamed with earnestness. . . . He spoke with a big voice and with many gestures." Receiving "the biggest hand of the night . . . he had to wave his calming right arm several times before the audience would stop its applause." That evening he declared socialism inevitable. Two weeks later, speaking as a free lance in Haverford, Pennsylvania, he described "two kinds of 'bums,' the kind that loafs around city parks in ragged clothing and gets arrested for vagrancy, and the kind that rides in 8-cylinder automobiles." Nearing proposed putting "the 'automobile bum' . . . to work on county farms on a diet of thin soups. They would at least be earning their own keep." [2]

Shortly thereafter Nearing and his family moved to Toledo. Born a year after its new recruit from Philadelphia, the municipal university was among the first to be established in America, although Nearing regarded it warily as "the scene of a bitter factional quarrel; it is more or less in politics." Strife was so rampant that its president could not enter his office in 1914; a carpenter had changed the lock and a policeman blocked the door. The victor of this coup d'état was A. Monroe Stowe, who followed the advice of Dr. John S. Pyle, one of the nine directors of the institution, and hired Nearing as professor of economics and sociology and—in an inspired piece of casting—as dean of the college of arts and sciences.[3]

Two distinguished Progressives, Sam "Golden Rule" Jones and Brand Whitlock, had governed Toledo more effectively than Blankenburg had served Philadelphia; and the Central Labor Union dominated the University's board of directors by the margin of one vote. Pyle, for example, was a Socialist. "We had an exceptionally nice student body," Nearing fondly recalled; classes were small, and relations between students and teachers intimate. Nearing taught everyone from freshmen to graduate students while fulfilling the duties of a dean, but he could not refrain from comment on civic and international affairs.[4]

"When I find a church in Toledo that preaches Christianity," Nearing told an audience in Chautauqua, New York, "I will attend that church." At least one infuriated minister parried confidently that, out of the more than 140 churches in the city, "there are a dozen pulpits in Toledo where Christianity has been preached."[5] When Nearing told a Cincinnati meeting that "freedom and justice for all, as recited by innocent children, is humbug," the Anthony Wayne chapter of the Sons of the American Revolution denounced his remarks as "utterly repugnant to the intelligent, loyal, and patriotic people of Toledo." When Nearing announced that "the flag belongs to the capitalists," the Grand Army of the Republic wondered why "the City of Toledo would employ a man as a public educator who makes statements which not only humiliate the surviving soldiers of the Civil War, but also insult . . . an emblem of liberty." And the Toledo Real Estate Board launched a campaign to drive Nearing from the University.[6]

Nearing's fear of war flung him increasingly into the maelstrom of controversy. When American investors in Mexico demanded military intervention against the government of Victoriano Huerta, Nearing raised an alarm and reported that the New York *Times* knew of business pressure to send the Marines. In turn the newspaper complained that the "reckless and libelous" dean could not "make a speech without incorporating in it false and foolish statements . . . greedily swallowing . . . every slander that was attractive to his omnivorous and undiscriminating ap-

petite." Because he considered military preparedness an un-
debatable topic, ex-President Roosevelt refused Nearing's
challenge to share a podium in Detroit. Undeterred, the
economist became program chairman of the City Council's
Committee of Public Forums in order to galvanize public
opinion. Such a role did not apparently compel him to with-
draw into a studied neutrality. "There is more danger to national integrity in the $10-a-week wage than in the Kaiser's
army," he calculated, while insinuating that President Wilson "is for preparedness because he is a tool of the U.S.
Steel Corporation." [7]

Nearing's denunciation of poverty as the matrix of "sin,
trouble, and crime," coupled with his demands for ampler
rewards for toilers, made him considerably more popular
with the Central Labor Union than with, say, the Toledo
Real Estate Board. When the economist's contract came up
for renewal late in the spring of 1916, a member of the
machinists' local warned that "the owning class is leading
every effort to drive Professor Nearing out of the University" and suggested that, if fired, Nearing should become a
local labor organizer. But fears that the dean would be eliminated in the guise of an economy move proved un-
founded, though President Stowe felt obliged to complain
that "so many people confuse social science with socialism.
Dr. Nearing is not a member of the Socialist party." [8]

When war threatened more ominously early in 1917, the
conflict between interventionists and pacifists became more
frenetic. In February more than a thousand citizens heard
Nearing deny the possibility of "a sufficient provocation for
war" and proclaim: "We need protection, but not against
Berlin, or London, or Paris, or Petrograd, but against Wall
Street." Referring to the Ludlow massacre of the families of
striking miners in 1914, the principal speaker criticized a
double standard: "One American is killed on the high seas
and we go wild about it. But when American soldiers

burned women and children in their tents in Colorado, was that not a stain on Americanism?" [9]

When the publication of Arthur Zimmermann's telegram drew the nation to the brink of war, an even larger peace rally was organized under Nearing's direction. Charles E. Ruthenberg, a Cleveland Socialist, called for fair play: "This President has put the foulest blot on his record by making public, to influence Congress, the German plot with Mexico and Japan." Nearing was more philosophical, reaffirming the right embedded in the Declaration of Independence to overthrow an unrepresentative government.[10]

Four days later more than two hundred professional and business men welcomed to the Commerce Club the members of the local cavalry troop from service in Mexico. Six speakers denounced pacifists in general and Scott Nearing in particular. Among them was a pugnacious priest named Patrick O'Brien: "God forgive me, men, if it is un-Christian, but I feel tonight like taking him by the nape of the neck and hanging him to the nearest tree." The guests yelled back, "Good for you, father," stood on their chairs, waved menus and napkins, and cheered for several minutes. O'Brien anticlimactically challenged Nearing to a debate; when he subsequently accepted, the priest withdrew the offer. Amidst the patriotic frenzy, a Protestant minister reminded the audience of the value of the First Amendment: "A dog always barks before it attacks, and we are thankful for that now, because we can tell what our traitorous brethren are planning. . . . We must be thankful for the free press. It has served its purpose well in this crisis." [11]

Faced with a mounting attack upon his deepest convictions, Nearing offered to resign whenever the University's board of directors considered his service detrimental to the institution. Local Socialists buoyed him by circulating petitions calling for his retention and by bringing Congressman Meyer London to town to praise this "great man who fights in American universities for the principles of socialism and social justice." Although the Toledo *News-Bee, Blade,* and *Times* called Nearing's pacifism a danger to the community and urged the immediate acceptance of his resignation, every labor organization supported the professor whom the *Union-Leader* labeled "the idol of the workers." He was equally popular with students, who conducted more than twenty street meetings and collected more than 1500 signatures for petitions in his behalf. On April 11, five days after the Congressional declaration of war, the board of directors voted by a 5–4 margin to reject Nearing's conditional resignation.[12]

Six days later, however, the board reconsidered. Two of Nearing's supporters, a former president of the Central Labor Union and a lawyer who described Nearing's fault as excessive adherence to the Sermon on the Mount, inexplicably failed to attend the directors' meeting. By a 4–3 vote, the board thereupon ousted Nearing from the University, demonstrating that a representative board could exclude a dissident from its institution as readily as a self-perpetuating body of aristocrats.[13] And against a democratic decision there could be no appeal to popular retribution; against the board's formal correctness the AAUP was helpless.

Over a decade after he had determined upon the vocation of teacher, Nearing was forced out of conventional academic life, to which he grew so hostile that he eventually exulted in his pariah status. Soon after resigning from Toledo University, he published the first statistical analysis of the governing boards of educational institutions. Studying the occupations of the trustees of 143 colleges and universities enrolling over 500 students, Nearing concluded that America supported a system of "plutocratized education." [14] Nearing's article in *School and Society* was his last technical contribution to the discipline of economics, for the golden retriever of statistics on wages and income decided to follow the spoor of the oligarchy in politics as well. But his letter of resignation revealed a more immediate commitment to the extirpation of militarism, "the madness of the past, dragging us down and destroying us." Nearing counted himself among "those who are willing to overcome evil with good" in order to achieve "the full promise of manhood." [15]

THE MOVEMENT TO KEEP AMERICA OUT OF THE WAR WAS NOT confined to isolated individuals scattered throughout the cities and hamlets of the nation; it coalesced into several organizations, of which the most conspicuous was the American Union against Militarism. When President Woodrow Wilson had announced a tour of the heartland early in 1916 in order to enlist enthusiasm for a more lavish military budget, three Socialist delegates visited the White House to protest the preparedness campaign. Wilson told them to hire a hall, which is what Meyer London, Morris Hillquit, and James Maurer did; and the AUAM was born.

Beginning with a huge rally in Madison Square Garden, a bevy of orators accompanied by a papier-mâché dinosaur named "Jingo" duplicated the Presidential expedition and denounced the proposals for conscription and increased military expenditures. Boston, Kansas City, Cincinnati, and other cities warmly greeted antimilitarists like Maurer, the president of the Pennsylvania State Federation of Labor; Amos Pinchot, an attorney whom Penrose defeated for the Senate in 1914; Rabbi Stephen S. Wise, formerly Oregon's commissioner of child labor; and Nearing. They all feared the havoc that bombs would wreak on the trajectory of reform movements. The AUAM spent $50,000 in less than two years to prevent American intervention in Europe; but despite the bravura of the "dinosaur campaign," the Congress doubled the size of the army.[16]

When Nearing spoke in St. Louis, a social worker named Roger N. Baldwin heard him for the first time and remembered the Toledo dean's "very sharp and didactic and positive way of expressing himself in an almost strident voice." His speech was "couched in such simple and forceful language that it really made quite an impression on the audience. . . . His voice just rang with not only conviction but almost self-righteousness." Baldwin, who was then the local representative of the AUAM, contrasted Nearing with Maurer, a "pleasant man who made fun of things, and . . . had the audience in stitches. . . . But [in Nearing] there was always that ring of self-confidence and assertiveness. . . . It's not hard to feel that he was almost a religious figure, almost a preacher." [17]

Nonetheless the social workers and religious pacifists who dominated the organization did not underscore Nearing's desire to merge antiwar activism with drastic economic reform; and although he served on the AUAM's executive committee and its committee on Constitutional rights, he exerted little influence. Nor did he share the faith of other members in the President's impulse to promote liberal reform at home while avoiding trench warfare in Europe. Confidence in Wilson's good intentions crippled the AUAM and dissipated its antiwar drive in 1917. In February ex-Secretary of State William Jennings Bryan told Lillian D. Wald, the settlement worker who headed the organization, that he would "oppose a declaration of war until the declaration is adopted. . . . My opposition will then end." [18] Such respect for majority rule caused the collapse of the AUAM when the Congress voted to make the world safe for democracy.

As the power of the AUAM waned within the peace movement, another organization emerged in embryo from the First American Conference for Democracy and Terms of Peace, which was held in May 1917. Its founder was

Rebecca Shelley, who had once camped on Henry Ford's doorstep until his wife promised to try to persuade the industrialist to launch a "peace ship" toward Europe in order to negotiate an armistice. Shelley, a leader of the Emergency Peace Federation, proposed the Conference in order to trigger massive endorsement of a "peace without victory," which Wilson articulated in January, and of a peace without annexations and without indemnities, which the Petrograd soviet formulated after the March Revolution in Russia. In the idyllic days before the November Revolution, American and Russian war aims could easily be depicted in identical terms; and hopes were aroused that such unanimity might spike the guns that had blazed so terribly for three years.[19]

But when the various representatives of the Emergency Peace Federation, the American Neutral Conference Committee, the National Conference of Labor, the Woman's Peace Party, and others arrived at Madison Square Garden, they found that the atmospheric pressure had risen since the dinosaur campaign. Policemen surrounded the building; and "on the roofs of buildings facing the Garden," Maurer observed, "were strong searchlights behind which, I was told, were machine guns." Inside the hall the keynote speaker, Rabbi Judah L. Magnes, invited "all Secret Service men . . . to come to the platform so that they may see and hear better." More policemen, sailors, and soldiers were sprinkled through the hall; but athletic Irish volunteers passed hecklers over the heads of members of the audience until they landed outside.[20]

As chairman of the industrial standards committee, Nearing helped shape the economic thinking of the Conference and of its organizing committee. Besides advocating a price freeze and a minimum wage, he adumbrated a style of pacifism which was to be as recognizably his own as his signature: "Our line of attack is not against the war. Our line of attack is not against the present Administration. Our line of attack must be fundamentally against the system of plutocratic oligarchy that dominates the United States and makes war necessary as a consequence." [21] Echoing Nearing's praise of the soviets were Max Eastman and John Reed of the *Masses* and Morris Hillquit, the attorney, tactician, and theoretician who was the triple threat of the Socialist party.

Similar rallies flared concurrently in other cities. The hall in Chicago was so crowded that Congress Street was blocked and the audience overflowed into Grant Park. A school teacher named Berg served on its organizing committee; later, under the name of Michael Borodin, he became the top Soviet agent in China. Nellie Nearing addressed the rally in Toledo, during which at least two scuffles and an arrest occurred. For example, when a bearded partisan announced with an accent, "I am for Mr. Nearing," the *News-Bee* noted with laconic satisfaction that "a swift punch to the jaw put him out of commission." From the New York conference and its provincial imitations emerged more permanent groups modeled upon the workers' and soldiers' soviets. Translated from the Russian as "councils," they comprised the People's Council of America for Democracy and Peace. But the White House refused to acknowledge the peace proposals that the Council sent, and Wilson's secretary did not meet its delegation when it arrived in Washington. [22]

Wilson's discourtesy was mild, however, compared with the repression his administration promoted thereafter. In this connection it has become obligatory for historians to quote Wilson's poignant and perhaps apocryphal remark that the war would inject "the spirit of ruthless brutality . . . into the very fibre of our national life, infecting Congress, the courts, the policeman on the beat, the man in the street." Less familiar is a philosopher's contemporaneous explanation for that spirit: "You cannot expect to incite people to the emotional level at which they willingly give their lives or the lives of their sons, and at the same time have them view with cool magnanimity the indifference or obstructiveness of their neighbors." For employers relishing the chance to quell ostensibly unpatriotic labor agitation, for moral Manicheans asserting their certitudes without shading and their absolutes without complexity, for nativists anxious to strengthen political loyalty and social homogeneity among the approximately one-third of the population that were immigrants or their children, neighbors could be incited in an already more charged atmosphere than in peacetime. A nation that had experienced half a century of comparative security thus tasted what General Erich Ludendorff was the first to call "total war." [23]

IN STEPHEN VINCENT BENET'S "THE DEVIL AND DANIEL Webster," a New Hampshire rustic is forced to confront a jury composed of the seediest characters in American history. But since all of these stranglers, pirates, renegades, and other representatives of our least attractive impulses populated America before the Great War, the diabolically selected venire list should be updated to include the following violators of the spirit of decency:

1) The leader of a Butte, Montana, lynch mob that tortured a crippled labor organizer, and then hanged him from a railroad trestle in 1917.

2) The vigilante chiefly responsible for tarring and feathering a Nebraska citizen whose crime was simply refusal to contribute to the Red Cross.

3) The judge who sentenced Rose Pastor Stokes to ten years in prison for having written in the letters-to-the-editor column of the Kansas City *Star:* "I am for the people,

while the Government is for the profiteers." When her sentence was protested as unjust on the grounds that the editor who had printed Stokes' initial article had not been indicted, President Wilson wanted the editor jailed too.[24]

4) George Creel, the chairman of the Committee on Public Information, formerly a muckraking opponent of child labor, who boasted: "I have procured the suppression of scores of books that, while not pro-German in any degree, have at the same time given false . . . impression of America's war aims." [25]

5) The New York City school administrator who fired a teacher for having conducted in a neutral tone a class discussion on anarchism.

6) The American liaison officer who persuaded the French to circulate *Secret Information Concerning Black Troops,* warning Frenchmen that their "indulgence" and "familiarity" with American Negroes angered the saviors of democracy, that they must not "commend too highly" black soldiers, and then please, please keep their women away.[26]

7) The military guard who, after his associates had tortured to death a member of the Dukhobor sect imprisoned for conscientious objection, put the corpse in a military uniform to present to the widow.

8) Judge Kenesaw Mountain Landis, who tried to trip up pacifists with "What would you do if the Hun were to attack the honor of your daughter?" When a couple of defendants replied that the murder of even a rapist was sinful, Landis cried to a bailiff, "Take them out of the courtroom! These men hold their measly little shriveled souls of more importance than they do the honor of their mother, wife, or daughter." [27]

9) Postmaster General Albert S. Burleson, who withdrew second-class mailing privileges from seventy-five radical organs, including one that criticized labor conditions on his Texas land. "The use of the mails is almost as much a part of free speech as the right to use our tongues," a dissenting Justice Holmes argued in criticism of Burleson's exercise of

power. "To refuse the second-class rate to a newspaper is to make its circulation impossible." Among the targets of suppression were a Robert Browning poem, an issue of the *Nation* that rebuked Gompers, and Thomas Jefferson's statement advocating a republican form of government for Ireland.[28]

10) The vigilante who read aloud, "In the name of the poor women and children of Belgium this man should be whipped," after which numerous lashes were laid on the bare back of a Cincinnati minister affiliated with the People's Council.

11) Walter Douglas, the president of Phelps Dodge Company, who took a leaf from "Tsar" Nearing's book. When his copper miners struck in Bisbee, Arizona, in 1917, Douglas had vigilantes round up over 1200 "slackers" and "Wobblies," hurl them into cattle cars, and dump them into a desert in New Mexico. He was never indicted.

12) The judge who sentenced a movie producer to ten years in prison for showing a film that, in depicting the American Revolution, showed the future imperial ally in a bad light. The case was entitled *United States* v. *The Spirit of '76.*

In such an ambience of malevolence and ignorance, a British visitor told crusading Americans: "It does not seem to me that you have a surplus of democracy here—certainly not enough to warrant exporting any of it." For Nearing, who had assumed that the prewar forums, debates, open-air meetings, and lectures were permanent ornaments of American culture, the blow to free expression struck with special force. In 1917 the Macmillan Company, which had published his works for nine years, removed his name from its list, sold his surplus volumes to another firm, and offered several hundred dollars in lieu of royalties. The summer of 1917 was the last in which the Chautauqua society invited Nearing to teach in its program.[29]

Another shock came in September, when Federal agents swooped down upon his home in Toledo, ostensibly to confiscate antidraft literature in conjunction with another raid upon Wobbly headquarters in the city. Nearing had spent over a decade accumulating the material, which consisted mostly of economic and sociological data in the public domain, and feared that "the agents . . . have undone in a night the work of years. . . . There is something about such an act that savors more of czarism than of our boasted American democracy." Literature was returned a year later, but he had "no idea how much" and decided not to keep records thereafter.[30]

"OVER THERE" BECAME THE REQUIEM MARCH NOT ONLY OF American liberalism but of radicalism as well, but Nearing bucked the rising tide of repressive intolerance by joining the Socialist party in July 1917.

Organized in 1901, the party had become a force to be reckoned with in local elections and a few Congressional races, in several trade unions, and in journalism and social thought. In the decade or so before the war, "a vague terror went over the earth and the word socialism began to be heard," Justice Holmes recalled; and Ambrose Bierce's *Devil's Dictionary* defined grapeshot as "an argument which the future is preparing in answer to the demands of American Socialism." Far more cheerful was the *Appeal to Reason*, one of the world's most popular weeklies, whose serialization of *The Jungle* helped achieve a meat-inspection act: "Socialism is coming. It's coming like a prairie fire and nothing can stop it . . . you can feel it in the air. You can see it in the papers. You can taste it in the price of beef . . . the next few years will give this nation to the Socialist party." [31]

More than two million readers devoured over 300 similar newpapers and magazines. More than a thousand comrades held political office. Socialists helped to found the National Association for the Advancement of Colored People and the International Workers of the World, and in 1912 the Socialist opponent of Samuel Gompers got almost a third of the votes for president of the American Federation of Labor. Chapters of the Inter-collegiate Socialist Society could be found on seventy campuses, and its one-time president was a best-selling novelist who signed his name with a flourish: "Yours for the revolution, Jack London." Walter Lippmann, whom Roosevelt considered "the most brilliant young man of his age," presided over Harvard's Young Socialists and then clerked for the Socialist mayor of Schenectady, where the electrical wizard Charles Steinmetz also held office as a party member.[32] Although Leon Trotsky later gibed that the typical American Socialist was a dentist, a casual organizational structure enabled the party to enroll a pungent variety of characters: urban immigrants and former Populists, workers and intellectuals, sharecroppers and small-town merchants, gradualists ("opportunists") and immediatists ("impossibilists"), free-thinkers defiant in their materialism and clergymen enlisting "the Golden Rule against the Rule of Gold," advocates of dynamite and, yes, practitioners of dentistry. Not even wealth was a disability, as the canny discoverer of radical chic, Mr. Dooley, noticed: "Mrs. Vanderhankerbilk give a musical soree f'r th' ladies iv the' Female Billyonaires Arbeiter Verein. . . . Th' meetin' was addhressed be th' well-known Socialist leader, J. Clarence Lumley, heir to th' Lumley millyons. . . ."[33] And in 1912 Eugene V. Debs attracted nearly a million ballots in a Presidential campaign that siphoned much of the discontent that percolated through American society.

Even Adam and Eve were dissatisfied with Paradise, or at least with an aspect of the conservation policy there; and socialism found adherents because America was considerably east of Eden and certainly less than ideal. But to understand such a society and then to transform it was one of the toughest assignments in the dialectical history of class struggles, for reasons that are now familiar: the paucity of class consciousness; the ideal of individual mobility; the sense of prosperity and relatively high standard of living; the residual ethnic, national, racial, and sectional animosities; the tenacity of religious faith; the inclusion of nearly all white adult males in the suffrage; the tradition of the two-party system; the larcenous behavior of the major parties toward the good ideas of third parties; and the appeal of bread-and-butter trade unionism. Many of these factors Professor Louis Hartz subsumed in *The Liberal Tradition in America,* a tradition so native and so nearly exhaustive as to make our political history unique in its unarticulated major premise in Locke. To oversimplify Professor Hartz's famous argument: because no Loyalist could be a feudal lord, Norman Thomas could not be a President. Yet the liberal tradition, however compelling, could not slake everyone's thirst for justice; and in order to hone the intellectual weapons with which to assault the institutions and *sancta* of capitalism, the Rand School of Social Science was created.

The story of the origins of this school, whose most popular teacher turned out to be Scott Nearing, belongs more to a romantic dime novel than a tract on historical materialism. An elderly widow named Carrie Rand had been so taken by George D. Herron that she presented the radical young Congregationalist minister with an endowed chair at Iowa College. But Herron's brand of Christian Socialism proved too potent for his superiors; and he was hounded from his lecturn and his pulpit, only to fall in love with the daughter of his patroness. The former professor of applied Christianity persevered through the scandal of a divorce to marry her. When his mother-in-law died, Herron and his wife, who was also named Carrie, had to battle other heirs to secure the funds to establish a workers' school in New York. The creation of the Rand School in 1906 was among their last acts before ostracism drove them into exile. Leaving the American Socialist Society to operate the school, they sailed for Italy, where Carrie Rand Herron died seven years later.[34]

Initially designed to provide workers and labor organizers with a systematic comprehension of socialism, the Rand School soon extended itself into a panoply of liberal arts courses and extracurricular activities. Its faculty included few of the custodians of culture who graced the Ivy League colleges; but the Rand School got by, at various times, with Charles A. Beard, Clarence Darrow, John Dewey, Frank Harris, Morris Hillquit, Sidney Hook, Alexander Kerensky, James Harvey Robinson, Bertrand Russell, Gaetano Salvemini, Norman Thomas, and Lester Frank Ward.[35] Yet none of them taught larger classes than Nearing, who first lectured there in 1913, four years before he officially became a Socialist. By 1915 admission cards had to be allocated for his lectures on "The Human Element in Economics," and the school had to hire a nearby high school auditorium in order to provide seating for 1200 students. Yet crowds still had to be turned away, for Nearing was "an uncommonly effective speaker," with a "clear voice and attractive personality," according to Louis Waldman, a Socialist state assemblyman. He communicated not so much through emotional appeals as through the force of factual accumulation, skillfully organized and presented.[36]

The Rand School offered the sort of shelter from persecution that universities no longer provided. The AAUP Committee on Academic Freedom in Wartime accepted the proposition that freedom of expression could be curtailed more fully within the academy than outside, and its Committee on Patriotic Service was formed to facilitate the war effort. Lovejoy wrote that conscientious objectors' "sense of moral and social values has been perverted by an obsession" and that they played "an unpleasantly parasitic part in the history of human progress." The Johns Hopkins philosopher also urged the academy to clean its own house of political undesirables, "whether or not they have already come within the reach of the law." [37] Another member of the subcommittee that investigated Nearing's dismissal, Franklin H. Giddings, blamed pacifists for "doing their best to put civilization back a thousand years." In a debate on freedom in American universities with the chairman of Committee A, Nearing blasted the philanthropic largesse of the Carnegie and Rockefeller Foundations and delineated the plight of the teacher who must "stifle his own conscience, repress what he knows to be right, and knuckle under to the powers above him." But when he pinned on some instructors what the Brooklyn *Times* delicately called "a phrase descriptive of women of the streets," E.R.A. Seligman responded: "I want nothing to do with a man who uses such a phrase. He has no right to demand recognition from any well-meaning individual in this community." [38] The line between the professor and the agitator had been drawn again.

The University of Pennsylvania established the first ordnance school of its kind in the country and released over 200 faculty members for war work. It also released Patten because, as one trustee argued, "it was impossible to deal with the Nearings . . . until you have reckoned with the teacher of the Nearings." After Patten introduced a pacifist academician to a Philadelphia audience prior to the Congressional declaration of war, the board told him to retire at the conclusion of the semester.[39] The decision raised "anew the question of free speech," the venerated economist asserted, "and is akin to the case of Dr. Scott Nearing." But Penn and Toledo were hardly unique in removing teachers for insufficient loyalty; and Amos Pinchot, "knowing how dear to you is the Anglo-Saxon tradition of intellectual freedom," urged Woodrow Wilson to reaffirm its value. But the former professor washed his hands before the multitudes, refusing to make a statement that "would undoubtedly be taken advantage of by those with whom" he was not "in sympathy at all." [40]

The Young Scott Nearing at the University of Pennsylvania
UNIVERSITY OF PENNSYLVANIA ARCHIVES

Yet the Rand School itself could not escape the blast of the Great War. From Italy, of all places, George Herron announced that "there are no neutrals in this war" and condemned Hillquit as "pro-German. . . . Your neutrality or impartiality is a delusion." In the 1916 elections the Socialist party for the first time failed to register an increase, as its Presidential vote plummeted to half a million. In Debs a cast of nobility was imposed upon a common man. Allan Benson, the 1916 nominee and an ardent advocate of a war referendum, was simply a common man, and thus typified much of the shallowness of socialism, American style. Converted to socialism by an encyclopedia article, thrilled by lucrative commissions from the Hearst press, he caused Nearing, who had supported Debs in 1912, to vote for Wilson four years later.[41] Even Eastman and Reed voted for the Democrat; and so did W. E. B. DuBois, not because he shared Tom Watson's eccentric conviction that Wilson was "ravenously fond of the negro," but because Wilson most resonantly expressed ideals of peace and social justice.

But when he no longer kept us out of war, the Socialist party stood firm; and its fidelity to Marx's internationalism marked its virtual uniqueness among the Socialist parties of the world. In a special convention in St. Louis, its members adopted a resolution that Hillquit, Charles E. Ruthenberg, and Algernon Lee of the Rand School had written. The party denounced the Congressional declaration of war as "a crime against the people of the United States," promising that "in support of capitalism, we will not willingly give a single life or a single dollar." [42] This position was consistent with traditional principles but disastrous in its consequences, for the St. Louis Declaration constituted the suicide pact of American socialism.

With the majority of workers convinced that they indeed had a country, the party's trade-union base disintegrated. Even more conspicuous was the exodus of publicists and intellectuals like Sinclair, Algie M. Simons, John Spargo, J. G. Phelps Stokes, and William E. Walling. Allan Benson left the party less than a year after running as its candidate for President. Herron also resigned, horrified that the Rand School had published the St. Louis Declaration without presenting the minority, pro-war resolution. He called Hillquit and Algernon Lee "tragically mistaken . . . [and] taking the course that is destructive to the cause to which you have given your lives. . . . I know I am expressing the mind of her (of her mother also) to whom the destiny of the Rand School was so dear, ere she spread the wings of her flight from this mad and intolerable world." [43]

With the departure of so many writers and propagandists, Nearing's arrival was especially welcome; for he was an important new energy source in a party more anxious to control the printing presses than to control the barricades. At the request of the American Socialist Society, Nearing immediately contributed a couple of pamphlets on war, *The Menace of Militarism* and *The Great Madness,* parts of which were excerpted in the New York *Call* that summer. With doughboys on the way to the Western front, Nearing offered a course in the Rand School on the philosophy of Tolstoy.[44]

He did not then realize how ominously Socialist affiliation might be regarded, or the sinister interpretation that might be grafted onto *The Great Madness.* Although a Justice Department official later denied having paid "any more attention to the Socialist party than we did to the Republican party," leaders of the G.O.P. nevertheless roamed freely by the end of the war, while almost a third of the Socialists' National Executive Committee was behind bars.[45] Part of the reason was the Socialists' intimate association with the cutting edge of radical pacifism, the People's Council of America, an organization that helped drive Nearing so far to the left that he could never again return to liberalism.

CHAPTER FOUR

FOR DEMOCRACY
AND PEACE

"THE DEPLORABLE STATUS CONFRONTING US,"
A. W. Ricker complained in June 1917, "is . . . that we
have so many peace organizations each fathered by some
erratic individual who wants to do things in a certain pre-
scribed way and is wholly lacking in the spirit of cooperation. When you get into the Socialist party," he added, "you
find a bunch of cheap politicians who are afraid of any cooperation lest they lose their political halos." [1]

The publisher's assessment soon needed revision. The Socialists admitted suspicions of traditional pacifists whose indifference to economics therefore implicated them in the
maintenance of capitalism. Most pacifists before the Great
War felt compelled by religious principles to oppose killing
and compliance with the military, but their consciences did
not strike them with similar force against the general authority of the government in economic and social policy.
The connection between military engagement and commercial expansion that Socialists drew either escaped most traditional pacifists or seemed to them irrelevant. Con-

sequently the New York Socialists' *Call, Daily Forward,* and Workmen's Circle emphatically backed only the radical People's Council of America for Democracy and Peace.[2] But the problem the pacifists faced was actually the collapse of its traditional and liberal foundation. Instead of too many recalcitrant groups, too few resisted the drumbeat of war.

Of the thirty-five peace societies active in 1914, almost all either supported the war or disintegrated under the strain. The Carnegie Endowment for International Peace even turned its offices over to the Committee on Public Information. Sometimes withdrawals from the struggle against war were coupled with criticism of remaining militants. Wise, who had promised during the dinosaur campaign never to support war, was working in a naval shipyard more than a year later; and he denounced the People's Council for including "Socialists, not of the parlor or drawing room variety, but of the basement and cellar type." David Starr Jordan, who had agreed to serve as treasurer of the Council, hastily resigned upon discovering the inclusion of "other purposes than those of peace." Emily Greene Balch, an economist and future recipient of the Nobel Peace Prize, nevertheless avoided affiliation with this "Frankenstein of a People's Council" because "protest is such a sterile spirit." Jane Addams was also pleased to have "escaped any special identification" with the Council, which embraced both "fine people with whom one would be glad to cooperate and certain others who are more or less self-seeking." She subsequently lectured under the auspices of the Committee on Public Information and, while criticizing conscription, nevertheless opened Hull House to military recruiters.[3]

But her friend Lillian Wald, and the AUAM which she directed, were most vulnerable to the exigencies of liberal pacifism. The organization prided itself on ties with official Washington: one of its board members, the brother of the President's son-in-law, gave the AUAM a life line into the

White House itself. "I have not for a moment thought that my efforts in the American Union against Militarism were an embarrassment to the country," Wald claimed, "and I have assurances from those most high in authority that our efforts to retain the fundamental rights of our democracy chimed in with the wishes of the President." After the Congressional declaration, she decided to oppose the excesses of militarism and the threat to freedom of expression, not the war itself.[4]

Upon the suggestion of Roger Baldwin, newly arrived from St. Louis, a civil liberties bureau was created within the AUAM; and Baldwin and Crystal Eastman, a labor attorney prominent in the Woman's Peace Party, directed its activities. Reverend Norman Thomas, who had studied under Woodrow Wilson at Princeton, also actively defended the rights of conscientious objectors, including his brother Evan. Baldwin wanted the bureau to split from the AUAM in order to attract pro-war liberals and conservatives to the defense of the Bill of Rights, but Wald wanted to retain control of the new agency. "Mr. Thomas . . . is reasonable and has judgment," she confided to Addams, "but Crystal . . . and Roger Baldwin, much as I like them personally, are more than I can manage single-handed." The chairwoman was outvoted, however, and in September the National Civil Liberties Bureau was created.[5]

That month the People's Council held its constituent assembly, but Wald argued against sending an AUAM delegation because of the Council's reputation for "impulsive radicalism." Again she was overruled, and Baldwin and Thomas were selected to represent the organization. When an interlocking directorate with the People's Council was established, she resigned. The "angel" of New York's Henry Street Settlement subsequently joined three committees of the Council of National Defense and made one of the settlement houses available to the draft board. The symbolism of the AUAM needed revision: not "Jingo" the dinosaur but rather the liberal organization itself was composed of papier-mâché.[6]

"All the people of prominence have deserted," a Seattle secretary of the AUAM lamented. "Only a handful of Socialists and Wobblies left." As she looked at the empty tables where once militant pacifists had sat, Anna Louise Strong, a children's welfare worker whose ancestors touched shore in 1630, realized that " 'our America' was dead! The profiteers, the militarists, the 'interests' had violated her. . . . Nothing . . . so shook the foundations of my soul." The war and the futility of preventing it struck Nearing with equal force, and he irretrievably lost faith in American democracy and American beneficence. He warned Rabbi Judah Magnes that "there will be no more free speech in the U.S. while the economic tyrants hold power. Our 'sweet land of liberty' playing its new role as mistress of 20th century imperialism is very unfamiliar to some of us who thought of her in another way. We must get wise." [7]

Like Hillquit, Maurer, and other Socialists, Nearing concentrated his antiwar activities within the People's Council, although he rejected its offer to become a $600-per-month labor organizer on behalf of peace. Along with Baldwin, Thomas, and Socialist Jacob Panken, Nearing addressed a major rally in Philadelphia in July; but when its local branch protested against mail interference to the President, he confessed to ignorance of the Council.[8] Within a week, however, Wilson had apparently learned enough to call its minions "for the most part a bad and mischievous lot." Other Americans learned still more about what the New York *Times* called "the Kaiser's Council" when it attempted to hold a national peace convention on September 1–6, 1917.[9]

THE COUNCIL'S ORGANIZING COMMITTEE DELEGATED THE task of hiring a hall for the convention to Louis P. Lochner, a feisty publicist from Wisconsin who had helped to launch Ford's "peace ship." Minneapolis was picked as the convention site because of the Socialism of its mayor and police chief. But when the county sheriff predicted that the meeting "would result in bloodshed, rioting, and loss of life," Governor Joseph Burnquist declared halls off-limits, adding that the convention "could only aid enemies of the United States." [10]

Instead of a hall, Lochner hired tents and a 35-acre tract of land on the outskirts of Minneapolis. "At the last moment," Rebecca Shelley reported, "the tent-owner refused to allow the use of the tents, [fearing] . . . that they would be destroyed by patriotic mobs." Lochner and his staff miraculously raised $5000 within three days to purchase the tents, only to recoil as the mayor capitulated to the governor, who threatened to remove him under a new state law designed to intimidate the Socialist official.[11]

The People's Council then tried North Dakota, the hotbed of the Non-Partisan League; but there the political situation was reversed. The governor welcomed the pacifists, but the only town in his state big enough to house them was Fargo, whose militia-led mob had run Max Eastman out of town earlier that summer.[12]

The indefatigable Lochner went to Hudson, Wisconsin, instead. After inquiring about a hall he returned to the lobby of his hotel; there he met a "mob of grim-looking men . . . whose leader carried a heavy rope tied in a noose." Allowed to escape, Lochner and his staff hopped on the next train, which had conveniently waited for them in the station "to make sure they got rid of us." The New York Times, defining ballistics as a branch of politics, explained the motivations of the provincial patriots: "Every pacifist speech is a German bullet. . . . They tell these servants of the German cause that they shall not fire those bullets in Hudson." [13]

To avoid the appearance of a shooting gallery, Wisconsin soon imposed a statewide ban on the People's Council. With Utah's governor already declaring his state off-limits, Lochner appealed for protection to the President and to the Secretary of War. Neither cat replied to the canary, but the police chief of Washington, D.C., squelched rumors by warning that the People's Council would be treated like Coxey's Army if it came within the shadow of the Capitol.[14]

But by then trains carrying the large New York contingent were already churning westward. Joseph Freeman, then a Columbia undergraduate, recalled that "the trip had its personal exhilaration. At last I was out of New York seeing the 'real' America." The uncertain destination of the trains was amusing to the New York *Sun,* whose correspondent heard an order to *"vorwaertsgehen"* and overheard "conferences heavy with German gutterals" between "Herr" Hillquit and those stock characters of antiradical polemic: a "group of short-haired women and long-haired men." The *Sun* guffawed that the caravan might become "the Flying Dutchman of the railroads," but the delegates were spared such a fate when one city in the "real" America offered a haven: Chicago.[15]

Mayor William Hale Thompson would not have loved freedom of speech and assembly so much had he not loved tweaking King George's nose more. But because he was out of town, his police force dispersed the first session of the convention, held in a deserted room of a factory on the edge of the city. Afterwards Thompson returned home to proclaim: "Pacifists are law-abiding citizens. I shall not have it . . . that Chicago denies free speech to anyone." [16]

His honor's attitude alarmed the Chamber of Commerce, which warned Governor Frank O. Lowden that the peace convention would be "antagonistic to our national purposes in the present world crisis." Lowden needed little nudging: "The People's Council is a treasonable conspiracy which must not find refuge under the guarantee of freedom of speech." Also alerted was the State Council of Defense, whose British-born chairman, Samuel Insull, was hardly the sort to allay Nearing's suspicions about the nature of the war. Sailing under the star-spangled banner instead of the more apt jolly roger, the utilities magnate delegated the task of countering pacifist propaganda to a young attorney, Harold L. Ickes. Lowden backed up Ickes by dispatching four companies of militia from Springfield. It was the first time militia had been summoned in Illinois since Debs' American Railway Union had joined the 1894 strike against George Pullman, whose daughter Frank O. Lowden had married.[17]

Taxis swollen with defenders of the city raced through the streets, but that ended the resemblance to the First Battle of the Marne. For the People's Council was in no mood for confrontation. While the Wobblies sitting next to Freeman "grumbled about the 'yellow socialist rats' ready to disperse without a fight," the assembly hurriedly passed resolutions that called for "progressive disarmament of all nations, repeal of the Selective Draft Law by the U.S. Congress, a concrete statement by the Administration of its war aims, and peace without conquest, annexation, or indemnities." And the delegates' final salvo was a pledge "to hold no further meetings in Chicago under present circumstances," as though they had any choice in the matter. A Polish wedding party that had previously scheduled the hall quickly replaced the radicals, and into these festivities Governor Lowden's troops charged.[18]

Thompson's threat to challenge the militia with his own police force did not materialize, and the Council's executive committee disappeared into an expensive hotel suite to escape detection and to complete its agenda. For the position of executive chairman, the committee chose Scott Nearing *in absentia;* he had landed in Minneapolis and never showed up in Chicago. Lochner was chosen executive secretary.[19]

The city council, the governor, and the attorney-general rebuked Thompson for his unpatriotic defense of civil liberties, and the local chapter of the National Security League assessed impeachment tactics. The Society of Veterans of Foreign Wars hanged the mayor in effigy; and "the cheering which broke out when the fat figure was strung up was of such volume that it roused residents of all the hotels facing Michigan Avenue, who had to be assured . . . that it was not an actual lynching," the *Times* reported.[20]

Repercussions of the convention were felt on campuses on both sides of the continent. Because he had been a participant-observer at the convention, Professor Allen Eaton was fired from the University of Oregon. Professor Henry Wadsworth Longfellow Dana was forced out of Columbia because of his involvement with the Council and his opposition to conscription. The dismissal of Dana and others led Beard, although pro-war, to resign in protest against "trustees who have no standing in the world of education, who are reactionary and visionless in politics." The *Times* wished Beard and Dana good riddance and drew a moral from the Nearing case: "Infallible wisdom does not perch upon the back of every chair occupied by a professor. . . . Academic freedom has two sides . . . [for] freedom to teach is correlative to the freedom to dispense with poisonous teaching." [21]

Considered desperadoes rather than legitimate dissenters, members of the People's Council could not successfully appeal for a conscription upon wealth, for a speedy conclusion to the war, for an exact statement of diplomatic aims against which a future peace treaty might be judged. Instead the pacifists were forced to concentrate upon the means, "focusing sentiment of civil liberties and democratic institutions," while the objects of political action got lost in the shuffle of rifles and nooses.[22] Unlike the earlier Abolitionists, whose gravestones and wrecked printing presses slowly aroused Northerners to the evils and disadvantages

of slavery, the pacifists had too little time to make their martyrdom the catalyst in turning swords into plowshares. Civil
liberty was necessary but not sufficient if radical pacifism
was to advance, and the People's Council failed because
what was necessary had become uncommon. The story of
this organization must therefore take the form of autopsy
notes.

WHEN NEARING BECAME CHAIRMAN OF THE COUNCIL, HE
was thirty-four years old, eager and competent to take on "a
thankless job" that "took a lot of time, a lot of energy, and
. . . got me into a peck of trouble." Although Eastman later
dismissed him as "a fanatic" and his "intransigeance" made
Baldwin uncomfortable, Nearing generally commanded the
admiration of those who served with him. He became chairman at the urging of Hillquit and Magnes, who called Nearing "one of the most straightforward, one of the most honest men I know. There can be no mistaking what he says, or
what he means. . . . He has a wonderfully sweet smile
which betokens a gentle heart that knows no rancor."
Lochner described him as a "brilliant, thoroughly honest
fellow . . . one of the most persuasive speakers I ever
heard." Freeman recalled that Nearing's words were always
"crisp and authoritative, like gospel truth" and that his sincerity "moved people even when they least agreed with
him." Paul Douglas, who worked briefly with the People's
Council and later debated Nearing, remembered him as "a
brave fellow. . . . I always had a high opinion of his
courage and basic purpose." A. J. Muste, forced from his
pulpit when the war struck, called Nearing's "outspoken-
ness, the sharpness of his views and . . . fearless eloquence
. . . an inspiration to other anti-militarists, including myself." [23]

"He would not have risen so far had he not been so good-looking," Margaret Mead speculated; the daughter of teachers at Penn, she also remembered Nearing as the first adult she called by his first name. Nor was his ascendancy on the left hurt by his ancestry, which could be traced on both sides of his family to the eighteenth century. Like Thomas, Princeton '05, whose father and grandfather had also been Presbyterian ministers; like Baldwin, Harvard '04, whose family had arrived on the *Mayflower,* Nearing faced few social obstacles. Unlike Hillquit, he never apologized to a Socialist convention "for being born abroad, for being a Jew." [24] And even for the Workmen's Circle of the United Hebrew Trades, the organizational backbone of the People's Council, Nearing's leadership may well have symbolized a blend of the socialist dreams of the Old World with the assimilationist aspirations of the New.

Within the Council itself, Lochner directed a dozen volunteers and paid staffers in the New York office. Neither an absolute pacifist nor much of a Socialist, Lochner was an efficient administrator; and Nearing "rarely interfered with the office . . . [or] staff meetings." He defined his own role as primarily oratorical, for Nearing much preferred to have an audience than a staff. Yet the need for money soon preoccupied him, as if he were a Penn trustee; and he once complained: "It seems a shame for me to be wasting my time raising money. However it must be done." [25] Already in September Lochner worried about "double rent for meeting places . . . [and] double printing expenses." The hurried exit from Chicago had prevented a mass fund-raising affair, nor could a financial angel be located: for purposes of peace, J. Clarence Lumley and Mrs. Vanderhankerbilk turned out to be quite fictional. Nearing himself drew no salary. Trying to reduce an initial debt of $17,000, he first sought donations from local councils, but "terrorization by the police and secret service" dried up this source of revenue.[26] Nearing then asked supporters to send a dollar a month for ten months, and this program helped reduce the debt to about $3000 by October 1918. By then the operating budget of the leading antiwar organization was a little over $700 per month.[27]

How imposing a force the People's Council was is difficult to determine, since the evidence consists mostly of its own fluctuating claims of size and significance. Loosely organized even in its prime, the Council consisted of local branches and affiliated labor unions, single tax societies, peace fellowships, and individuals. Extant records make it difficult to reconstruct the extent to which these groups meshed into a movement. But the secretary's claim that 200 branches were operating in December 1917, and Maurer's calculation of 2,500,000 members in September 1917, must be taken, in Max Beerbohm's phrase, "with a stalactite of salt." [28]

It was enough of a threat, however, to scare Samuel Gompers, who had renounced his professed pacifism to become a member of the Council of National Defense. Afraid that even a tincture of disloyalty would so discredit labor that industries seeking to drive wages down would be able to write a free-wheeling immigration policy, he became a patriotic zealot. Because the People's Council prided itself on working-class support, Gompers did more than denounce its members as "conscious or unconscious agents of the Kaiser." He sought to outflank it with an organization of his own.[29]

The American Alliance for Labor and Democracy was created *ex nihilo* in the office of Ralph Easley, the secretary of the National Civic Federation, with Spargo also a partner in the scheme to outbid the People's Council for labor support. Although Easley provided the first $700, the Committee on Public Information paid for office rent and publicity. Further funding gushed from the President's $100 million "secret fund," about which Gompers was most reticent but which did not prevent him from accusing the Council of taking "immense sums from the government of Germany." He deserves recognition as an early perpetrator of black humor. But when Minneapolis aborted the birth of the People's Council, Gompers wired a protest in behalf of freedom of assembly, because he needed a counterpoint to the Alliance convention scheduled—not quite by coincidence—in St. Paul early in September.[30]

Into the city converged two groups: anti-Socialist trade unionists like Gompers and attorney Frank Walsh, and pro-war exiles from the Socialist party, who had formed the Social Democratic League. What unified them, despite past suspicions, was dependency upon the power and wealth of Creel, who advised Walsh: "The principal resolution should concern itself with the war. Declare it a *war of self-defense*— recite the three years of forbearance that were blood-stained by the brutal aggressions of the Imperial German Government. . . . Save radical resolutions until [the] last day," he added, and "stick close to Gompers." Algie Simons, the former editor of the *International Socialist Review,* was reminded of "one of the first Socialist conventions. All the best brains of the movement are here. There is nothing left in the S. P. worth taking." [31]

Walsh agreed that the "conference was a great success" and predicted that the antiwar radicals "will continue to look cheaper . . . until they finally disappear." But his participation angered Nearing: "You knew about Paterson and Ludlow. You knew who was behind them. You know that these same forces are throttling democracy in America to-day. . . . You are lending them your name and your influence. The plutocrats are using your power to rivet the chains. How can you do it?" [32]

Woodrow Wilson, who had chosen Walsh to head the Commission on Industrial Relations, was delighted with labor loyalty to his Administration. When he addressed the AFL convention in November, the President announced his opposition "not to the feeling of the pacifists, but [to] their stupidity. My heart is with them, but my mind has contempt for them. I want peace, but I know how to get it and they do not." Flanked by a cordon of soldiers, Wilson praised Gompers for knowing "how to pull in harness. The horses that kick over the traces will have to be put in a corral." Within the first six months of operation, the American Alliance for Labor and Democracy had established 150 branches and had distributed nearly two million patriotic pamphlets, mostly inside the pay envelopes of workers.[33]

AGAINST SUCH OPPOSITION NEARING'S PROMISE TO MAKE the People's Council "a clearing house for liberal and radical elements" could not be fulfilled. "We are neither obstructionists nor law breakers," he announced. "We desire to distinguish sharply between the military aspects of the war and its political and economic aspects. It is exclusively with the latter that our work is concerned." The distinction was as elastic as the enunciation of Papal infallibility only in matters of faith and morals, for the People's Council continued to oppose conscription and to call for disarmament. When asked whether his program committed the Council to socialism, the executive chairman replied, rather disingenuously, only that he favored industrial democracy.[34]

Within two weeks of assuming office, Nearing dashed off an *Open Letter to Profiteers*, tactlessly addressed to the New York *Times:* "You and your masters want the war to continue so that ten billions of fabulously profitable war contracts may be given out." A somewhat formal reply came from the Librarian of Congress, who placed the *Open Letter* on the Army Index, thus prohibiting the pamphlet from camp libraries. By the Armistice fewer than a hundred titles had been listed on the Index; the other authors included Henri Barbusse, the late Ambrose Bierce, and G. K. Chesterton.[35]

Meanwhile the Council's landlord, George A. Plimpton, a former trustee of the World Peace Foundation, evicted the notorious tenants from his building. In early October the branch office in Chicago was raided. Later that month Nearing, Maurer, and the Socialist mayoralty candidate, whom one newspaper constantly labeled "the unindicted Mr. Hillquit," spoke at a mass meeting to protest the threatened suppression of the New York *Call*. The next month its second-class mailing privileges were revoked; but Hillquit, running on a platform that did not disavow the St. Louis Declaration, polled 22 percent of the city-wide vote in a frenetic campaign that distracted Socialists from the work of the Council.[36]

Nearing himself served on Hillquit's finance committee while organizing a petition and letter-writing campaign under the rubric of "Peace by Negotiation—Now!" A second national office was opened in Washington, and plans were laid to organize campus chapters of the People's Council.[37] But the stacks of letters and petitions could not paper over internal dissension and dissatisfaction with Nearing's extremism. The civil rights attorney Louis Marshall warned his brother-in-law, Rabbi Magnes, to avoid association with Nearing, Hillquit, and the "half-baked political economists and sociologists" of the People's Council. But Magnes and Hillquit remained Nearing's closest collaborators within the executive committee. Were the government to "put Lochner and me in the coup [*sic*]," the chairman confided to them, "we are counting on you" to prevent moderates from trying to "wreck the whole machine." [38]

Assured of Hillquit's and Magnes's confidence, Nearing embarked on a cross-country tour which would teach him, in Michael DiSalle's *aperçu*, that "the whole United States is just an extension of Toledo." Nearing's first stop was Chicago, where the overflow crowd was deceptively large. Policemen in plain clothes and in uniform mingled among the antimilitarists: and the chief of police and Department of Justice agents were among the platform guests because, upon the acting governor's orders, Insull had informed the police chief to stop the rally in case of sedition. Two companies of the Eleventh Infantry were alerted; but despite the chief speaker's demand to end the war and to let the rich pay for it in any case, the meeting was not dispersed. Towards the end of the evening, however, what was probably a stink bomb routed some of the participants.[39]

Two days later, to insulate against the chilling effect of government stenographers, Nearing decided to make his Duluth meeting a very private affair. Only antimilitarists were to receive passes in the form of cards bearing his name. But the local Department of Justice representative tipped off the police, whose card-carrying stenographer slipped into the back of Woodmen's Hall and recorded the speeches. At the moment when Nearing uttered the phrase "immediate peace," one of fifty policemen who had eased into the hall laid a hand upon the speaker's shoulder and, amidst hoots from the crowd, took him and four companions into a patrol wagon and jail. Afraid that Governor Burnquist's ban on Council meetings was still effective, anxious about his schedule of rallies and caucuses across the continent, Nearing pleaded guilty the next day to a charge of disorderly conduct. He was fined $50.[40]

Then the chairman of the People's Council plunged deeper into the "real" America. In San Francisco, he reported, "the hall for the Tuesday evening meeting was withdrawn Tuesday afternoon. An injunction suit failed to secure any result. The hall for the Wednesday evening meeting was locked by the police Wednesday afternoon." On the next day police raided the local headquarters of the People's Council and transferred the materials to military headquarters nearby. In Pasadena, Upton Sinclair, who favored the war but not repression, claimed that meetings of the People's Council were difficult even in private homes. In Los Angeles, in Salt Lake City, in Colorado Springs, in Denver, in Kansas City, in St. Louis, in Louisville, in Cincinnati, in Detroit, in Milwaukee, in Washington, in Baltimore, meetings were held either in hotel rooms or in private homes.[41] Thus only in Chicago did Nearing conduct a public gathering, but he was probably too busy licking his wounds to appreciate the irony.

The executive chairman blamed the disaster upon "a nation-wide conspiracy among certain organizations which are financed in whole or in part by the big business interests." Behind policemen he saw vigilantes; behind vigilantes he saw oligarchs. Two private organizations were implacable opponents of the People's Council and vowed to track it to its death. One was the American Defense Society, the lengthened shadow of Col. Roosevelt, who called pacifists "sexless creatures," "slackers pure and simple, or else traitorous pro-Germans," and "pink-tea . . . people who like to think of themselves as intellectuals." [42] The National Security League's organizer was S. Stanwood Menken, an arch-conservative who showed some method in what Nearing called "the great madness": "The people must be made to realize that not only is victory essential . . . but that they must understand economic and political questions so as to avoid . . . the errors of the past." The import of "errors" in the Progressive era did not have to be decoded for corporation lawyers like the vice-president of the League, George Wharton Pepper, who also chaired the National Committee of Patriotic and Defense Societies. Easley, another active loyalist, also conveyed the capitalist overtones of patriotism in a pamphlet that alleged that "the Germans simply took

over the methods and the machinery of the I.W.W.'s." [43]
The thesis of Easley's *Sabotage* might have raised a few eye-
brows in the *Generalstab* in Berlin.

Since a field secretary for the National Security League
proposed "the firing squad just before dawn" for "men of
Scott Nearing's ilk," the executive chairman might well have
wondered exactly what government officials were con-
templating. Yet Nearing did not accuse the Federal government of an active role in crushing the People's Council, of
anything worse than neutrality on the side of local janis-
saries of jingoism. Creel masked his role in the American
Alliance for Labor and Democracy, and used private means
to assert that the People's Council was infested with "traitors
and fools, and we are fighting it to the death. . . . Have patriotic societies and civic organizations . . . condemn . . .
the People's Council as pro-German and disloyal. . . . See
all the newspapers and see to it that they get the point of
view and action that I am giving you now. . . . Tear this letter up." [44]

One Federal official did make his hostility obvious, however. On the night of January 9, 1918, Marshal Thomas D.
McCarthy attended a New York meeting in which Nearing
and Steffens were the main speakers. After that accounts
vary. McCarthy recalled fearing the effect of Nearing's oratory upon "the audience . . . composed of 2000 men and
women. People of Jewish blood composed perhaps 95 percent of the audience. They were of the poor, uneducated
type." The marshal then offered the executive chairman
"some friendly advice that I believed might be of service to
him," politely urging him to display greater loyalty. "This
was all said in a spirit of contempt and pity. . . . Nearing
and I parted on the friendliest of terms." [45]

The New York *Sun* got a different impression. "You are
just the kind of bird I want to get," McCarthy allegedly told
the pacifist, a newly endangered species. "If I ever do get

you, I will send you so far that you will be a long time getting back." The marshal also ventured to predict that "there may be hemp picnics in Central Park on Sunday mornings for just such as you." The official sworn to uphold law and order, however, promised to "stand on the fringe of the crowd and clap." [46]

Nearing, the *Sun* reported, remained firm and reminded the marshal, "Should there be any such violence or resort to lynch law, we expect to hold you liable for it." The pacifist mailed the newspaper's version of the incident to Attorney-General Thomas Gregory, and urged him and the President to remove McCarthy from office. Baldwin, the director of the National Civil Liberties Bureau, also sent a letter to Gregory in support. But the Attorney-General, who had recently warned that "an avenging Government" would swoop down upon "moral and physical degenerates who believe nothing is worth fighting for," was in no mood to dismiss anyone *plus loyaliste que la loi* for the moment permitted. The absolved marshal even expanded political ornithology beyond hawks and doves to include "the buzzards! They're educated buzzards, and they know how to spread sedition without saying the actual words that would land them in jail. . . . After Nearing and his bunch got through, I doubt whether $5000 of Liberty Bonds could have been sold in the whole crowd." Only later did an amendment to the Sedition Act make it a crime to obstruct in any way the sale of Liberty Bonds, although brokers giving bearish advice on purely financial grounds were exempted.[47]

Within two weeks of the encounter with McCarthy, Nearing described the condition of free speech as better than the People's Council had ever known; and the organization boasted "a good staff, excellent lists . . . and a moderate pledged monthly income." The chairman's unusual contentment was based upon his desire to make a quick, graceful exit; he wanted to return to his "chosen work—study, teaching, writing and speaking." He had also been disappointed with what he considered the slackened interest of Magnes and Hillquit in the People's Council. The rabbi of New York's Temple Emanu-El assured Nearing of his personal friendship and reassured him that the People's Council had seen its worst days: "It is impossible to attack it more violently than it has been attacked." Nearing's resignation was indefinitely tabled; and Magnes, Hillquit, and Amos Pinchot were among the chief speakers when the Council sponsored a National Conference of Labor, Socialist, and Radical Movements in February 1918.[48]

Although the American Defense Society urged the government to quash the meeting, Nearing presided over sessions devoted to selecting and instructing delegates to European congresses under the aegis of the Bolsheviks. "The Russian people are in the lead," Nearing proclaimed, a month after Lenin abolished the Constituent Assembly, "and we must humbly follow." He expressed his admiration for the policy of "no fight but no peace" and predicted, a month before the treaty of Brest-Litovsk, that "Bolshevik printing presses" would subvert any German occupying army. Besides denouncing militarism, capitalism, and repression, Nearing also read excerpts from the secret treaties that the new Minister of Foreign Affairs, Leon Trotsky, had undiplomatically broadcast upon taking office. Yet the principles that the three hundred delegates adopted blended Wilsonian liberalism with Bolshevism: free trade, freedom of the seas, national self-determination, civil liberty, open diplomacy, world federation, complete disarmament, and popular control of banks and the means of production.[49]

Only when Nearing and Lochner presented a plank favoring free Chinese and Japanese immigration was a sour note injected. Maurer, the unanimous choice to attend the Inter-Allied Labor and Socialist Conference, protested: "It's all very nice to be an idealist. . . . It's all right for your philosophers to tell us what to do." But as a Knight of Labor by the age of sixteen, Maurer had "suffered from the competition of cheap foreign labor, and I know what it means. My wife and my family starved at one time because of cheap foreign labor." Nearing called the unionist's position "narrow minded" but left himself open to a charge of idealism by conceding that if Asians "can get more out of our industrial resources than we, then in heaven's name they are justly entitled to it [sic]." Although Maurer was unmoved by Nearing's generosity, the delegates overwhelmingly supported unrestricted immigration.[50]

The radical convention in February was the last significant project of the Council. In the previous month Wilson had ostensibly incorporated the radical pacifist demands for no annexations and no indemnities into the Fourteen Points, and some pacifists therefore eased into support of a war whose aims had become clarified and acceptable. The continued German invasion and occupation of Russia, along with the harsh treaty of Brest-Litovsk, had a similar effect upon the antiwar American Socialists. The editors of the *Appeal to Reason* and of the *Masses* thus switched to support of the war; Congressman Meyer London addressed war bond rallies; and Thomas, in an anguished letter to Wald in March, still called war hideous on religious principles. But "the Russian situation and the progressive abandonment of imperialistic aims by the Allies . . . remove the reproach of hypocrisy from us. Meanwhile the German people seem to be more completely under the dominance of their cynical Junker class than I had thought." Thomas confessed that he no longer knew "what to think. I wish Mr. Wilson could have taken the liberal stand he now has last summer." [51]

Other pacifists retained their convictions and remained within the Council, which found its propaganda channels— for all Mr. Wilson's liberalism—blocked as never before. Lochner even called a special meeting to pass out antidraft

literature to cadres who were to distribute it either in person or in unmarked envelopes. The *Bulletin* of the People's
Council was sometimes delayed for several weeks pending
the *deus ex machina* of a postal bureaucrat willing to release
it, and the trickle of voluntary contributions forced the *Bulletin* to become a bi-monthly by the summer. Often Nearing
placed no more than two letters in each mailbox in order to
prevent detection of the sender. A secretary learned that
Western Union office operators were submitting copies of
telegrams to the Department of Justice, adding credence to
the Attorney-General's boast that America was "never so
thoroughly policed in its history." [52]

Intolerance and political estrangement induced a couple
of journalists to promote compromise. Already in October
1917, the ubiquitous Steffens outlined an arrangement with
Colonel E. M. House: freedom of speech, if exercised with
moderation; curtailment of labor prosecutions and pardon
for "class war prisoners"; and a plea to pacifists "to stop
fighting the war and to work for permanent peace terms."
The grey eminence agreed to pass the suggestion to Wilson,
while Steffens tried to persuade Nearing and Big Bill Haywood of the Wobblies. But his attempt at conciliation
failed.[53]

The following spring A. W. Ricker proposed that radicals
support the Democratic party in exchange for the restoration of civil liberty. "Nearing is about the hardest of all," but
even he saw advantages, Ricker told House. Nearing even
calculated that in the elections of November 1918, "the
Non-Partisan League, the Socialists, and the radical labor elements will probably elect from a dozen to 25 Congressmen. . . . This group will hold the balance of power in the
House of Representatives." He agreed with Ricker that the
Administration might secure radical support by assuring
"freedom of speech and press, looking to the Courts rather

than the Post Office Department to enforce the laws." [54] But the proposal was quixotic. The radicals were too shattered to tease foes with swing votes: the Republicans carried both houses of Congress in November and refused to seat the Milwaukee Socialist Victor Berger, sentenced to twenty years at Fort Leavenworth and triumphant in a fair election. Given Nearing's recalcitrant opposition to capitalism, he might have been among the first to break even a pledge of conditional support; and the Red Scare that followed would surely have eroded his touching faith in the judiciary.

Radical buttressing of the Administration, as Ricker explained to House, was especially dependent upon a gaunt, bald sexagenarian who mounted a Canton, Ohio, platform over a month after the compromise was proposed. Perspiring heavily, weaving back and forth, stabbing a bony forefinger into the summer air, Eugene V. Debs had come to talk about what the war had done to his friends, to Haywood and Ruthenberg and Tom Mooney and Kate Richards O'Hare and Alfred Wagenknecht. This was a new martyrology; and when Debs called Scott Nearing "the greatest teacher in the United States," the crowd burst into applause. Debs attributed the Penn dismissal to "great capitalists [who] found he was teaching true economics to the students of the university, as the same forces said of a Judean carpenter nineteen centuries ago. They said of Jesus Christ, who was a workman and a teacher . . . 'He is preaching a false religion,' and their lineal descendants say, 'He is preaching economics.' " Debs continued, as further applause punctuated the eulogy: "The truth is always unpalatable to these plutocrats, who make their living by the sweat of the working class. . . . They must see that our vicious doctrines don't reach your ears." After over a year of equivocation and silence on the war, he had come to answer the question, O Debs, where is thy sting? The government's response to Ricker's proposal was indictment in late June under the Espionage Act.[55]

The afternoon before the September 9 trial, Nearing visited the Socialist spellbinder and marveled at the rectitude of "so radiant a spirit." Yet the executive chairman still wanted to resign his post, for "there ought to be at the head of the organization" a pacifist "not so much in disrepute as most of us." Thirteen months after becoming chairman, he acted upon his decision, his secretary reported, to "wash his hands of all Peace activities, excepting through the Socialist Party. This was a blow to all of us . . . a keen disappointment." Lochner's concurrent resignation was not accepted, however, and he succeeded Nearing as executive chairman.[56]

The death of the People's Council was protracted, like a fifth act in which the tragic hero's mortal wounds do not stanch lengthy soliloquies. In 1919 Nearing's scorching pamphlet *The Madness at Versailles* was circulated under the auspices of the Council, which could still collect an audience of 6,000 inside Madison Square Garden to hear Berger, Lee, and others cry for amnesty for political prisoners. Woodrow Wilson implicitly conceded early in September 1919 that these radical pacifists had been right all along: "The real reason that the war . . . took place was that Germany was afraid her commercial rivals were going to get the better of her. . . . This war was a commercial and industrial war." A year earlier anyone making such remarks risked jail. A month later the People's Council of America abolished itself.[57]

About 1500 of the 5000 Socialist locals had already been destroyed, and it was no consolation to the adherents of the St. Louis Declaration that the Social Democratic League and the American Alliance for Labor and Democracy also disintegrated at the same time. Behind their interlocking directorates were only a few dues-paying members, whose ideals had become merely an incantation as they strained to be Socialists without also being radicals. Others jettisoned the pretense of faith altogether. The novelist Ernest Poole worked gamely for the Committee on Public Information. William English Walling welcomed the imprisonment of antiwar Socialists, whom Charles E. Russell skewered as "dirty traitors." Simons, whose political star rose with the Marxist *Social Forces in American History,* served the Wisconsin Loyalty League and ended up in the Bureau of Medical Economics of the American Medical Association. Spargo became an adviser to the State Department and among the first anti-Communist intellectuals of the left. He also carved an epitaph for the Social Democratic League, "a paper organization" of tired radicals, "some of whom are no longer Socialists, and most of whom have tied themselves to Sam Gompers." [58]

Nor was it comforting to generalize that wars are easier to start than to stop. Having failed to reduce the number of corpses, the radicals had little hope of influencing the diplomats. When the guns stopped smoking, insurrection engulfed Central Europe and its first anniversary was celebrated in Soviet Russia. But in America not revolutionaries but Republicans gained the power to advise and consent in the shaping of the postwar world.

CHAPTER FIVE

ON TRIAL

On MARCH 21, 1918, THE MAN THE NEW YORK
Times called "one of the most prominent 'peace at any
price' agitators in the United States" surrendered himself in
a Federal courtroom. Flanked by Hillquit and Lochner, he
was released on $5,000 bail that Baldwin had quickly col-
lected and that Thomas was ready to match in case the need
arose.[1]

The indictment was based upon *The Great Madness,* the
43-page pamphlet that the *Call* had serialized in the summer of 1917 and that the American Socialist Society had
published in two editions of 10,000 copies each. The pamphlet was priced at 10¢, and all but a thousand copies had
been sold by the spring. For having printed it the Society was
indicted as Nearing's co-conspirator in crimes punishable
under Section 3 of Title I of the Espionage Act of 1917:

[1] Whoever, when the United States is at war, shall willfully make
or convey false reports or false statements with intent to interfere
with the operation or success of the military or naval forces of the
United States or to promote the success of its enemies [2] and
whoever, when the United States is at war, shall willfully cause or

attempt to cause insubordination, disloyalty, mutiny, or refusal of duty, in the military or naval forces of the United States, [3] or shall willfully obstruct the recruiting or enlistment service of the United States, shall be punished by a fine of not more than $10,000 or imprisonment for not more than twenty years, or both.

Among the directors of the Society were Hillquit, who was also the attorney of record in the case; Lee, the Rand School's educational director; Herron, who firmly supported the war; Job Harriman, who might have been elected mayor of Los Angeles in 1911 had trade unionists not confessed to blowing up the Los Angeles *Times* building; and Benjamin Hanford, creator of the mythical Jimmie Higgins, who scrubbed Socialist offices while intellectuals discussed the labor theory of value. "The indictments . . . mark the first move through the criminal branch of the Federal courts against these agitators," the *Times* observed. "Nearing is the recognized spokesman for this group." [2]

Despite the group's notoriety, prosecution had been brewing for little more than a month. Henry A. Wise Wood, the chairman of the Committee on National Preparedness, feared that "pamphlets such as Nearing's . . . incite pacifists and fanatics to burn factories and otherwise aid the Kaiser's cause"; and as the son of the Copperhead mayor of New York, Wood was unusually sensitive on the subject of treason.[3] His critical review of *The Great Madness* attracted the attention of Easley, the industrious director of the League of National Unity who still served as secretary of the National Civic Federation. Although he wore a couple of hats, Easley nonetheless had only one head, which he used to ferret out subversive sentiments in the heads of others. The board members of his organizations included Gompers, Lowden, Pepper, Seligman, Stotesbury, Walling, Wise, and Wood, but Easley hounded Nearing with a relentless dedication all his own.

To the Attorney General he sent Wood's February 1918 statement that *The Great Madness* was "the most seditious pro-German propaganda that the Kaiser's aids [*sic*] have had the audacity to attempt." And he thereupon paid a visit to the Department of Justice a few days later to discuss "some matters" that deserved Gregory's "personal attention." [4] Easley announced his agenda amidst a crescendo of attacks on Nearing from Wood, who urged the Attorney General either to arrest the People's Council chairman or to resign, and from Stanwood Menken, who also clamored for Federal prosecution. John Lord O'Brian and Alfred Bettman, the assistant attorneys general in charge of Espionage Act prosecutions, maintained a discreet silence; and O'Brian later discounted Easley's influence upon the Department's decision to prosecute. [5]

But within a week of Easley's visit, the Attorney General called *The Great Madness* "a pretty raw production" and told O'Brian to "see if we can base a successful prosecution on it." After reading the Bureau of Investigation dossier, Bettman identified Nearing as an incipient commissar, "attempting to make himself the leader of a revolutionary movement analogous to the Bolsheviki movement." But the assistant attorney general suspected that Nearing might court arrest: "He has a passion for the limelight and may even desire to emulate the position of the revolutionary political prisoners in Russia who are freed from prison by revolutionary forces and placed at the head of such forces." Rather confusingly Bettman termed the pamphlet "absolutely frank, open, and direct," yet conceded that it did "not expressly urge anyone to refuse military service or other help to the United States." But because Nearing presumably "knew he was violating the law," Bettman agreed that the author's desire for martyrdom should be satisfied. [6]

Until the passage of a second Espionage Act in May 1918, Gregory usually allowed United States Attorneys free rein in selecting targets for indictment; the Nearing case was an exception. Though the idea originated in Washington, its execution was the province of Francis G. Caffey of the Southern District of New York. Born in Lowndes County, Alabama, the U.S. Attorney had once been among the dozen trustees of the National Child Labor Committee. Pleased that the Great War "has taught us to think more alike, to feel more alike," praising conscription as an example of American self-government, Caffey was not the sort to recoil in horror at the prospect of prosecuting Scott Nearing.[7]

He nonetheless asked to see the Department's complete dossier on Nearing. Because the Post Office had exercised its right to read the mail as well as deliver it and had refused to circulate *The Great Madness* and *The Menace of Militarism,* the pamphleteer had attracted notice. The U.S. Attorney found Nearing's social philosophy "absurd and visionary" but wondered whether prosecution on the basis of *The Great Madness* alone would be successful. Nearing might easily demonstrate that his pacifism preceded the war; his booklet was therefore consistent with a constitutionally protected ethos rather than an incitement to interfere with war operations. In urging Marshal McCarthy's removal a month earlier, Nearing had described himself "as an American citizen who believes in the maintenance of law and order"; and Federal agents found nothing incriminating in the spoor of People's Council propaganda nor among the documents scooped up in the Toledo raid. Despite Caffey's doubt that *The Great Madness* was itself sufficient evidence of criminality, he agreed to bring an indictment, girded by O'Brian's assurance that the pamphlet presented "a prima facie case of matter violating the Espionage Statute." As though echoing a Penn trustee, the assistant attorney general clinched his case by noting that Nearing had not attempted "a scientific presentation." [8]

ON THE NIGHT THE INDICTMENT WAS RETURNED, THE FORMER professor was the embodiment of equanimity as he addressed a cheering audience on "industrial democracy" without even mentioning his brush with the law. But the People's Council laced its statement condemning the prosecution with quotations from the executive chairman: "A jail sentence, imposed on such grounds, will do more to arouse an intelligent spirit of revolt in the American people than a thousand lectures and a library full of books. I count this a greater honor than a degree from any American university." Repression thus certified his own political effectiveness: "The plutocrats fear us because the people are listening to what we have to say." [9]

Nearing then went to Philadelphia, where the University Club was rocked by the scandal of his entry into its portals. The doorman, not recognizing the indicted pacifist, guided him into the visitors' room and informed ex-Professor Patten that "a gentleman in the reception room" awaited him. According to the club secretary, Patten "out of politeness asked him to . . . talk while he finished his breakfast"; and the headwaiter later assured the Club's investigative committee that the notorious Nearing did not actually eat anything. Club president John Cadwalader, a trustee who had voted for dismissal three years earlier, and his secretary called "the situation . . . embarrassing to any club." Like Tantalus, Nearing could attract attention by not eating. A week later a fund-raising dinner in his honor at New York's Central Opera House was suddenly canceled, and the *Times* left him to his own just desserts: "Not a single friend of Professor Nearing put in an appearance. A squad of police, which was at the hall as early as six o'clock, dwindled to the proportion of a single uniformed patrolman an hour later." [10]

Nearing's friends had not forsaken him, however; and the two radicals who had stood at his side in the docket launched a financial and legal rescue operation on April 2. Lochner unfurled an open letter in behalf of the man who "staked his liberty upon our cause, without gain to himself." To members of the People's Council, he wrote: "At the request of Dr. Nearing, we are not at this time asking you to contribute to his defense, though we cannot refuse you the privilege if you desire it. But we do ask all locals to increase their activities." [11] By late summer, money was flowing "in a heartening manner" and over $6,500 had been collected.[12]

Hillquit meanwhile filed a demurrer to the indictment, charging that the co-defendants had been "improperly joined" and that "no overt act on the part of either is specified." The immediate result was simply another indictment on May 13, to which the attorney and director of the American Socialist Society filed another demurrer.[13] But on August 1, 1918, Judge Learned Hand of the Southern District of New York dashed whatever hopes Nearing's partisans still cherished of saving him from a trial.

"The manner and diction is intolerant and violent after the common tradition in revolutionary propaganda," the comparatively tolerant judge announced. "It is obviously inflammatory to the feelings of such readers as believe themselves unjustly treated by the existing order, which it presents as unqualifiedly noxious to the body politic and proper only for immediate destruction." With demurrers overruled, four counts of the indictment stood: 1) Nearing and the Society had conspired to disseminate *The Great Madness* to unknown men in uniform who committed overt but unstated acts; 2) Nearing and the Society similarly conspired to obstruct conscription, recruitment, and enlistment; 3) Nearing wrote the pamphlet, and the directorate of the Rand School published and sold it, with the intent to cause insubordination in the armed forces; 4) the same substantive violations of the Espionage Act occurred with respect to conscription, recruitment, and enlistment.[14]

Hand's decision was especially unsettling, if not quite unexpected, because of his earlier attempt to make the Espionage Act congruent with the common law definition of responsibility for incitement. In *Masses Publishing Company* v. *Patten* the previous summer, Hand had reasoned that the Congressional law was designed to punish specific incitements to resistance and mutiny rather than general criticism of public policy. "To establish criminal responsibility" at common law, he later explained, "the words uttered must amount to counsel or advice or command to commit the forbidden acts." But the Court of Appeals for the Second Circuit had overruled Hand's attempt to circumscribe guilt within "the character of the words themselves," and a new test of culpability was formulated: "If the natural and reasonable effect of what is said is to encourage resistance to a law, and the words are used in an endeavor to persuade to resistance, it is immaterial that the duty to resist is not mentioned. . . . One may willfully obstruct the enlistment service, without advising in direct language against enlistment." The Court of Appeals thus enshrined the doctrine of remote bad tendency in the Espionage Act, and district judges like Learned Hand complied.[15] The government would merely have to construe the likely effect of *The Great Madness* upon some impressionable young draftee; it would not need to produce Nearing's mutineering protégé, Billy Budd's Billy Budd, to secure a conviction.

Despite the odds against acquittal, Nearing looked forward to his trial: "It didn't make any difference whether the Rand School and I were convicted, but here was an opportunity to get a million dollars worth of publicity for the Socialist movement." In the same spirit of refusal to assign a priority to victory, Socialists like Nearing were more fascinated by what was said on the soapbox than by what was done in the ballot box. "I have raised hell all over this country!" Mother Jones shouted to women seeking the suffrage. "You don't need a vote to raise hell! You need convictions and a voice!" Hillquit explained that ineluctable historical forces would achieve an economic maturity facilitating the transition from capitalism, but that only education and propaganda could win the masses over to socialism. A Socialist who served in the New York State Assembly recalled: "We were so happy campaigning that we wished there would never be an election day." [16] Impelled by the love of struggle rather than the will to power, New York Socialists in the summer of 1918 nominated an indicted pacifist for the United States Congress.

MANHATTAN'S FOURTEENTH CONGRESSIONAL DISTRICT RAN from Fourth to Fourteenth Streets and from river to river. Despite the proletarian cast of the constituency, the Fourteenth Congressional was not exactly socialism's burned-over district: although the predominantly Jewish East Side had gone 60 percent for Hillquit in his 1917 mayoralty race, the largely Irish and Italian West Side had given the attorney only 8 percent of its vote. Unlike Socialism west of the Hudson River, writers and lawyers did much to stamp the New York movement; and the garment unions had been a bulwark of the People's Council as well as the party itself. But merely because the New York contingent had lived constantly on pens and needles was no reason to nominate in wartime a radical pacifist charged with a four-count violation of the Espionage Act, a comrade so recently affiliated that the state organization had to exempt him from its normal requirements for candidacy. Party literature simply averred that "this fiery apostle of social justice, who spent many an evening in IWW halls and AFL unions, rather than with the social set of the university," had been "a Socialist long before he became a member of the Socialist party." [17]

The specter of Nearing, incumbent Meyer London, and "the unindicted Mr. Hillquit" in quest of national office from New York was enough to drive Democrats and Republicans into fusion. With the National Security League urging unity against Socialism, with William Randolph Hearst and Adolph Ochs becoming political bedfellows, and with Robert F. Wagner arranging the details, a team of patriotic candidates was selected. It was simpler this way, Nearing believed—"the workers against the capitalists." [18]

The fusion candidate in the Fourteenth District was the incumbent, Fiorello H. LaGuardia, who was then representing his constituents from the cockpit of a Caproni biplane on the Italian front. But his political ingenuity was intact. Though he had courageously opposed the Espionage Act in 1917 and would do so again after the election, Major LaGuardia planned to seek reelection on "an anti-yellow, anti-Socialistic, anti-German and true-blood American platform." [19]

The incumbent's confinement to Europe would have been a bonus to a more conventional opponent, but Nearing electioneered as though he wished to blow his advantage. His first campaign speech was a lecture on economics, spiced with a call for workers to "take over the machinery of production, and declare their independence of big business, just as our ancestors in 1776 took over the machinery of politics and declared their independence of royalty." The *Times* characteristically urged an insufficiently vigilant Department of Justice "to keep an ear open for the disloyal and treacherous purposes of these accomplices of Germany," and even Allan Benson disavowed the candidate's objectives: "Scott Nearing is an idealist. Nearing didn't mean to be anything like [*sic*] as confiscatory as he reads."

From J. G. Phelps Stokes, a millionaire Socialist who became a sergeant in the Ninth Coast Artillery, came another gratuitous clarification: "What Scott Nearing meant to say was that industrial exploitation of the type that involves robbery or oppression of the working people must be stopped in democratic ways." Stokes' wife, a baccalaureate of the Lower East Side workshops, nevertheless signed up as treasurer of Nearing's campaign; and Lochner loyally agreed to serve as his campaign manager.[20]

LaGuardia took no chances. On September 25 the Department of War cabled General Pershing to send the stocky major home, ostensibly to provide bombing instructions. His return a month later was carefully orchestrated in order to explode into headlines. "Who is Scott Nearing? " the incumbent innocently asked upon arrival, professing surprise that his opponent was not Upton Sinclair. "If he is a young man, I shall ask what regiment he comes from." Suddenly informed of Nearing's peculiar background, Major LaGuardia, his uniform emblazoned with decorations, solemnly told reporters: "The question of patriotism must not be introduced into this campaign." After feigning ignorance of the indictment, he reminded the citizenry that "under the laws of this country, a man is innocent until he is proven guilty." [21]

The Socialists responded to such tactics by taking the high road and by securing an endorsement from Terre Haute. "We have not had a comrade," Debs wrote while awaiting appeal, "who would enter . . . [Congress] with a better mental and moral equipment to combat the capitalist enemy and to serve the interests of the working people. For the very reason that Scott Nearing has been so mercilessly persecuted and so brutally hounded by the ruling class and its minions and mercenaries—for this very reason the workers and their sympathizers should . . . send him to Congress." The imprimatur included praise for Nearing's "heart and soul; he has keen insight and broad vision; he has the fundamental facts and the gift of speech." [22]

Speech was perhaps the most valuable endowment of all, for the conditions of political life might have taxed the lungs of an heroic tenor. "As the speaker stood on his more or less precarious wooden platform," an assemblyman who worked actively in Nearing's campaign remembered, "street-cars went clanging by, heavy horse-drawn drays rumbled over cobblestones, and every conceivable street noise seemed to be organized in a conspiracy to drown out his voice." The candidate in 1918 sometimes spoke three or four times in a single evening, and held house meetings in the daytime surrounded by women voters. "The people have voted him a great success as a . . . rough-and-tumble speaker," Lochner exulted. [23]

LaGuardia in turn lashed the Socialists for subservience to a foreign power—sometimes Germany, sometimes Russia. He came on as an alley fighter against the "silk-stocking university professor who condescends to come here and attempt to foist Bolshevism on America." He asked the pro-Bolshevik to love America or leave it: "If Scott Nearing wants to work out his beautiful theories, why doesn't he go to Russia? " And LaGuardia's rhetoric was unusually colorful as he blistered the "yellow dog Socialists" and painted Nearing "not red but yellow." [24] The primary color of his campaign was of course khaki.

Nearing's response to LaGuardia's assault was to flesh out a Socialist critique of an oligarchic society and to quote the section of the Declaration of Independence that affirmed the right of revolution. But special wrinkles were introduced into his campaign. Art Young of the *Masses* drew cartoons at one rally; and a book of his drawings, *Art Young's Political Primer*, became a campaign volume. Because of his "large personal following among the students," the Rand School held a fund-raising dance for Nearing. And a Yiddish theatre staged a benefit performance of "Mrs. Warren's Profession." Between acts Nearing addressed his tailor-made constituency but, in perverse defiance of the conventions of New York politics, came out strongly for— Irish independence.[25]

The campaign peaked on the night of November 1, when LaGuardia and Nearing debated at Cooper Union after the Socialists promised to foot the bill. The challenger, blond and thin, was dressed in plain mufti. The incumbent, a roly-poly bowling ball of a man, was of course resplendent in his uniform. One reporter also contrasted the epicene and the virile: "While Nearing's gestures are airy and graceful, LaGuadia's convey simply the impression of strength and fighting energy." Against Nearing's impeccably American origins, LaGuardia enhanced his already diverse ethnic appeal with decorations like the Italian War Cross; while a whispering campaign inaccurately noted Nearing's birth in Germantown, Pennsylvania.[26]

A contingent of policemen attacked some members of the crowd trying to get into the hall, and the moderator threatened to commit some of the disorderly for contempt. Otherwise the debate was conducted with dignity. Nearing repeated the themes of his campaign: he urged an immediate peace and demanded that the rich pay for the war; he vilified Wall Street, which was not in the Fourteenth District anyway; and he advocated recognition of the Leninist regime. LaGuardia retorted that Socialism had been a failure, that he went to war because he opposed war, that he could do more as a Congressman than could the Socialists with their talk "on the corners of the East Side." [27] That was presumably why Socialists wanted to talk on Capitol Hill. In any case Nearing considered LaGuardia "a very competent discussant of political issues." Informed after the debate that Nearing was an economist, this most unprosaic Congressman replied, "It's a mistake. He's a poet." [28]

The day that Socialists hoped would never arrive was November 6. In the barber shops and funeral parlors where voting booths were arranged, "it was a common occurrence for toughs and gangsters to lounge about," according to Louis Waldman. After block captains checked their lists of registered voters who were sick, absent from the district, or dead, "a stream of strangers would then flood the polls and, under the tolerant eyes of the party regulars," become "cemetery voters" and "mattress voters." To underline the people's choice, ballot counters sometimes placed small pieces of lead beneath fingernails in order to mutilate and therefore disqualify ballots, which might also be torn to be discounted.[29]

Major LaGuardia won in a landslide, 70 percent of the district's vote; Hillquit, London, and Lee went crashing to defeat; and despite the margins the educational director of the Rand School cried foul. Besides the usual intimidation, Lee told Hillquit, "a new and ingenious sort [was] applied chiefly to women. Mothers and sisters of men in deferred classifications were warned clearly enough, and yet in such ways that it would be hard to get legal proof, that, if they gave offense, the boys might be reclassified. . . . Inspectors brazenly opened ballots before putting them into the box. . . . Protest was useless." Nearing was more philosophical: "Elections are but incidental to the big thing—educational propaganda to make the worker develop his common sense and intelligence." [30] With similar pedagogic aspirations, he stood trial for violations of the Espionage Act three months later.

PRESIDING IN THE CASE OF *United States* v. *Nearing et al.* was Julius M. Mayer, a graduate of Columbia Law School, a former attorney general of New York, a Republican, and a "short, stocky . . . businesslike . . . stickler for the dignity of the court." He seemed the sort of magistrate whom radicals hoped to avoid. Mayer was one of the three judges on the Circuit Court of Appeals who had toughened the Espionage Act in *Masses* v. *Patten*. He admired the "splendid" work of the National Security League Flying Squadrons, which Nearing regarded as the cutting edge of the plutocracy. Mayer had learned his politics at the feet of the author of the Platt Amendment, which made Cuba a client state of the Yanquis. In contrast, the author of *The Great Madness* claimed that the purpose of the American military was "to menace neighbors" and "to guard the hundreds of millions of dollars . . . invested in 'undeveloped' countries." Mayer branded the St. Louis Declaration "vehement and violent," but also favored prosecution of pacifists using an "insidious and shrewd, indirect method . . . to paralyze the army." Nearing was presumably the sort of orator who cleverly called a spade a metallic instrument for excavation.[31]

Hillquit and Seymour Stedman, who had presided over the Chicago convention of the People's Council, prepared the case for the defense. But the legal efforts on behalf of Debs and Victor Berger had exhausted Hillquit, and pulmonary tuberculosis forced him to follow the latest Espionage Act trial from a sickbed in Saranac Lake, New York. Stedman therefore called upon the legal assistance of two other Socialists, I. M. Sackin and S. John Block, and of Walter Nelles of the National Civil Liberties Bureau. Their task was made easier on February 11, the day the trial began, when the first two counts, the conspiracy charges, were dropped. When Nearing was sworn in as the only corporeal co-defendant, the *Call* reported, "by a singular freak of refraction . . . a flow of the outer sunlight rested on his face, which was lighted already with the smile with which he faced his questioner." [32]

His questioner was Assistant U.S. Attorney Earl B. Barnes, who explained to the jurors that "nobody is being prosecuted because he is a Socialist. That would be abhorrent to our Constitution." Not having to produce a witness to claim that *The Great Madness* led to insubordination or draft resistance, Barnes merely contended that the pamphlet "was designed and intended to dull the enthusiasm" for the war that—he failed to add—had cost the lives of 8,540,000 Europeans and Americans. But conviction depended upon bad intent as well as bad tendency, and the prosecutor conceded that "the hardest point always in any case of this kind is proving the intent." But he reminded the court that "a man is presumed to intend natural, ordinary, and reasonable consequences of what he says and does." [33] To explain his own motivations, Nearing agreed to take the witness stand.

The strategy that he and his attorneys devised was *de rigueur* in political trials: "We decided that I would deny nothing, I would say yes to everything, and we would put the ideas of Socialism across." Nearing wanted not exculpation but a forum; he hoped to be the catalyst of conversion experiences outside the courtroom as well as within the jury box. Among the hundreds who lined up from early morning, jostling for a place in the crowded room, was Arturo Giovannitti, an Italian by birth, a Wobbly by conviction, a romantic poet by temperament. Having earlier dismissed Nearing as "a pampered intellectual trying . . . to make a little squeak of his own," Giovannitti came to scoff and remained to say to readers of the *Liberator* that the defendant "turned the courtroom into a classroom, the witness stand into a chair of revolutionary economics, the judge into an invited guest of the faculty, and the jury into a bunch of still unhazed freshmen. . . ." Nearing spoke "hour after hour with a clear, resonant voice that carried to every corner of the hall, unhaltingly, directly, aggressively, never stopping a single second to select his words or to qualify his statements." [34]

Barnes had already read to the jury the entire pamphlet by the time Stedman elicited in considerable detail Nearing's economic theories. Defining the plutocracy as "an instinctive cohesion of great wealth," the witness showed how its desire for preparedness was disseminated through the Navy League and the National Security League. He brought along a chart showing the interlocking directorates of the great trusts. He quoted from government documents, from conservatives like Professor Seligman, from liberals like President Wilson, from his own pamphlets like *The Germs of War* and *The Menace of Militarism*. "By the time his statement was finished," Charles Ervin noticed, "you could hardly see him from the stack of books." [35]

On February 14 Barnes interrogated the witness, who was so eager to elaborate his views that Stedman complained, "Mr. Nearing, you answer so quickly, I don't have a chance to object. . . . I either get caught by the inability to tell when the prosecution has finished a question, or by the football rush of the witness to answer." Uncontrolled by his own attorney, Nearing explained American intervention in the World War: "There is a definite ruling class psychology that dominates not only rulers themselves, but those who work intimately with them . . . I believe that the members of the capitalist class as a rule would prefer war to the disestablishment of capitalism." Although his pamphlet condemned the absence of a popular referendum, Nearing conceded, under Barnes' grilling, that the declaration of war had been constitutional. The defendant added, however, that the President had lured America into the conflict despite pledges to the contrary, and he attributed popular acceptance of an imperialist adventure to propaganda and other "methods which were notorious at the time." Nearing refused to concede that pro-war Congressmen were representative of their constituents.[36]

Nearing also assailed the wartime policy of the American Federation of Labor, for he wished that the trade unions had been as militant as they were belligerent: "The war is an incident to the economic conflict. . . . The problem of establishing industrial democracy is a problem that goes on continually with the wage earner." From the witness chair he even denigrated the Red Cross: "I never contribute to any private or philanthropic or charitable institution. . . . I regard the Red Cross as a method of making war more endurable, and I do not care to make war more endurable, because it is a crime."

Yet Barnes forced Nearing into the graceless position of conceding that Socialists had been accomplices in the crime, that his own pamphlet had made no impact. Among Europeans as well as Americans, he admitted, "the millions of socialists who fought in this war . . . were not any less subordinate than the other fellows." Far from intending to cause mutiny or insubordination, Nearing claimed merely educational value for *The Great Madness:* "I wrote this pamphlet to try to educate people. . . . I wanted the people to understand what was going on." Had he aimed at an audience of conscripts, he would have chosen some other weapon, "a different kind of leaflet. I would not have sold it through the Rand School where it went out for general circulation to a very small number of people."[37]

Asked about conscientious objection, Nearing called this ethical question too personal to be answered with counsel for other citizens. A high-risk employee himself, he avoided "advising a man even to jeopardize his job. I think it is up to a man to make up his own mind on these matters." In the summer of 1917 Nearing had urged conscientious objectors to register with Selective Service and to cooperate with the law as much as their values permitted. On the witness stand, the comrade of Roger Baldwin, whom Judge Mayer had recently sentenced to prison for draft refusal, disclaimed belief in civil disobedience to conscription. With a touch of disingenuousness in his answers, Nearing caused even the *Times* to concede that he was "his own best witness." [38]

The address to the jury is normally the climactic scene in a political trial, and Nearing's peroration eloquently established the case for freedom of speech. Since no evidence had been produced that *The Great Madness* had decelerated the slaughter, Nearing concluded that his liberty was endangered because of an expression of opinion, including his denunciation of "the existence in New York and other American cities of starving children side by side with fabulous wealth and idle people." He reminded the jurors that even the expression of unpopular opinion supposedly fell within the penumbra of the First Amendment and that he had expressed his views openly. "Never in my life have I gone out and done anything indirectly," he announced. "If I have wanted to say a thing, I have said it . . . and taken the consequences." Nearing described himself as "a student of public affairs. I am a Socialist. I am a pacifist. But I am not charged with any of those things as offenses. On the other hand, I believe that as an American citizen I have the right to discuss public questions . . . to oppose the passage of a law [and] . . . after the law is passed, to agitate for . . . a repeal of that law." [39] No banshee of violent revolution would thus lecture on the meaning of the American Constitution.

THROUGHOUT THE TRIAL NEARING HAD CONDUCTED HIMSELF with a courtliness that Mayer appreciated, for he was guarded by six detectives in order to discourage radical attempts on the judge's life. Mayer also thanked the attorneys for their "courtesy, clearness, and force." He then charged the jury: "With the principles of the Socialist party you have no concern any more than the court. . . . But you have a right to look at . . . documents to see what was in the mind of both of the defendants," in order to determine intent.[40] The jury was then sequestered.

Meanwhile a reporter found Nearing "alert, active, and cheerful . . . conferring with his counsel and chatting with relatives and friends. Mrs. Nearing sat at the counsel table all day, smiling and talking to companions." The relatives included Louis Nearing; the friends included John Reed, the Rover Boy of radical journalism; Rabbi Magnes; Lee, a defense witness; and other sachems of New York Socialism like Thomas, Bloor, and Waldman. Nearing commented that "the trial has been good-humored but grim. The Government is out to win and is doing its best to provide me with a long prison term at public expense." [41]

The jury returned after an absence of thirty hours, convicted the American Socialist Society, and acquitted Scott Nearing. The Espionage Act, which did not net a single German spy or saboteur, had not caught Nearing either. But the verdict occasioned puzzlement; the co-defendants had, after all, been charged with the same substantive offenses connected with the authorship and distribution of *The Great Madness*. Professor Zechariah Chafee duly noted that the jury's conclusion was "interesting," but left it unexplained, a task that must therefore be attempted here.[42]

The judge himself accounted for the seeming inconsistency by assuming that a jury is naturally more sympathetic to a person than to a corporation, especially if the person exudes dedication and idealism: "The human being may lose his liberty if convicted, while the worst that can happen to the corporation is the imposition of a fine." Hillquit similarly speculated that "the jurors had compassion for Scott

Nearing, a person in the flesh, whom they saw and heard, but they had little sympathy with . . . a mere abstraction without physical existence." Walter Nelles and Nearing himself agreed with this interpretation of the verdict.[43]

Such an explanation ignores the political context of 1919, when jurors were unlikely to presume the innocence of Socialists charged with obstruction of the war effort. Of the 1,956 citizens indicted under the Espionage Act, 877 were convicted. But except for the two trials of the *Masses* editors, whose antimilitarism had been considerably muffled during the course of the war, no other prominent Socialist whom the government prosecuted could escape the wrath of juries. Even O'Brian belatedly recognized jurors' "instinctive aversion toward anyone ever under suspicion for disloyalty." [44]

Others suspected that Nearing had talked his way out of a trip to the penitentiary. Bettman told Thomas that "in New York City it's very hard to convict any of your folks who can make a good speech to the jury." Nelles claimed that his client had been "so lucid, so forceful, and so honest that he could make even political adversaries see that what he meant was not something sinister and covert, but just exactly what he said." Admittedly eloquence helped; and a famous precedent could be found in an 1849 sedition trial in Cologne, in which the foreman of the jury that rendered an acquittal thanked Dr. Marx for his most instructive lecture on German social conditions. But searing rhetoric was often futile, and Nearing's lacked the sublimity of Debs' plea to an unconvinced Cleveland jury that "men are fit for something better than slavery and cannon fodder; and the time will come . . . when men will marvel that there ever was a time when men who called themselves civilized rushed upon each other like wild beasts and murdered one another. . . . I can hear the shrieks of the soldiers of Europe in my dreams." [45]

The jurors who listened impassively to Debs averaged seventy-two years in age and more than $50,000 in personal wealth. Nearing confronted a more varied group, which the *Times* learned had "stood ten to two in favor of . . . [conviction], the two men holding out because they believed Nearing was entitled to his convictions"—but not to a conviction. Francis Caffey told essentially the same story to Gregory, adding that the two holdouts had been born in Russia. If so, Sam Gordon, an importer-exporter, and Solomon Marcus, a retired tradesman, saved Nearing from the fate of other Socialists and caused the U.S. Attorney to complain about "the cosmopolitan character of the population in this District." [46] The verdict thus makes sense if seen as a compromise, as the only way for the majority to prevent the declaration of a hung jury.

But when counsel for the defense moved that the entire verdict be set aside as inconsistent, Mayer could only uphold the decision within the rules of logic. The jury may have construed the motives of Nearing differently from the corporation that published his pamphlet, the judge reasoned; for unlike the solitary literary figure, the American Socialist Society may have designed a "program whereby its anti-war attitude in various aspects should be consistently . . . expressed by means, among other things, of the publication and distribution of pamphlets." [47]

When counsel for the Society appealed Mayer's finding of consistency, the Circuit Court of Appeals for the Second District explained that "Nearing must have been acquitted on one of two grounds, viz. either that the pamphlet itself was innocuous or that he had no intent to obstruct the recruiting and enlistment service of the United States." Nearing could not have been acquitted on the basis of the harmless tendency of *The Great Madness,* Judge Henry C. Ward reasoned, because then its publisher should also have been acquitted. The court therefore felt "justified in finding that the acquittal was on the second ground," the criminal nature of the intent.[48] But Ward, speaking for the appellate court, slipped on something he himself had thrown away. For in order to uphold the conviction on the basis of bad intent, he conceded as a premise that the pamphlet was harmless. Therefore, if the publication had no bad tendency, why was the Society guilty, since both elements of effect and intent comprised the tests of criminal responsibility? Ward's own assumption undermined his conclusion of culpability.

If judicial logic was not impregnable, Mayer should at least be credited with surprising fairness, which provided a brief respite between the last spasms of wartime hysteria and the first convulsions of the Red Scare. As a patriotic conservative, he may have welcomed a *Walpurgisnacht* for radicals; but in the daytime drama of the courtroom he was more tolerant than they had reason to expect. Nearing was given an ample forum from which to expound the principles of Socialism and pacifism. The conviction of the Society on the third count, the attempt to cause insubordination in the armed forces, Mayer set aside for lack of evidence. On the fourth count, the judge told the jury to consider the likely effect of *The Great Madness* only upon recruitment and enlistment, not upon conscription. The next month, in the *Debs, Schenck,* and *Frohwerk* cases, the Supreme Court was less lenient, and defined the draft as a form of recruitment subject to the full force of the Espionage Act. Admittedly Mayer's general interpretation of the Act, in his charge to the jury, presaged the March 1919 decisions; but Nelles had little justification to denounce Mayer's "venom" in *United States* v. *Nearing et al.*[49]

Otherwise radicals were ecstatic about the verdict. The *Call* perceived "a sign of returning sanity," adding that "every member of the robber class, all those who legally loot and pile up ill-gotten millions, would have rejoiced" had the Socialist agitator been convicted. The *Messenger,* a "mag-

azine of scientific radicalism" that A. Philip Randolph and
Chandler Owen edited, hailed the "unassuming, poised,
and brilliant" defendant who "answered every question
without evasion. . . . He has placed his wonderful powers
at the service of the lowly, the humble, the poor. . . . Race,
creed, color, and sex produce no prejudice in Nearing."
Giovannitti was more casual: the former professor "was not
an accused on trial before his judges, not a thinker defending a new unorthodox theory before a synod of academicians, nor was he even the usual agitator haranguing a hostile crowd." Nearing was merely a "scientific investigator
who had arrived at the true diagnosis of a social sore and
was telling it to his patients." Nelles hailed Nearing as "a
dedicated person, wholly indifferent to personal consequences," and attributed the success of the defense tactics to
"a personal quality of the size of Scott Nearing's to put itself
across." [50]

When the Supreme Court refused to review the conviction of the American Socialist Society, the Rand School gaily
collected three thousand one-dollar bills and deposited
them in the office of the U.S. Attorney. But Waldman re-
trospectively punctured the euphoria of the moment, for he
noted that "the trial embittered Nearing and made him less
valuable as he lost moderation." [51] The trial culminated
three years of personally intensive effort in behalf of pacifism and Socialism, an ordeal that seemed to generate more
frustration than achievement, more hostility than comradeship. The rare courage that rendered Nearing invulnerable
to patriotic pressure would soon sour into such assurance of
his own rectitude that he would abandon the attempt to
learn, to open himself to the processes of correction, to let
perception ripen into wisdom. Soon the beliefs to which he
bore witness during the war congealed into platitudes without nuance, which he mechanically summoned for all occasions. His excoriation of oligarchy became automatic, like

a tic. Because he considered the wartime persecutions unjust, and his postwar trial illegitimate, Nearing would soon define himself in terms of the enmity he aroused, as though unpopularity substantiated the viability of his creed and the worth of his character. He too was one of the casualties of war.

CHAPTER SIX

ON REVOLUTION

JIMMIE HIGGINS, THE SOCIALISTS' ARCHETYPAL factotum, was cast as the title character of an Upton Sinclair wartime novel and was scheduled to die during the Meuse-Argonne offensive. But when the United States engaged in an undeclared war during the Russian civil war, Sinclair hastily added two chapters. As one of the soldiers shipped to Archangel, Jimmie Higgins realizes that President Wilson has ordered him into an illegal and immoral war, and he is reawakened to the vile character of capitalist imperialism. At the end of the novel, he goes insane in an Archangel jail.[1]

The United States had been the first power to recognize the Russian provisional government after the March Revolution, and it was to be the last major power to recognize the Bolshevik government established after the November Revolution. With the collapse of the Eastern front, American troops landed in Siberia in the late summer of 1918 for a variety of purposes, few of them purely anti-German: to restrain the economic and geopolitical appetites of the Japanese, to maintain the Open Door in the Far East, and to demonstrate Wilson's expressed desire to help the Russians. "What Russians?" was Lenin's pointed reply. The American claim of noninterference in internal affairs became increasingly difficult to maintain, especially after the Armistice and Wilson's illness, as the State Department openly adopted the British and French policies of support for the White reactionaries under Admiral Alexander Kolchak. The Administration added to the miseries of war with the imposition of a food blockade. Yet, as Winston Churchill concluded, "enough foreign troops entered Russia to incur all the objections which were patent against intervention, but not enough to break the then gimcrack structure of the Soviet power." [2]

Thus Allied intervention provoked charges of hypocrisy from radicals like Debs: "We were not too proud to recognize the Tsar . . . whilst Siberia was in existence and human beings were treated like wild beasts; when women were put under the lash and sent to Siberia and brutalized and dehumanized. . . ." [3] Nearing fully shared the outrage that radicals felt toward American policy, and he enunciated his support of Bolshevism with characteristic bravado. Unlike Jimmie Higgins, he needed no reminders of capitalist perfidy; and on November 7, 1918, he celebrated not only the Revolution but the recent triumph of the Republicans: "The political structure of a nation should reflect its industrial organization. Under the domination of a set of despots, bourbons, and tories, such as no other country possessed, our political structure will exactly reflect our industrial structure." Sharing the platform with Reed, Eastman, and others, Nearing received the most thunderous ovation of the evening when he predicted that American workers would dispose of their "tories" just as Russian workers had done. [4]

The night after the signing of the Armistice, Nearing suggested to another Manhattan audience that "expressions of good cheer and messages of encouragement are not the things that the Russian and German workers want from us.

They want from us a Workers' and Soldiers' Council in New York City. They want from us a Workers' and Soldiers' Government in the United States." In the same week he joined Rose Pastor Stokes and Ludwig Lore in Harlem to celebrate the German revolution, which Lenin considered indispensable for the survival of Bolshevik Russia. He also became a contributing editor to *Revolutionary Age,* which Louis Fraina edited on behalf of Left Wing Socialism and to which Lenin sent "A Letter to American Workingmen," predicting different paths to revolution. Nearing and Reed were the only two native Americans on the editorial staff of *Revolutionary Age,* as the party itself shifted from gradualist doctrines and from its prewar base west of the Mississippi.[5]

In April the man the *Times* labeled "our leading revolutionist and sociologist" debated Professor Albert Bushnell Hart on the Fourteenth Point. The New York hall was so packed that crowds spilled into the aisles and onto the stage as Nearing blasted the "league of highwaymen" and proposed "another remedy as against the League of Nations. I suggest revolution! . . . . The next six months will see the combination of Russia, Germany, Austria-Hungary, and other portions of Central Europe that will be far more effective as a method of preventing war than any other League of Nations now in existence." The Harvard historian was startled: "Had I supposed that I would be obliged to listen and hear my country called a robber nation, to hear the industrial system of the United States called an abominable system that ought to be put down by revolution, I would not have set foot in this hall." Hart had set foot in Nearing's territory; for when he rhetorically asked whether America really wanted the devastation of revolution, a burst of applause and cheers greeted the professor.[6]

The disciple of Tolstoy did not praise the methods of the Red armies and the Chekist police; and upon the request of

Lochner and others, he dashed off a pamphlet in 1919 aimed at workers, *Violence or Solidarity?* In it Nearing argued that force made social advance more difficult and urged resort to solidarity and reason. In another pamphlet a year later, he held up the example of the plutocracy: "The manufacturers, merchants, brokers, bankers, and lawyers stand by one another in their efforts to conserve and protect property. They have given one of the most effective demonstrations . . . of the extraordinary results that may be expected to follow from a well-conceived policy of social cooperation." [7] Specific manifestations of proletarian solidarity were not advocated, however, though *The One Big Union of Business* lends substance to the suspicion that hatred and protest may be transmutations of envy.

Nearing soon enough got a taste of what he perceived as the class consciousness of American capitalists, when Attorney General Mitchell Palmer, a legislative father of the Federal drive to abolish child labor, manipulated the Red Scare. In January 1919 a Senate committee investigating German propaganda had already placed Nearing in a rogues' gallery of a hundred American radicals. The list was so laden with errors that the Senators cut half the names, but Nearing's survived among the hard core of insurrectionaries. [8]

The author of the list was Archibald Stevenson of the Military Intelligence Service, who soon rose to the rank of field commander of a raid upon the Rand School. Armed with a search warrant addressed to John Doe, Richard Roe, Thomas Poe, and Mary Roe, the raiders also brought along a safecracker to blow open the most nefarious designs of Socialist subversives. But when the Lusk Committee of the New York legislature, which authorized the raid, brought suit to revoke the character of the Rand School, the State Supreme Court dismissed charges of subversion for lack of evidence. The committee was then reduced to raising a whiff of perversion in announcing that the School's book store had displayed a copy of Marie Carmichael Stopes' *Married Love.*[9]

Stymied in its efforts to quash radical dissent through litigation and innuendo, the Lusk Committee then decided to expose its evidence of subversion by publishing four volumes entitled *Revolutionary Radicalism.* The name of Lenin, who was presumably not subject to prosecution in New York State, appeared most often in its pages; second was a citizen of Chicago, Jane Addams. But Nearing was not forgotten, for the committee sardonically noted that he provided "intellectual stimulus" for the Amalgamated Textile Workers of America. "Agitation was a profitable calling to at least one of the lecturers in the Rand School, namely Scott Nearing," the investigators concluded, because within one monthly period he earned $616.[10]

Nearing refused to comment publicly, because he considered capitalist journalists "frankly enemies." But to Upton Sinclair he explained his financial arrangements: "My contract with the Rand School called for a salary of $35 a week and a bonus of $15 for each class in which the attendance exceeded 250 . . . I agreed to teach about five or six classes. . . . The publicity incident to the trial brought a host of students into the Rand School." He added that he "did some lecturing for the Rand School outside. . . . In such cases the school took 20% of the fee and I got 80%." Though Nearing offered "no defense . . . for taking as much as $15 for a lecture . . . most lecturers get a good deal higher fees than I do for the same grade of work. Personally, I believe they are overpaid." Nevertheless, he conveniently argued, if one lecturer "cuts the rates on the others, it seems a good deal like scabbing on the profession." [11]

The Red Scare itself reduced his opportunities to lecture, however. In May 1919 Nearing was prohibited from addressing a Socialist rally in New York City. In November an injunction prevented him from disseminating Socialism in Lafayette, Indiana, thanks to a new organization named the American Legion.[12] That month Waldman and four other Socialists elected to the New York State Assembly became the ticket that exploded when, though Hillquit and Charles Evans Hughes provided counsel, they were denied their seats. Nearing not only plunged into the defense of the Albany Five but worked for the release of "class war prisoners" and other victims of the war and Red Scare. The National Civil Liberties Bureau organized the Liberty Defense Union to demand amnesty for some 1500 Socialists, Wobblies, religious pacifists, and assorted other radicals who awaited trial and languished in jail. Charles Ervin of the *Call* served as chairman and Nearing as a member of its executive committee. The Liberty Defense Union quickly dissolved, however, and from its ruins emerged the Workers Liberty Defense Union, whose leaders were Ervin, Nearing, and Elizabeth Gurley Flynn, the already immortalized "rebel girl" of Wobbly troubadour Joe Hill. With subsidization from trade unions and radical organizations, the amnesty campaign continued until 1923, when the last victims of the wartime attack on the IWW walked out of prison. Not until Christmas 1933, however, were pardons issued to all those convicted under the Selective Service and Espionage Acts.[13]

With Bolshevik braggadocio John Reed had assured Baldwin that the aroused working class would imminently free him from the penitentiary. Although such hopes were dashed, and he was sprinkled with Armistice confetti on his way to jail for refusing to fight the recently defeated Germans, Baldwin was treated well, cultivated a garden on the outside, and was even released daily to arrange the files of the National Civil Liberties Bureau.[14] "I enjoyed the whole experience," he recalled. "I liked many of the prisoners, no better nor worse than those outside." They included a couple of other draft resisters: Louis Fraina, who helped found the Communist party later in 1919, and Ralph Cheyney, the son of the Penn historian who rose to Nearing's defense. Nearing, sometimes bringing along his elder son, Johnny, was probably Baldwin's most faithful visitor. After one visit the prisoner chased Nearing for a couple of blocks in order to continue a discussion, leaving Johnny quite confused about the meaning of incarceration.[15] When Baldwin wrote to an assistant from his prison cell, he mentioned Nearing along with Thomas and Elizabeth Gurley Flynn as helping to prepare the "big cause" that became the American Civil Liberties Union in 1920. Nearing became a charter member of the organization but did not hold office or serve on its board.[16]

Another "class war prisoner" whom Nearing befriended was Ralph Chaplin, heir to the bardic mantle of Joe Hill. Sentenced to two decades in Leavenworth, with his wife and son in danger of eviction for failure to meet mortgage payments, Chaplin accepted Nearing's advice to publish his verse. With the bully-boy posturing that marked the Wobblies, Chaplin did not "want anyone to try to make me out a 'poet'"; but Nearing arranged for the publication of *Bars and Shadows* and wrote a fervent introduction to express outrage at Chaplin's imprisonment and to call for a more humane social order. Nearing actively promoted the book, the Chaplins' home was saved, and his sentence was commuted in 1923.[17']

The most famous convict was Atlanta Penitentiary's No. 9653, Eugene Debs, for whom Nearing also engaged in an amnesty campaign. Because the "same lawyer-business element that controlled Palestine 2,000 years ago controls the United States today," Nearing told the Inter-Church World Movement, he eagerly signed up for a national speaking tour coordinated with the Socialists' 1920 Presidential campaign. Since Debs' last hurrah was restricted to a weekly

United Press bulletin from Atlanta, the active responsibility for conducting the campaign was expected to fall to the Vice-Presidential nominee. Speculation centered upon Kate Richards O'Hare, *la pasionaria* of the Corn Belt and choice of the rank and file; Maurer, whose recent election as president of the Pennsylvania State Federation of Labor kept Federal agents from arresting him at the end of the convention; and James Oneal and Nearing, two of the party's most reliable publicists. But at the Socialists' national convention, the delegates chose Stedman, perhaps because they found one endorsement especially persuasive: "Nobody but a lawyer can run for Vice-President on the Socialist ticket at this time. . . . He knows just exactly what to say, say it well, and keep out of jail at the same time." [18]

After listing the handicaps of a "candidate in prison, the party outlawed in many places, meetings difficult or impossible," Nearing nevertheless detected "a great current of unrest rushing and surging everywhere." Only 26,766 comrades paid their dues that year, but they campaigned with a win-one-for-the-Gipper frenzy. Nearing contributed to party coffers with two pamphlets, *A Nation Divided* and *The New Slavery,* of which 40,000 were put on sale; and the ticket attracted an unprecedented 915,302 votes. But the Nineteenth Amendment sliced the proportion of the Socialist total from 6 percent in 1912 to 3.5 percent in 1920; and since party membership continued to decline after the election, many Americans apparently preferred to protest Debs' incarceration rather than help realize his dream.[19]

LABOR JOURNALISM WAS ANOTHER MOVEMENT TO WHICH Nearing devoted considerable energy and attention. Immediately after the war he helped organize the short-lived International Labor News Service, whose purpose was to provide news material to trade union journals that the "bourgeois" press might disregard or inappropriately slant. Its replacement was the Federated Press, a cooperative news service that delegates to a farmer-labor conference organized in 1919 to "report objectively all matters of interest to the workers everywhere." Over seventy trade union and radical journals received mimeographed stories daily, and each was granted one vote in the determination of policy.[20]

Robert Morss Lovett served as president of the Federated Press, but its virtually indispensable man was Carl Haessler, a former Rhodes scholar who had taught philosophy at the University of Illinois. He had also headed its Socialist club, which Dean Nearing had addressed; and his incisive hostility to the leisure class had impressed Haessler. The philosophy instructor had blamed American intervention on "commercial imperialists" and refused conscription, not for "private, secret, personal, impulsive, religious, pacifist or pro-German" reasons, but as "a patriotic political objector." Fired from the University of Illinois, he was sentenced to Leavenworth, where he organized a school for political prisoners. After a stint on the Socialist Milwaukee *Leader*, Haessler became managing editor and secretary-treasurer of the Federated Press in 1922.[21]

Headquarters were established in Chicago, with bureaus in New York, Washington, and Europe, where Lochner moonlighted as bureau chief while serving as an Associated Press correspondent in Berlin. Other correspondents included Chaplin, Leland Olds, Carl Sandburg, Anna Louise Strong, Mary Heaton Vorse, Ella G. Wolfe, and Art Young.[22] "I am giving all of my spare time and energy" to the Federated Press, Nearing told Sinclair; he also gave the news service the serial rights to his pamphlet, *Oil and the Germs of War*.[23] In return, press credentials provided him with a sanction and an opportunity for travel.

When Lenin once learned that British strikers and bobbies had been playing soccer together, he reputedly blurted out that England would never experience a revolution. Nearing was more optimistic, and in 1920 represented the Federated Press at the Trades Union Congress in Portsmouth, where he predicted that England would be the scene of an imminent revolution. To exclude Nearing from participation in it, however, Sir William Joynson-Hicks, who served as Home Secretary in Stanley Baldwin's Conservative Cabinet, rejected the visa application of the orator who had in Canada recently described "The Crumbling British Empire." While the Federated Press lodged a formal protest against the "boycott against labor correspondents," others intervened more effectively. George Lansbury had met Nearing in Philadelphia in 1913 and had "pictured him ending his days as a prosy old man, teaching young men how to be respectable by not being too enthusiastic or too revolutionary." Lansbury was subsequently elected to the House of Commons and, with the aid of another Labour M.P., Ellen Wilkinson, assured the Home Secretary that Nearing would not destroy the British Empire. A visa was issued, and Nearing attended another Trades Union Congress.[24]

Closer to home other conservatives expressed equivalent fears of the persuasive power of radicals. Baldwin, for example, was denied the right to address New York City high school students and, in 1925, was indicted in Paterson, New Jersey, for attempting "to destroy and wreck the city hall, to the great terror and disturbance of the citizens." During a dock strike in San Pedro, California, in 1923, Sinclair was arrested for reading aloud from the First Amendment. The American Civil Liberties Union itself was prohibited from using a New York high school auditorium to present a program on " 'Old Fashioned' Free Speech." No chauvinist organization was more hostile to Baldwin's agency than the National Civic Federation; and Easley, who coined the term "free-speech faker" to denigrate the motives of radical champions of the Bill of Rights, refused even to debate representatives of the ACLU.[25]

At the University of Wisconsin the Social Science Club wanted to invite Nearing to speak in the gymnasium in October 1921. With the approval of President Edward A. Birge, a faculty committee rejected the club's request; and a storm erupted. The students' *Daily Cardinal* released all of its dammed-up syntax: "The student body deems it its right to demand that it be not everlastingly coddled with pussyfoot ideas so that its vision will be warped and its will and reason become walled against progressive thought. . . . The student body wants to know reality, not veiled and mystified with hollow phrases, but . . . unvarnished, naked, and bare, from the lips of men and women who have lived and met with the jars and jolts of the world." Slightly more sedate was the *Wisconsin State Journal:* "Offer bibs and sugar teats to a football nurtured student body and you are sure to provoke an intellectual riot. . . . Doubless student intelligence will be able to spot the nigger in the woodpile, if nigger there be, and the chance to do so is good practice." [26]

Although the Madison *Capital-Times* blamed the ban on free speech on "special interests," Nearing could somehow not be prevented from speaking off-campus in a high school auditorium. A packed and enthusiastic house welcomed him to the capital of midwestern Progressivism; and a reporter found him "a youngish-looking, smooth-faced, alert man, democratic in appearance and deportment. He talks with great rapidity and brilliance of diction." Nearing's speech emphasized the manner in which American surplus wealth was converted into foreign investment, and only in his conclusion did he specifically advocate socialism. Later President Birge criticized the Social Science Club as a "propagandist organization for socialistic doctrines," and in January the State Board of Regents affirmed its "ultimate control of university buildings and a measure of responsibility for the speakers who speak from a university platform." Control was exercised more moderately thereafter, and the *Wisconsin State Journal* inquired: "How long would a Nearing have lasted in this level-headed country had he not been booted out of colleges and denied freedom for his politically licentious tongue? . . . . And since his departure, what has all the hubbub been concerned with? His speech? Not a score can remember what he said." [27]

Five months after Nearing left Madison, he came to Worcester, Massachusetts, at the invitation of the Liberal Club of Clark University to speak on "The Control of Public Opinion in the United States." After about an hour of his address, while Nearing was citing Veblen's *Higher Learning in America*, President Wallace W. Atwood slipped into the back of the hall. Having given cursory approval to the meeting, Atwood was shocked to hear the lecturer's "malignment [*sic*] of the moral integrity of the American people . . . the unscientific method of presentation, and the intemperate manner." Atwood did not apparently know that Nearing was quoting Veblen; Nearing did not know that Atwood was Veblen's brother-in-law.[28]

So the president leaped from his seat and strode across the hall to demand that the president of the Liberal Club stop the "disgusting" speech. After a brief conference, the pair walked upon the stage, and the school's leading liberal whispered to the famous saboteur of the status quo, who then politely ceased his address. Choking with emotion, Atwood announced three times that the meeting was adjourned. The audience of about 300 persons, who had paid 25¢ each, began hissing and stirred only when the president ordered the lights off. The motto of Clark University, ironists in the hall might have observed, was "Fiat Lux."

Grumbling members of the audience filed out; and some

professors dispersed toward the platform to shake hands with the speaker, who accepted an invitation to complete his discussion of the plutocratic control of American institutions at the Kappa Phi fraternity house. Until early morning students and teachers clotted in animated discussions on the campus, although several officers of the Liberal Club confessed their disappointment at the blandness of the speech. In fact, Nearing told the press, "it was one of my mildest speeches . . . [but] this is the first time that a university president ever went to the trouble to prove by a public act that he was unwilling to let students hear our side of the case." [29]

In rubbing raw the nerves of one man, Nearing aggravated the temper of a university. Beginning with an indignation meeting at the Kappa Phi house, what passed in the age of normalcy for a student revolt flared on the Clark campus. Representatives of all undergraduate organizations disclaimed adherence to Bolshevism, socialism, or anarchism, but demanded "the inalienable right of self-expression within the environs of the University." The vice-president of the Liberal Club was struck in the face after accusing another student of supporting Atwood, and the president of the club intoned what must have constituted the ultimate threat: "If we could raise the money, we would engage Upton Sinclair." [30]

While asserting his belief in "absolute academic freedom within the university," Atwood found no inconsistency in warning that future meetings of campus organizations would need his explicit approval. "If the Liberal Club attempts to conduct meetings in an outside hall," he continued, "they [sic] will have to deal with the United States Government." The champion of "absolute academic freedom" also insisted that speeches "be made without passion, without any intention of furthering misunderstanding, or of arousing antagonism or hatred in the minds of one

group of people against any other group." Atwood feared
the influence of "Reds" among college youth, and cited evidence of subversion in a series of magazine articles written
by no less an authority than Calvin Coolidge.[31] The president ordered plainclothesmen and uniformed policemen on
campus, and he received a letter that he interpreted as a
death threat. He managed to find solace, however, in the
babbitt warren of the local Rotary Club, which hailed his
"patriotic stand against radical propaganda." [32]

Others were more critical—like the American Civil Liberties Union, whose protest campaign fizzled. An editor of the
New Republic interviewed Atwood, a "captain of erudition"
much like the object of his brother-in-law's barbs. Also onto
the Clark campus marched an AAUP committee of inquiry
under the command of Professor Lovejoy, to determine the
extent of the university's "maladministration." The committee devoted over ten pages of its subsequent report to "the
Nearing incident," and condemned Atwood's "failure to understand either the spirit of a university or the ordinary
workings of human nature." The AAUP committee also criticized presidential paternalism and the "irrelevance" of Atwood's "attempt to raise the issue of 'Bolshevism.' " Because
he interpreted the students' and teachers' insistence upon
free speech as the genesis of a revolt, the Lovejoy group
concluded, "the most regrettable consequence of the incident . . . was its effect upon the mind of Dr. Atwood
himself." Nearing's brief entrance and exit, stage left,
merely worsened an already poor relationship between
president and faculty.[33]

Although a dean at UCLA denied Nearing permission to
speak because of his "abnormal mind," although the Sons of
the American Revolution almost prevented him from coming to the University of Utah, at least the Rand School val-
ued his services. "The growth of the school is really remarkable and . . . encouraging," Lee reported late in 1918,

adding that the "most pressing problem. . . is that of teachers" for the several thousand students of both sexes, of whom most were adults of proletarian origin.[34] Nearing taught everything from economics to education, from statistical methods to the philosophy of Tolstoy, from sociology to oratory; and the limitations of space kept half the applicants away. Most distinctive was the pedagogy he devised to suit working-class radicalism. His course in public speaking, for example, included assignments not required in the Ivy League: how to introduce Debs at a rally, how to deliver an attack on profiteering, how to propose a toast at a public dinner to Lenin and Trotsky. Because of the 5½-day work week in the garment district, Nearing also offered a special course at the Rand School on Saturday afternoons: for 25¢ a worker could hear the famous economist unravel the meaning of the week's news.[35]

Besides Nearing and Lee, the regular members of the faculty were Alexander Trachtenberg, the director of labor research, and David P. Berenberg and Benjamin P. Glassberg, who had been expelled from the New York City school system for their pro-Bolshevik attitudes. Such sympathies became incompatible with the social democratic Rand School; and three years after Lee had expressed such optimism for the growth of the institution, Trachtenberg and Glassberg depleted it with their departure. And then, in 1922, Nearing's favorite teacher died, after Penn had denied him an honorary degree. At the end Simon Nelson Patten felt convinced that only government intervention and coercion could sway men from "old antagonisms" and "senseless stupidity" and thus assure the benefits of abundance.[36]

WITH THE CREATION OF AMERICAN COMMUNISM IN 1919, the choreography of the left became an intricate maze of couplings and divisions, surprising solo performances, odd displays of technical skill, ungainly and awkward splits, inchoate patterns, sudden twists and turns, unexpected exits, highly expressive gestures in stationary positions, occasional comic pratfalls, and many slow-motion imitations of the styles of the Ballets Russes. In the heroic period of the Revolution, all the dancers favored their left sides; even Hillquit, whom Trotsky deemed the "Babbitt of Babbitts," defended the "dictatorship of the proletariat." When the Socialist party wanted to join the Bolsheviks' Third International, however, stringent conditions of membership were imposed, including the primacy of the Central Committee, subservience to the Comintern, the extirpation of "reformism," and the specific repudiation of Hillquit. These demands would have transmogrified American Socialism; but suppose, for the sake of international unity, the party had agreed to the Twenty-One Demands? "We would find a twenty-second," Comrade Zinoviev replied.[37]

As some Socialists became disenchanted with the course of Leninism, as others chafed at the moderation and anemia of the believers in the cooperative commonwealth, the danse macabre played itself out. Trachtenberg and Glassberg quit the Rand School in 1921 to join the Workers Party, as the Communists called themselves until 1929. Although Nearing was a member of the educational committee of the School, he did not involve himself in questions of policy and curriculum; and he played a lone guileless hand in the affairs of the Socialist party itself. He even skipped its 1920 national convention, although attendance required only a subway ride uptown into Harlem. Nearing preferred to adorn the party rather than to influence its character; without the politician's talent for identifying self-aggrandizement with the aggrandizement of party, he accomplished neither. Unlike the earlier fallen angel whom John Milton cast in important partisan struggles, Nearing exhibited little desire to "reign in hell" once more-respectable employment had been denied. He scrupulously avoided factional disputes and frequently criticized the schismatic proclivities of the left, which the rise of Communism exacerbated.[38]

Yet Nearing, too, felt the sapping of Socialist energies even as he thrilled to Bolshevik achievements. As the suspicions between the two movements froze into hatred, the teacher who loved to quote the Declaration of Independence realized that his party had become "a counter-revolutionary force . . . attacking the Communists. . . . They were the shock troops for capitalism. The [Socialists'] *Daily Forward* was more vituperative than the New York *Times* against the Bolshevik Revolution." [39] His own attitude was stated most cogently in a 1924 debate in New York on the applicability of the Soviet polity to the West, in which he associated change in Russia with progress and identified the historical greatness of the Revolution with its goodness.

Nearing adopted the Marxist idea that "the forms of government correspond to the stages in social development." Because the social order collapsed first in Russia, she was the first to develop a new form, "a bridge over the abyss, working toward communism and away from capitalism." Nearing then listed the three most serious political contributions of the Bolsheviks: the idea of economic rather than geographic representation; the scientific organization of the economy; and the application of the principle, "He that will not work, neither shall he eat." The man Baldwin called a "puritan revolutionist" praised the Russians with their "millions of living units of suffering agony, while we have been going to the movies and living on the fat of the land." The credo of economic determinism taught Nearing that Western capitalism had to disintegrate, to be replaced with "the dictatorship of a group of industrial workers under a highly organized and disciplined party like the Communist party in Russia." [40]

His debating opponent that evening had been jailed for penning an anticonscription leaflet during the war, when some American pacifists called him "the Scott Nearing of England"—a comparison that showed their ignorance of *Principia Mathematica*. Bertrand Russell was also the author of *The Practice and Theory of Bolshevism*, written after a disillusioning five weeks' visit to Russia in 1920; and he was as clever as a host of Huxleys.[41] Nearing's premises were not fully acceptable, but "since they will allow my conclusion, I will accept them for a moment," John Stuart Mill's godson confidently began. Since tsarist Russia followed a different economic pattern, heavily founded upon peasant industries and handicrafts, its political form was bound to differ from the West's. Russell further argued that revolutions are most likely to erupt when military defeat has been inflicted upon a nation, a prospect he did not foresee for England and especially not for the United States. Furthermore Russian history includes "a Byzantine tradition of centralization and despotism, a tradition from which people with our Western tradition are separated by a great gulf."

Having shown that Nearing's premises could lead to an opposite conclusion, Russell then proceeded to batter his premises. Dismissing the primacy of economic causation, the aristocrat observed that China and Russia had similar economic structures yet very divergent civilizations. He also disputed the authenticity of economic representation in Russia: "It is a government by the Communist party . . . this is to say, by people having certain opinions." The Russians were unscientific because of their fidelity to a "dogma" that was "too simple"; and they were subverting the ideal of justice, which could "never be realized by methods of violence and by methods of force."

Russell conceded that "as a transition in an uneducated country, I think the Bolsheviks have chosen probably the better way." He implied that it was wrong to deny Western peoples—but not Russians—their political and civil rights, and added: "Where people are accustomed to participation in politics . . . it is a totally impossible method. . . . If you tried the methods tried in Russia, you would find . . . that it would be the Fascisti who would emerge," he warned. "In the French Revolution you got not only the Committee of Public Safety in the middle of it, you got Napoleon at the end of it." Nearing's rebuttal reiterated his faith in economic determinism and in the inevitable passing of capitalism. He also expressed with candor his own tactical goal: "The change that I have suggested must come . . . by the appointment of a Committee of Public Safety." [42]

Robespierre was a lawyer without clients, Marat was a doctor without patients, and Nearing was increasingly becoming a teacher without students. He formally resigned from the Socialist party in 1922 because of its hostility to Bolshevism; but he continued to serve on the faculty of the Rand School, where he and his wife also worked for its Labor Research Committee.[43] But he complained to Lee that "the school is getting away from labor education toward the same kind of cultural education that school boards in various cities provide." Eager to train cadres to shift the American Federation of Labor to the left, the Rand School's most popular teacher quit the institution that had sheltered him in 1917. He abandoned the movement because it could not inspire "the class conscious worker who should have but one object in view—the dictatorship of the proletariat." [44]

"I LIKE TO GO OUT IN THE COUNTRY AND BLOVIATE!" WAS President Harding's contribution to what might be termed neological positivism. About the same time, the Nearing family left New York City to live in bucolic Ridgewood, New Jersey. During the war Louis and Minnie Nearing had

moved from Morris Run to Ridgewood so that he could oc-
cupy his seat on the New York Stock Exchange. But despite
the rising market, the former grocer and liquor dealer had
managed to lose some of the fortune that he had inherited
from Tsar Nearing. For about two years Louis' son and
family occupied the basement, which consisted of two
rooms, a kitchenette, and bathroom, until the garage was
converted into a new home. Louis was a Democrat, Minnie
a Republican; and their son's unconventional politics were
normally not topics of conversation. Warmth between father and son still could not be kindled, but Nearing continued his close relationship with his mother. He did not
maintain affectionate ties with his siblings; all three of his
sisters married into the upper strata of the bourgeoisie, one
brother became an engineer for the New York Central
Railroad, and the other pursued a variety of interests, particularly botany, an interest that Minnie Nearing shared.[45]

Whatever warmth the family hearth failed to supply the
heat of political controversy generated, for the Ridgewood
guest book bore as many notorious names as a Red Scare
subpoena. Solon De Leon, the son of the founder of the Socialist Labor Party and a Rand School researcher, helped
erect the Nearings' roof and called his month's visit "one of
the loveliest vacations in my life." Cartoonist Robert Minor
wished "that the Nearing family will be in on the Dictatorship"; and, somewhat tamer, Harry Laidler of the
League for Industrial Democracy expressed his appreciation for a "royal week-end with rustic revolutionists. What a
treat." Anthropologist Melville Herskovitz hoped that the
Communists would not be "the lamb to be led to the slaughter." Other guests included Socialists like Paul Blanshard,
Nathan Fine, Algernon Lee, Jacob Panken, and Norman
Thomas; liberals like Stuart Chase, Lewis Gannett, and Rex
Tugwell; radical pacifists like Jessica Smith and Harry F.
Ward; Robert Morss Lovett and Carl Haessler of the Fed-

erated Press; Roger Baldwin, Robert Dunn, and Joseph Freeman of the American Civil Liberties Union; writers and editors like Margaret Anderson, V. F. Calverton, Ralph Chaplin, and Louis Lochner; and anthropologist Margaret Mead, then a graduate student whom Nearing warned of an early death unless she worked less.[46]

Despite this lengthy list of companions, it is difficult to envision Nearing as a master of the revels, as a radical version of Jay Gatsby. He was such a compulsive worker that he was also perhaps less involved in raising his sons than fathers less anxious to report the vagaries of social revolution. Nearing's sons attended a variety of schools in the United States and Switzerland: while Bob enrolled in "a very ritzy progressive school" in Greenwich, Connecticut, Johnny romped in an East Side Quaker institution with the children of Magnes, Panken, Thomas, and Elizabeth Gurley Flynn. Nearing seems to have made no direct attempt to foist his political opinions upon his sons, who would undoubtedly have resisted such influence anyway. "Everyone I met either would compliment me on being my father's son, or reproach me with his opinions," the elder son recalled, "and I decided that I'd like to be someone myself." While attending the University of Wisconsin, he decided to drop his patronymic. He went to a Madison lawyer, who lectured him instead on the importance of filial piety; the attorney's own name was Philip LaFollette. It thus fell to a lawyer down the hall to make him simply John Scott. Bob Nearing attended an agricultural school, became a farmer, and much later worked in a bank. Neither son established especially close ties with his father, who pledged allegiance more conscientiously to the human family than to his own.[47]

The years in Ridgewood also coincided with the disintegration of Nearing's marriage. A suffragist with a doctorate, Nellie Seeds Nearing pursued interests and causes that her husband did not necessarily share. Mead found her "friendly, warm, with a sort of wry humor, always seeing to the heart of flamboyant political pretensions"; while Nearing took himself quite as seriously as the causes he championed. Nor could she fully share her husband's untrammeled idealism, which she deflated with her "impatience with impracticality." [48] Though their relationship remained cordial, in 1925 they separated.

Leaving Ridgewood, dropping her married name, resigning her post as associate director of the Rand School, Nellie Seeds became the director of a boarding school in Pawling, New York. The Manumit School was almost unique among the experimental educational institutions that developed in this decade; nearly all of its forty students, from fifth grade through high school, were the children of trade unionists. Some of its income was derived from the special tuition fee charged to the few bourgeois students, who were given the "privilege of associating with the children of workers." A. J. Muste, the director of Brookwood Labor College, served as chairman of board of Manumit; and Henry Linville, who founded Local 5 of the American Federation of Teachers, served as its co-director. In a curriculum meeting primarily for parents, Nearing urged Manumit to create a specifically socialist and proletarian art. The workers themselves, nevertheless, objected to this early closing time in the museum of conventional bourgeois culture; they wanted their children's education directed toward getting them into college.[49]

Nellie Seeds also participated in the Socialists' League for Industrial Democracy and in the Progressive Education Association, at whose 1932 convention she introduced a resolution calling for a committee to "promote, within the schools and their affiliated bodies, thoughtful and systematic study of the economic and industrial problems confronting the world today." The resolution was adopted; and the committee included the historian Merle Curti, the philosopher Sidney Hook, and George Counts, whose study of class bias in school boards superseded Nearing's 1917 article. But little came of the project except the stigma of radicalism, just as her earlier attempt to investigate the status of Russian women failed to materialize. Nellie Seeds resigned from Manumit in 1932 and, with her younger son, went to live on a farm in Clinton Corners, New York.[50]

MEANWHILE NEARING'S MORE-MILITANT SOCIAL CONSCIENCE was driving him further into the vortex of revolution, at least in theory. He praised Lincoln Steffens' novel *Moses in Red,* which depicted its hero as a Bolshevik and his brother Aaron as a hesitant Menshevik; Nearing especially admired the "vigorous" introductory section on revolution. Nearing's own contribution to the understanding of drastic social change was a class of about twenty students that he organized in the autumn of 1923. Every Saturday afternoon papers were presented and discussed in anticipation of reaching "tentative conclusions that will prove of very real advantage to those classes or groups whose emancipation depends on the success of social revolutionary movements." Nearing wanted to formulate "the laws of social revolution," and to determine why some outbreaks succeed and others fail, when conditions are ripe for revolution, and what constitutes their social and economic effects. The students began with slave revolts and peasant uprisings, traced the bourgeois revolutions of Europe, Japan, and the United States, and concluded with the Paris Commune and the Bolshevik victory in 1917.[51]

Nearing and the most advanced students then summarized the group's investigations in *The Law of Social Revolution,* which appeared in bold red covers in 1926. The book was creditable and original in conception, but in execution verged on caricature. The chapter on the American Revolution, for example, is interesting only as a clumsy imitation of Charles Beard: "Within the thirteen colonies themselves, there raged an economic struggle—in the North between the dominant merchant-capitalists and the oppressed rural and petty bourgeois elements, and in the South between overpowering agricultural capital and the small farmer. These conflicts were sublimated into a war against the mother-country. . . . The revolution may be said to have . . . ended in 1789 with the inauguration of George Washington . . . prophetically enough, in Wall Street." [52]

The participants in the study group included about a half-dozen women as much interested in the teacher as in his subject; Dale Zysman, who collaborated with Nearing on *The Economic Organization of the Soviet Union* under the Communist *nom de guerre* of Jack Hardy; and Ben Davidson, then known as David Benjamin, later the executive secretary of the anti-Communist Liberal Party of New York. Another student, whom Nearing met in the New York Public Library, not only translated *Bambi* and Franz Werfel's *Class Reunion* but became a courier in the Soviet espionage system. Whittaker Chambers' wry, fond remembrance of his teacher, caught in repose amidst a backdrop of revolutionary movement and yearning, may serve to close this chapter of his life: "Nearing's face was his fate. It combined intelligence with strength, was as native American as Gary Cooper and somewhat in the same style. . . . He had a good, plain, uncomplicated mind; the theoretical subtleties of Marx and the tactical flexibilities of Lenin were foreign to it. He was an extreme individualist, with a stubborn streak and used to getting his own way." Chambers further described him as *sui generis,* a "Christian socialist, moved primarily by pacifism," cogitating "in front of the social revolutionists, from time to time slapping into his mouth and chewing with audible energy handfuls of whole oats which he poured from a candy bottle that he always carried with him." [53]

CHAPTER SEVEN
"THE ONLY HUSKY PATIENT"

CHARLES GARLAND, A SHY, SERIOUS HAR-
vard dropout, could not justify the possession of private
property, except to satisfy immediate needs. What distinguished him from other readers of Tolstoy, Thoreau, and
the New Testament was his renunciation of the $815,000
inheritance that constituted a twenty-first birthday gift from
his father. In 1922 his shares of First National Bank of New
York and power companies, railroad bonds, and debentures
were donated to a nonprofit corporation, the American
Fund for Public Service.[1] "Through the Fund," its benefac-
tor wrote, "the money[would] be turned over to individuals
and to groups of individuals. These shall be trusted to use it
to the benefit of mankind—to the benefit of poor as much
as rich, of black as much as white, of foreigners as much as
citizens, of so-called criminals as much as the uncon-
demned." [2] Although Baldwin sold Garland on the idea of the
Fund and was its pivotal figure, Nearing also involved himself in the organization that encapsulated much of the history of the American left during the "prosperity decade."

The composition of its board of directors varied. In addition to Nearing and Baldwin, who served as secretary, it included Norman Thomas; Judah Magnes, whose residence in Palestine prevented him from active participation in the Fund; Harry F. Ward of the Union Theological Seminary; James Weldon Johnson of the National Association for the Advancement of Colored People; Robert Morss Lovett of the University of Chicago; Sidney Hillman and Clinton Golden of the Amalgamated Clothing Workers; Benjamin Gitlow and William Z. Foster of the Workers (Communist) Party; Lewis Gannett and Freda Kirchwey of the *Nation;* Morris Ernst, a libertarian lawyer; and Mary McDowell, a Chicago settlement worker who had addressed Philadelphia's Industrial Exhibition in 1906.[3] This board was as luminous in its field of endeavor as Penn's board of trustees.

The early beneficiaries of Garland's largesse typified the operations of the board and naturally reflected the interests of its members: the American Civil Liberties Union, the Rand School, the League for Industrial Democracy, the NAACP, the United Mine Workers, the Federated Press, Brookwood Labor College, and journals like the *Liberator* and the *World Tomorrow.* An investigator was also hired to probe into the case of a couple of obscure Italian-Americans charged with murder and robbery in Dedham, Massachusetts.[4]

Nearing and many of the other board members were committed to the destruction of an economic system that made even its enemies prosper, for the boom market of the 1920s quickly inflated the Fund's assets to $1 million, then to $2 million. Somehow, Nearing observed, "the more we gave away, the more we had." Although Ernst complained that "the Fund was afraid that easy money would corrupt the organizations seeking aid," Baldwin opposed the spendthrift proclivities of the board.[5] "The Fund has been pumping oxygen into a lot of hopelessly sick patients," he told Nearing in 1926. "The Workers party is the only husky patient we have got. . . . The less we invest now, the more we may have for perhaps more hopeful days two or three years from now, or perhaps we can find forces more likely to be militant than those now in the field. I am for hell-raising on principle, alongside more solid spade work." [6]

Nearing agreed with Baldwin's preference to err on the side of financial caution, but their minority position "became amusing to the other members of the board." [7] Even among this collection of dissenters, he dissented. On a memo proposing 5–6 percent interest on long-term loans and usually no interest on short-term loans, he cryptically scrawled: "I object to interest. It is bad social policy. Why should we favor it any more than we should favor capital punishment: It merely kills us." Nearing's position could also be contradictory; in a 1923 memorandum he opposed disbursement of "nickels and quarters . . . [which] are quite ineffective in the way of any permanent gain." Yet he also criticized the board's "presumption . . . in favor of giving to applicants." [8]

Nearing's confusion may have been due to the discomfiture of participation in "an immoral venture in corporate wealth"; yet Baldwin acknowledged that "he really pays scrupulous attention to Fund business." [9] Beginning in November 1924, he served two years as president of the Fund and tried to keep it on a leftward keel. Nearing helped bring Flynn onto the board as its assistant secretary, and opposed the nomination of economist Stuart Chase because he was "not part of the labor movement." Yet President Nearing did not seek to dominate the monthly meetings of the directors, and both manipulation and mediation were foreign to his nature. Baldwin noted that Nearing "expressed himself in very positive terms about what his views were and let it go. He didn't try to argue with you. He didn't try to compromise on anything. . . . He never was an organization man in any sense." [10]

The secretary suspected that Nearing joined the board of directors not only because of its value to the labor movement but also so that "his own interests might profit by it." In a five-year plan for the Fund, grandly entitled "Scott Nearing's Consistent Educational Work Looking to the Establishment of a New World Order," he argued: "What is most needed is . . . carefully worked out and consistent propaganda for social and economic emancipation. . . . The Fund . . . [must] participate . . . *educationally* without commitments to any factional or partisan groups." Nearing proposed four activities to free the proletariat through education: 1) a department of research and publicity, 2) a cooperative publishing house, 3) a monthly magazine, and 4) assistance for labor colleges. All four projects fell within the penumbra of his own talents.[11]

He supported funding for the Rand School's Department of Labor Research, of which he served as director; and the Fund agreed to underwrite it in 1925. Nearing also urged the Fund to support the Federated Press, which soon derived over a third of its income from the Garland Fund.[12] Nearing's second proposal was due to the reluctance of commercial houses to publish radical works. Sinclair had established his own publishing firm in Pasadena; and Nearing, whom reputable companies spurned by 1917, also resorted to private publication early in the next decade. The Fund spent $146,954 to operate Vanguard Press, to which authors usually paid $600 for 150 copies of their books, with Vanguard retaining the copyright and type. Out-of-print radical classics were also reproduced.[13]

While hardly as complex as Insull's empire, the Garland Fund became interlocking in its enterprises when the Vanguard Press published studies of American imperialism written under the supervision of another Fund creation, the Committee on Studies in American Investments Abroad. Nearing had advocated research into imperialism in 1923, and Thomas supported him. Although Baldwin preferred "militant propaganda work in that field rather than further research studies," he, Nearing, Gannett, James Weldon Johnson, and Robert Dunn of the Department of Labor Research soon constituted themselves as the Fund's Anti-Imperialism Committee. Harry Elmer Barnes, an historian and sociologist who had attended Nearing's syncopated lecture at Clark, was chosen editor-in-chief of studies of the flow of Yankee capital to Latin America. The advisory committee consisted not only of the Anti-Imperialism Committee but also of Ernst, Oswald Garrison Villard of the *Nation*, the U.S. Congressman Emmanuel Celler, and the future Senators Paul Douglas and Ernest Gruening. By 1929 books on Bolivia, Colombia, Cuba, and Santo Domingo had been published; and a study of Nicaragua, which was considered an apologia for the State Department, was sent elsewhere.[14]

Nearing himself proposed to summarize the findings of the scholars; and he collaborated with Joseph Freeman, then a Communist working for the American Civil Liberties Union, on *Dollar Diplomacy*. After several publishers rejected the manuscript, Benjamin Huebsch published it in 1925. Admittedly unoriginal, this successor to Nearing's *American Empire* (1921) was packaged as liberal scholarship, eschewing class analysis, utilizing government sources wherever possible, dispassionately presenting factual material, avoiding an explicitly radical conclusion. The authors traced the imperialist impulse to the "economic necessity" of advanced societies to utilize surplus capital and to control the source of raw materials. Focusing upon the American trademark in China, Mexico, and the Caribbean, *Dollar Diplomacy* observed that "a small, weak nation has no rights that a great, strong nation is bound to respect."[15]

Nearing's third proposal sought to satisfy the need for a journal that would "keep people straight in their economic and social thinking." The new monthly would be "sold at a very cheap rate . . . aimed at a comparatively small group of thinking people . . . [and] probably best . . . handled by a volunteer board of editors." He supported the financial aid application of *Dynamo,* which received money under its new name, the *New Masses.*[16] Its contributing editors included Nearing, Giovannitti, Sinclair, Sherwood Anderson, Van Wyck Brooks, Floyd Dell, Claude McKay, Lewis Mumford, Eugene O'Neill, and Edmund Wilson. To raise funds, the magazine charged Broadway musical prices for a debate on the Soviet Union between Nearing and an official of the National Security League. With Chambers and the poets Robinson Jeffers and William Carlos Williams, Nearing contributed to its first issue. His article apostrophized: "My country 'tis of thee; sweet land of a leisure class running treasure-island balls and throwing bathtub parties; of thee I sing, and thy skilled organized comfortable labor aristocracy defending the wage slave system. . . ."[17]

Nearing's esthetics were, in Freeman's opinion, "a blend of puritanism and socialism." He preferred the "determined, hard-hitting . . . sympathy for the class struggle" brandished in the *New Masses* to, say, the psychoanalytic twist to Marxism that permeated V. F. Calverton's *Modern Quarterly.* Yet Nearing encouraged Calverton's venture, supplied it with articles on education, and urged its editor to join the Workers party. Agreeing that "the life and thought of a period quite naturally reflects [sic] the productive and social system then existing," he nonetheless refused comment on Calverton's *Sex Expression in Literature.* Internationalist in politics, Nearing was rather provincial in tastes that did not transcend the genteel tradition.[18]

In that he was hardly alone. Paul Douglas had resented the old *Masses'* attempt "to pander to . . . passions . . . [that would] turn the stomach of the healthiest," and Norman Thomas had also found that journal excessively robust. Unlike the *Masses,* the avant-garde *Little Review* did not even try to fuse politics and culture, provoking Upton Sinclair to ask the editor to send him no further issues: "I no longer understand anything in it, so it no longer interests me." Margaret Anderson's reply widened the chasm between political and literary radicalism: "Please cease sending me your socialist paper. I understand everything in it, therefore it no longer interests me." Debs was no less philistine than other Socialists in his faith that, after the elimination of hunger and war, "we shall have a literature and an art such as the troubled heart and brain of man never before conceived. We shall have beautiful houses and happy homes. . . . We shall have beautiful thoughts and sentiments, and a divinity in religion, such as man weighted down by the machine could never have imagined." [19]

That supreme art might be rooted in neurosis, that authentic religion might be incompatible with comfort, that beautiful houses do not necessarily make happy homes, and that, while toil aborts art, its absence does not guarantee beauty—these problems few radicals wished to face. Those who sought to change the world did not engage the most plangent contemporary art to understand it. Themselves mostly reared within the stable and antiseptic middle-class culture of the late nineteenth century, they could not enter the world of modern creativity. They found too disquieting for comprehension its dissonance and complexity, its amorphousness and decadence, its juxtapositions and apparent disorder, its incessant surprise symphonies. Nearing's hazy advocacy of "proletarian culture" thus represented less the patronage of a new sensibility than the failure to confront the most intricate, painful, and permanent works that bourgeois artists of the period were then achieving.

The final component of Nearing's 1924 proposal urged extensive assistance for labor colleges, and he persuaded the directors to adopt a resolution favoring only "organizations and institutions which instill into the workers the knowledge and the qualities which will fit them for carrying on the struggle for the emancipation of their class in every sphere." A member of the Fund's Committee on Labor Education, he was among the first Americans to urge that the Soviets' "proletarian culture" go native. Public school indoctrination stifled the efflorescence of such a culture, Nearing charged; while labor schools affiliated with Amherst, Bryn Mawr, and other colleges signified a "counter-revolution in labor education." Nor did Nearing sanction independent schools that borrowed instructors from high schools and colleges, for that meant merely "transferring capitalist education to labor colleges. If the teachers were really class conscious . . . they would lose their official jobs in about nine cases out of ten." He therefore recommended the extension of the workers' "own schools supported by their own teachers and using their own . . . text-books." [20]

The most prestigious of the colleges that trained labor organizers and officials was Brookwood, in Katonah, New York, where a first class of resident workers was formed in 1921. By the end of the decade, the Fund had showered the school with more than $100,000, "far too much for its own good," in Baldwin's opinion. Nearing could also adopt the banker's flinty stare and had even opposed giving A. J. Muste, Brookwood's educational director, a paltry $1,200 to cancel a debt that Muste had contracted while organizing an Amalgamated Textile Workers strike in 1919. Facing bankruptcy in 1928, as well as the separate attacks of the A. F. of L. and the Communists, Brookwood requested further assistance.[21] Nearing opposed a grant that would "merely help to perpetuate an untenable and impossible situation," and disliked Muste's impersonation of a captain of erudition: "When we made our original $125,000 appropriation, it was understood that this would relieve A. J. *et al.* from the necessity of money-raising and enable A. J. *et al.* to *teach*. What did they do? Turned right around and organized a cam-

paign to raise $2,000,000 for Brookwood. . . . An appeal
from Brookwood for more money now constitutes an act of
bad faith." The country's most influential labor college was
eventually forced to shut down in 1937.[22]

Commonwealth College in Mena, Arkansas, received the
second largest grant from the Garland Fund. Nearing visited its campus at the Fund's expense, but the board overruled his recommendation to turn off the financial spigot. A
decade after Nearing's visit to Commonwealth College, the
president of its student body was Orval E. Faubus. Other
grants were provided to the Rand School and the Communists' Workers School in New York.[23]

Another appropriation was designed to support an experimental program that the United Mine Workers established in Taylorville, Illinois. Nearing helped plan the
curriculum for 200 miners enrolled in classes and for a
public lecture series; the required textbooks were those of
Beard, Oneal, and Nearing. The director of the program
explained that it was "based on the class struggle. . . . We
don't care to help our students to climb out of the working
class. We want them to learn to help put the owning class
out of business." [24] The program was nevertheless affiliated
with the Workers Education Bureau, an AFL subsidiary
that excluded the Rand School and the Workers School. At
the 1925 convention of the W.E.B., Nearing denounced the
AFL's repudiation of the class struggle: "I wonder what the
miners of West Virginia, locked out and in tents, think of
industrial peace; what the textile workers of New England,
unemployed or receiving wage cuts, think of industrial
peace; what the miners of Illinois, out of work or about to
have their wages reduced, think of industrial peace." Amid
hoots and jeers from the other delegates and during a decade in which no more than 12 percent of the nonagricul-
tural labor force belonged to unions, Nearing proposed an
alternative: "Industrial war must be the slogan of the work-

ers. . . . The Workers Education Bureau should . . . equip the workers for their emancipation from the capitalist system." But their educators were uninterested, and defeated a motion to go on record in favor of class struggle.[25]

A more likely group to convert from trade union consciousness to class consciousness was the American Federation of Teachers, whose largest affiliate was Local 5, the New York Teachers Union. Socialists like Henry Linville, the co-director of Manumit, and Abraham Lefkowitz were the driving force of the New York local; and, despite a drastic loss of membership, they persevered through the Red Scare and Lusk Laws of the early 1920s. While school authorities attributed subversive intentions to the union leaders, Communists and pro-Communists in Local 5 denounced Linville and Lefkowitz as "right-wingers" and "bureaucrats," thus mimicking the fission with which the larger left was reproducing itself.[26]

As a member of the Rand School faculty, Nearing joined the American Federation of Teachers; and his militancy, fluency, and prestige catapulted him to the top of the left-wing faction of Local 5. Most of his supporters in the so-called Progressive Caucus were well-disciplined Communists secretly taking cues from Benjamin Mandel, a high school typing teacher who became chairman of the membership committee of Local 5. Nearing, Mandel, and two other left-wingers also served on its executive board; and when Nearing received the most votes in the Local 5 delegation to the 1925 national convention of the American Federation of Teachers, and when Mandel was also elected, the right-wingers became alarmed. Linville accused the Progressive Caucus of seeking to wreck the union with extraneous issues, like the demand for affiliation with the Workers party. "Many American unions attempt to deal with the Communist sympathizers by throwing them out bodily," the founder of Local 5 warned in a pamphlet. "Our solution must be different. . . . We must see that the Board of Education has no excuse for punishing teachers for their opinions. But we must protect the union by informing our members of the situation." [27]

Delegate Nearing's response was immediate: "In order to show that I have no idea of helping to 'disrupt' or 'capture' the Teachers Union, I offer to resign as delegate to the Chicago convention." His resignation was quickly accepted; but the Communists themselves were recalcitrant, condemning "the stool-pigeon Abraham Lefkovitz [sic], tool of Tammany Hall and the Socialist party." Mandel demanded the right of rebuttal to the charges leveled against the Progressive Caucus. Linville recognized such a right but also instituted a successful recall petition against Mandel, who thereupon quit the union, quit the teaching profession, and became a Communist party organizer during the Passaic, New Jersey, textile strike.[28]

The expulsion of Nearing and the Communists did not make the union more glamorous, however, for only about 5 percent of New York's 30,000 teachers joined Local 5 by the end of the decade. Nearing's mordant opinion of bourgeois pedagogues was therefore amply confirmed: "Each strike, each gag-law, each red-raid, each act of imperial aggression, each threat of war offers the teacher . . . a new opportunity to take a stand. . . . Thus far, the overwhelming majority of American teachers have chosen silence, and by that choice have aligned themselves with the established order." [29]

IN 1925 NEARING VISITED THE NEW SOCIALIST ORDER, AND he was dazzled. "I wish Greenwich Village could be toured around in Russia for a few months," he wrote back. "There is more actual construction of stations, factories, houses, etc.

going on in Russia—twice over—than in any other country I have seen. . . . No one here needs to play golf to relieve the tedium of existence. The whole country is full of ginger." [30] Equally impressive were Soviet cultural achievements: "The whole country is filled with books. . . . I have never seen a country so completely saturated with literature. And most of it is economic and social science. There is a mania for science here." Russia, he wrote Baldwin, "is quite unique and very convincing." The euphoria that suffused his *Glimpses of the Soviet Republic* was enhanced by a stop in Weimar Germany, which he found "dead . . . hopes low; life hard; profiteering everywhere. They certainly are due for a shake-up." [31]

Upon his return to the United States, Nearing observed that the Communists were "the only live bunch in the U.S.A. right now"; and from his solitary perch he was to be swept into a movement of 10,000 ostensibly disciplined militants of the Workers party. The catalytic agent of Nearing's conversion, he recalled, was "one of the very fine group of young people who had . . . [built] up the Arden community." [32] Harold Ware was "quiet . . . gracious and friendly," according to Sinclair; and Ella Reeve Bloor observed that, when discussing agriculture, her son "forgot his shyness . . . and a flow of colorful, stirring talk would come from him, so persuasive that those who heard him were completely carried away." [33] In the aftermath of the Russian civil war, Ware had organized American farmers to demonstrate sophisticated methods to the peasants, thereby earning Lenin's gratitude: "You have achieved successes that must be regarded as truly outstanding. . . . No form of assistance is as timely and as important for us as that which you are rendering." Ware also established Russian Reconstruction Farms and wangled a $20,000 loan from the Garland Fund, though the Soviet government later took over the corporation and defaulted on the loan.[34]

One evening early in 1927, he and Nearing spent several hours discussing Communism in the underground passageway between the Pennsylvania Station and the subway. Harold Ware had quite a penchant for the underground. According to Chambers, Ware had returned from Russia with $25,000 to organize not only Dakota farmers but also espionage agents in Washington, D.C., including Alger Hiss.[35] The subterranean side of Ware's life was unknown to prospective open members like Nearing who, in Oliver Goldsmith's couplet, though "born for the universe, narrowed his mind,/And to party gave up what was meant for mankind."

But since intellectuals were the most explosive and fissionable material in the Party, his welcome was not especially warm. A novice of Nearing's stature could become the nucleus of a potential opposition movement or the future editor of a factionalist bulletin in an organization already racked with dissension. Workers no more dominated the Workers party than the medieval Schoolmen were academics or the *philosophes* were formal philosophers, but the functionaries who managed Party affairs preferred recruits lucky enough to have been born in a tenement to intellectuals for whom revolution was patently an acquired taste. So executive secretary Jay Lovestone, the author of the slashing pamphlet *Labor Lieutenants of American Imperialism,* solicited Nearing's specific views on imperialism, war, and revolution. The author of several books and pamphlets on these subjects was thus thrown into the brier patch, and he submitted a thirty-page document that not only analyzed social and economic conditions in several countries but urged the Party "to cultivate the highest standards of personal integrity—sound health, clean living; trained, vigorous, and courageous thinking; honest, straightforward dealing." Nearing hoped that the movement would "maintain in its internal life a standard of generosity and mutual aid that will make the Party, on a small scale, the kind of co-operative fellowship that we are seeking to establish upon a world scale." After a delay he was assigned to a New York local.[36]

The life of the Party was routine, centering around "how many comrades will take the paper this week, to get it around to some factory or some meeting; and how many comrades will take so many pieces of literature of the auxiliary organizations of the Party. . . . Then, how many comrades will take tickets to the next affair at which we are going to try to raise some money. Then the dues. Then . . . the voluntary contributions." Nearing, however, usually avoided such irksome duties and confined himself to his usual speaking, writing, and teaching. Amenable to calling himself a Marxist, Nearing joined the faculty of the Workers School, where the curriculum was officially "based on the assumption that Marx, Engels, Lenin in their works and deeds have given the proletariat a science of understanding, organization, and action which directs it along its march toward power and emancipation." Student enrollment hovered between a thousand and two thousand.[37] The directors of the school were Bertram D. Wolfe, the former publicity director of the Rand School, and Ben Davidson, who had imbibed the laws of social revolution from Nearing. Other faculty colleagues included Benjamin Gitlow, whose conviction under New York's criminal anarchy statute provoked the Supreme Court to hold the First Amendment applicable to state governments under the due process clause of the Fourteenth Amendment; William Weinstone, the Party's district organizer for New York and the brother-in-law of Carl Haessler; and Mike Gold, who "affected dirty shirts, a big, black uncleaned Stetson . . . smoked stinking, twisted, Italian three-cent cigars . . . spat frequently and vigorously on the floor," and tried very hard to be the poor man's Edmund Wilson. Courses were offered in *Capital*, materialist philosophy, the history of the American working class, Russian, English, and party training.[38]

Seeking to emulate the Workers School in New York, Canadian comrades invited Nearing to direct their Party training. He declined the offer, but the traveling salesman of Socialism did engage in an extended speaking tour of Canada in 1927. In collaboration with Harry Freeman, a *Daily Worker* staffer and brother of the co-author of *Dollar Diplomacy*, he had written the pamphlet *Whither China?*, and he converted the income from his Canadian lectures to third-class passage in order to see China for himself.[39]

His contact there was to be Ch'en Kung-po, a founder of the Chinese Communist party whose growing curiosity about social democracy instead led to his expulsion in 1923. The following year he had studied "practical economics" under Nearing in New York, while his former comrades joined the Kuomintang in order to accelerate the historical stage of the bourgeois national revolution. Ch'en himself became a member of the Central Executive Committee of the Kuomintang in 1926 and, though disillusioned with Marxism, rose quickly in the left wing of the Kuomintang and of its Wuhan government. He also secured Nearing's appointment as economic adviser to the Chinese Railway Administration.

But Ch'en also supported the Kuomintang decision to destroy the Communists, whose uprising in Nanch'ang was crushed even as Nearing was crossing the Pacific. When he arrived in Shanghai no one met him, so he went on to Peiping, where seventeen students had just been executed for putting up posters denouncing the purge. An anti-Kuomintang group arranged to hear Nearing at Yenching University and also avoid the police by keeping the lights off in the auditorium; only occasional muffled talk attested to the existence of an audience.[40]

After three precarious months in China, Nearing happily accepted an invitation to represent the American section of the Friends of the Soviet Union during the celebration of the tenth anniversary of the Bolshevik Revolution. Serving on the international press bureau, he attended the Moscow sessions of the Friends' congress, which warned constantly of the dangers of capitalist encirclement. There, too, Nearing saw the general secretary of the Communist party, who seemed accessible and industrious. Freeman recalled that Nearing, upon his return, described Joseph Stalin "with that peculiar reverence which he reserved for revolutionaries who worked unusually hard and lived with unusual frugality and had no thoughts but socialism." [41] In thus painting Stalin's portrait, Nearing was in fact sitting for his own.

Nearing also delicately shepherded Theodore Dreiser around Moscow between the novelist's consumption of vodka and his pursuit of Dorothy Thompson of the Philadelphia *Public Ledger*. Although Dreiser appreciated Nearing's attempts to be helpful, the journalist was more ambivalent, writing her future husband, Sinclair Lewis, that she was "getting tired of being educated by Scott . . . and being facetiously nudged by old Dreiser. . . . [but] one forgives even Scott his earnestness when he smiles, and he sometimes did." [42] After the festivities Nearing returned home by way of the Pacific, and startled the Philippine Secretary of Labor by traveling steerage in the company of coolies headed for work in Hawaii. [43]

Nearing thereupon plunged into the work of the All-America Anti-Imperialist League, a branch of the League against Imperialism and therefore one of the multifarious creations of an ingenious impresario for the Comintern, Willi Münzenberg. Newspapers, magazines, publishing houses, and cinemas were among the emanations of the "Münzenberg Trust"; but equally abundant were the prestigious committees laden with non-Communist progressive intellectuals, with Comintern agents operating in the background. Albert Einstein, for example, was honorary president of the League against Imperialism; and its members included everyone from George Lansbury and Henri Barbusse to Jawaharlal Nehru and Madame Sun Yat-sen. The American version of what Münzenberg called "the innocents' club" boasted a national committee including Baldwin, DuBois, Lovett, Debs' brother Theodore, and attorney Arthur G. Hays, plus Communists like Nearing and Foster. Its secretary, Manuel Gomez, was also a Communist.[44]

Nearing also served as chairman of the New York branch of the All-America Anti-Imperialist League and denounced the American intervention in Nicaragua as designed merely "to insure regular payment of dividends." At the same meeting the brother of guerrilla chieftain Augustino Sandino not only appealed for complete withdrawal of the Marines but also helped raise money to purchase medical supplies for the guerrillas. This did not constitute treason, the New Masses insisted, because "war has not been declared by the United States. The Marines are in Nicaragua only 'to insure a fair election' . . . in spite of the fact that hundreds of Nicaraguans have been killed, their homes burned, and their crops laid waste." The League distributed thousands of circulars, held mass meetings in three boroughs, and battled the Post Office, which refused to transmit mail affixed with stickers calling for "Protest Against Marine Rule in Nicaragua." Gomez continued to direct the antiwar demonstrations in front of the White House and the secret financial support of Chinese expatriates anxious to return to fight under the rubric of "Hands Off China!" The secretary of the League considered Nearing "sincere, earnest, stubborn, erratic, and personally aloof"; despite Party membership, he "did not help formulate policy in any way." [45]

If Nearing lacked muscle even within a front organization, he was willing to lay his voice if not his life on the line established in Moscow. But his voice would be compromised by the company he kept: once a prominent victim of intolerance, Nearing served a Party which was itself contemptuous of the rights of others. The most defenseless were other leftists, like the Russian Menshevik Raphael Abramovitch, whose lecture tour in 1925 was punctuated with the hoots of Communists seeking to disrupt his meetings. When Ralph Chaplin spoke in Chicago in behalf of what remained of the Wobblies, a Communist youth group drowned him out with stanzas of "Solidarity Forever," a song he himself had written a decade earlier. In Salt Lake City blacks and Filipinos dependent upon Communist soup kitchens were unleashed against a meeting that featured the Trotskyist tribune Max Shachtman. But at the moment when the crowd surged toward the platform, the chairman of the meeting and local leader of the ACLU pulled out a revolver and announced: "The first son of a bitch who wants [it] is welcome to come up here and try to take it." Shachtman later commented: "This was part of the educational work of bringing home to them the principle of free speech." [46]

Nearing did not condemn these tactics, perhaps out of a cynical assumption that whoever speaks, ultimately money talks. His own right to speak in public was still restricted. When Anthony Bimba, the editor of a Lithuanian-language Communist daily, was charged with blasphemy under a 1697 Massachusetts statute, Nearing came to Boston to advocate his cause. But the protest group was prevented from using a hall named after Thomas Paine; and when Nearing tried to harangue the crowd from a snowbank outside the hall, policemen led him away. Nearing was taken into custody but not formally arrested by the police, who received a commendation from the mayor of Boston.[47]

Two years later the Workers party sent the indefatigable

orator into West Virginia. Leaflets were distributed to the miners and foundry workers of the company town of Norwood announcing that Nearing would address them in the evening. But the proprietor of the hall found it wise to cancel the engagement when the local constabulary warned that he too would be arrested if any speakers showed up. Several days later, when a hall was successfully rented in Wheeling, policemen arrested the chairman at the outset of the meeting. A second traveling Communist then marched to the rostrum; he too was immediately arrested. A policeman behind Nearing cued him, "It's your turn now." He managed to utter, "Comrades and fellow citizens," before he too was grabbed and hauled to jail. They were charged with disorderly conduct and released on bail, but the charges were dropped after they left Wheeling. "Nearing Scores Police Terror," the Daily Worker quickly screamed.[48]

He could not bring himself to denounce police terror in the Soviet Union, however. When Emma Goldman lectured in Canada to raise money for Russian political prisoners, some Communists sought to impose a boycott; others recommended a debate with Nearing, who refused. "I didn't want to help her or anybody else defame the fair name of the Soviet Union," he later explained. "If I debated with her on the subject, I would be helping her carry on anti-Soviet propaganda." [49]

Oddly enough Nearing's definition of the function of debate did not prevent him from sharing platforms with democratic Socialists, even though they were petty bourgeois reformist opportunist social fascists. Thomas debated Nearing on "Socialism versus Communism in America" in March 1928, under the auspices of the New Masses and with Baldwin as chairman. With the audience clearly favoring Communism, the erstwhile advocate of nonresistance announced that if capitalism, war, and imperialism were to be smashed, force and the dictatorship of the proletariat were the only choice of weapons. His opponent had joined the Socialist party a year after Nearing did out of "a profound faith that the new world we desire must depend upon freedom and fellowship rather than upon . . . coercion." He compared democratic methods with the "armed minority of their own class" that ruled the workers' state.[50] By then both Thomas and Baldwin found Nearing's dogmatism so repugnant that ties of close friendship snapped. Nearing continued to correspond with Sinclair but was baffled by the novelist's political affiliation with "lawyers and real-estate speculators." [51]

That summer the Sixth World Congress of the Comintern announced the entrance of civilization into the "Third Period" of imminent revolutions and wars. The myth of Petrograd was expected to be etched on the map of Appalachia; the storming of the Winter Palace would soon be imitated in a hundred city halls, a thousand boondocks bastilles. The railroad tracks that would carry the American comrades to Washington would use the same gauge as those on which the sealed car had hurtled toward the Finland Station. When Robert Minor read a news item about a disturbance in rural Minnesota, he burst out to his colleagues on the *Daily Worker:* "It's the beginning of the American Revolution. We must play it up *big.*" Members of the Young Communist League sported khaki uniforms and practiced military drill, though not every schoolboy knew what one Young Pioneer proclaimed: "Our teaching is imperialistic teaching. In the public schools the children are taught to be against the workers' parties in China, Nicaragua, and Mexico." Another fifteen-year-old demonstrated against the Boy Scouts and was sentenced for six months to a house of corrections.[52]

Heightened militancy everywhere, which Nearing supported, coincided with utter subjection to Moscow, which Nearing also supported. He was an Ultramontane because revolutionary experience had forged "first-rate people in the Soviet Union," in contrast to "third-rate people in the United States." He continued to urge Communists to imitate the cohesion of plutocrats. "If you're going to play as a team, you've got to play as a team. And the Russians for obvious reasons were captain," he later explained. "There was no other power." [53] To this power a minority faction within the American delegation appealed during the Sixth World Congress, undercutting Lovestone's leadership with a denunciation of "the Right Danger." Among Americans criticized for overestimating the resilience of capitalism was Nearing, of all people, although he felt no repercussions of such a charge. While Stalin was crushing his own Bukharinite right wing, American Communism itself was irrevocably reduced to an appendage of Soviet foreign policy. Early in 1929 the Comintern deposed Lovestone, despite his claim of a nominal majority. When he protested to Stalin as though they were equals, the general secretary of the Russian party demonstrated that some general secretaries were more equal than others and warned that "there is plenty of room in our cemeteries." Lovestone, Wolfe, Gitlow, Mandel, and a couple of hundred followers thereupon formed the Communist Party (Majority Group), later called Communist Party of the U.S.A. (Opposition), still later called Independent Labor League of America. So alien was the American idiom to many Party members that the Yiddish daily *Freiheit* outsold the English language *Daily Worker;* and it was fitting that one victim of the minority faction who perceived Stalinism too late wrote in yet another language the epitaph of an indigenous movement: "Eben habe ich entdeckt, dass ich sieben Jahre lang den falschen Arsch geküsst habe!" [54]

Not threatening anyone's power, Nearing remained friendly, if not intimate, with the Party's assorted panjandrums. Without trying to emulate continental casuists, he devoted himself to agitprop and chose to run in 1928 for governor of New Jersey. Calling the state "one of the chief centers . . . of job ownership in the master class and of exploitation of the working class," Nearing and Senatorial nominee Albert Weisbord, the hero of the 1926 Passaic strike, nevertheless ran a listless campaign. The gubernatorial candidate toured few cities in New Jersey, working instead for Communist contenders in other states and for Presidential nominee William Z. Foster. After the climactic Madison Square Garden rally, the *Daily Worker* perpetrated a striking *non sequitur:* "The capitalist newspapers were able to count only 12,000 [in attendance]. The same papers managed to count 25,000 when Al Smith spoke." On the first Tuesday in November, the Republican candidate for governor received over 800,000 votes, the Democrat less than 700,000, the Prohibition and Socialist candidates a little more than 2,000 votes each. Nearing got 1,255 votes, about a third of his total against LaGuardia in 1918. Weisbord, who was also clobbered at the polls, quit the Party, which immediately expelled him as a deviationist.[55]

With the New Jersey proletariat mired in false consciousness, Nearing was drawn more deeply to the contemplative life. From the Garland Fund he received $3,000 for clerical assistance for "a research project which I believe is of fundamental importance to the American movement": studies of war, revolution, and imperialism; studies of internationalism; and their culmination in a grand synthesis. Of the twenty-one books and pamphlets which he promised, seven had already been published and four others were in manuscript, ranging from reportage to an eventual "restatement of the principles of sociology, the building and direction of society along scientific lines, a dynamic social science." [56] Architectonic in conception, Nearing's corpus might also be termed prophetic in impact, which means that his contemporaries in the American movement ignored it.

After visiting the southern states and northern ghettos, he wrote *Black America,* a subject that had scarcely interested him previously. Both the Progressive movement and the Socialist party had spotty records on the issue of racial oppression because both deemed the promotion of economic efficiency far more important than meeting the specific needs of blacks and other groups. Nearing was more comfortable with statistics than with direct social observation to support his generalizations; and his book, illustrated with his own photographs, could just barely be classified as reportage. *Black America* appeared in 1929, after the Comintern formulated a new national question: "In those regions of the South in which compact Negro masses are living, it is essential to put forward the slogan of the Right of Self-Determination for Negroes. A radical transformation of the agrarian structure is one of the basic tasks of the revolution." But Nearing wrote too soon to reflect the new line. One contorted sentence asserted that "Negroes are the victims of economic discrimination directed against blacks because they are blacks," but Nearing generally argued that oppression was "at bottom an economic phenomenon" that was not politically soluble. The ballot was "employed by the ruling classes in the exercise of class power"; instead Nearing urged blacks to join "trade unions, cooperatives, [and] a political party that represents working-class interests." Only a combination with "the white working masses in smashing the economic and social structure built upon . . . exploitation" could achieve justice. Those white working masses generally found repugnant such an alliance to promote that program. Nor were blacks then willing or able to follow his advice; and fewer still, as Nearing admitted to Calverton, even bothered to read his book.[57]

The appearance of *Free-Born* three years later was notable for several reasons. Along with Patten's *Mud Hollow* and J. K. Galbraith's *The Triumph*, it constituted a subgenre that literary critics have largely, and no doubt wisely, neglected: fiction written by professional American economists. It was also Nearing's only novel; privately printed, *Free-Born* was

subtitled "unpublishable." This story of a Southern black
who becomes the Marxist-Leninist leader of a Pennsylvania
coal strike is also, according to literary historians Sterling
Brown and Hugh Gloster, "the first revolutionary novel of
Negro life." In 1956 another literary historian called Nearing's description of the deaths of the protagonist's parents
"probably the most ghastly lynch scene in American literature"; it was, alas, based upon fact.[58]

Another part of the project was a history of imperialism
which argued that the process that had begun with nomadic
pastoralism would culminate in a world economy founded
upon the Soviet model. The author, therefore, urged
members of the vanguard "who have studied historic processes, who are familiar with social organization" to become
the social engineers of the postcapitalist system. Largely a
restatement of earlier views, the manuscript was presented
to Trachtenberg, who had become head of the Communists'
International Publishers. While submission of *The Twilight of
Empire* thus proved Nearing's submission to the authority of
the Party, Moscow denied its imprimatur because, as Trachtenberg explained to Nearing, Lenin's *Imperialism* "dealt
with the period from 1870 to 1915. And this then is the
period of imperialism. . . . You have gone before 1870 and
dealt with imperialism as though it existed in the period
before this definitive study of Lenin. . . . Who are you to
say that imperialism existed before 1870?" [59]

Nearing's reply was a letter to the Central Committee of
the Communist Party outlining his choices: 1) obedience, although the manuscript "presents an important historical
synthesis hitherto unstated"; 2) publication outside Party
channels, although it "might lead to additional inner Party
controversy"; 3) resignation, although he pledged nonetheless "to uphold the principles of the Party and to support
the Party work." Nearing chose his second and third op-
tions: the Vanguard Press of the Garland Fund published
The Twilight of Empire in 1930; and he quit the Party, not out

of disillusionment or boredom or anti-Stalinism or heretical impulses or desire for revolutionary spontaneity or philosophical commitment to freedom, but because his privileges as an author had been infringed.

No one resigns from the Party, however. Nearing was expelled in early January 1930, and his erstwhile comrades were quite unsportsmanlike about deviation on the question of periodization in the history of imperialism. Intellectuals like Nearing, the *Daily Worker* charged, are "little fit . . . to stand the pressure which the duties of the revolution put upon a revolutionist." His offer of friendship rather than membership was spurned in this, the Third Period: "To be a friend of the revolutionary working class is to be a fighter in its ranks. . . . Outside the ranks of the Party the 'friend' ceases to be a positive factor on the side of the working class . . . and, therefore, strengthens the enemy of the proletariat, the bourgeoisie." The "visibly sharpening struggles" that the Sixth World Congress had foreseen would "pass up such elements as Scott Nearing and deposit them on the scrap heap of revolution"—one of Trotsky's phrases that certified so many excommunications that by 1930 the scrap heap must already have reached mountainous proportions.[60]

But Nearing wanted the last word, so he penned a valedictory not only to the Party but to all other organizations he had joined. To the evil of plutocracy he added that of the gerontocracy of the left: "Long ago I sensed the danger of old men in power. . . . Tentatively I fixed on twenty-five years as the maximum of time that a man can usefully spend in the direction of public policy. It was in 1904–1905 that I began active work in Philadelphia politics. Since then I have come on from civic reform through the Socialist party to the Communist party." In order to help extirpate capitalist imperialism, Nearing promised to continue to write and speak but not to attend meetings or to serve on boards of directors. He advised the Garland Fund, for example, to replace him with "someone under 25. Avoid anyone over 30." Although he closed his letter with the fiery "All power to the organized workers," the *Daily Worker* was dubious: "The active services of the proletarian revolutionist continue until he is either physically or politically incapacitated." [61]

The comrades' skepticism was well-founded. Nearing's opposition to gerontocracy had been amply disguised before, and he was not to invoke this principle again, as Communist leaders aged throughout the world. His own energy remained undiminished, though it was to some extent rechanneled. The desire to avoid meetings is not uncommon; it meant for Nearing a refusal to be housebroken. He had been an unsuitable Communist and an ineffective Fund director because his ascetic mettle deprived him of the flexibility essential to political intercourse. As a Communist he believed in subservience, discipline, *partiinost*—but for others. His work on the board of the Garland Fund was conscientious and energetic but typified a remoteness from the arts of compromise and tolerance that are central to democratic procedure. "The flannel shirt he wore on his body," Freeman wrote of his friend, "was a symbol of the hair shirt he wore on his soul." Nearing's hunger for integrity established an irreducible definition of self that no group would be permitted to violate. What Communists denounced as bourgeois privatism, what Baldwin considered his puritan self-righteousness and quest for moral perfection, countermanded his advocacy of cohesion and class discipline.[62]

THE HUSKIEST PATIENT OF THE GARLAND FUND TURNED OUT to be hemophiliac, for Nearing's expulsion capped two frenetic years of heresy hunts and interdictions within the Communist movement. The departure of right-wing deviationists Wolfe and Davidson weakened the caliber of instruction at the Workers School. After Gomez withdrew from the Party, the All-America Anti-Imperialist League disintegrated, though it evolved into another front group, the American League Against War and Fascism. The pre-eminence of Party secretary Earl Browder, who had been a Comintern agent in China in 1927, assured the subservience of American cadres to Russian strategic objectives. It also solidified the bureaucratization of a movement that had once won the allegiance of Reed and Haywood.[63]

The crash of the stock market and the ensuing Depression forced the retrenchment of Garland Fund support for the labor movement, experimental education, civil rights, and civil liberties. The Vanguard Press was sold in 1932 after displaying the wrong kind of red. Garland himself attended the funeral service of the long-moribund Fund in 1940 and received a stack of I.O.U. notes. Since walking away from his million-dollar inheritance, he had lived on a farm, had married several times, had been imprisoned for adultery, and had become a suburbanite.[64]

During the decade in which prosperity had blunted the radical imperative, reformers made slow accretions; and American politics changed only to remain the same. Upon Penrose's death in 1922, Pepper became a United States Senator and even supported a Constitutional amendment to prohibit child labor. He also urged Harding to pardon a score of "political prisoners" and opposed the use of injunctions to cripple labor unions. The Congressman who led the fight against the labor injunction was LaGuardia. When Pepper's bid for reelection failed, his successor was a former garbage collector and Penrose ally whose financial prestidigitation induced the Senate to deny him his seat. The governor of Pennsylvania then appointed Grundy, who served a two-year term. By April 1929 more than 10 percent of Philadelphia's wage earners were out of work, and soon therafter investigators discovered a 25 percent rise in undernourishment among children in the state's rural areas. With the extensive unemployment of 1930, the archconservative Republican Senator was defeated.[65] *Sic transit gloria* Grundy and the legitimacy of the order he represented. The collapse of Vienna's Kreditanstalt sent shudders and then paroxysms through the body of capitalism, while Nearing tirelessly insisted that the only exit wound was through revolution.

He was content, however, to let the revolution start without him. His most popular debates in the decade had been on the topic, "Is the Human Race Worth Saving?", in which he had taken the affirmative position against attorney Clarence Darrow, a Sisyphean pessimist. Nearing had argued that life was meaningful in the Soviet Union, because common struggle and comradeship imposed purpose upon existence. But at the age of forty-seven Nearing was exhausted from his efforts within the organized left. He rearranged his life, retreating from urban activism to become a subsistence farmer, professing to seek both an alternative method to rescue humanity and insulation against Depression—which was in fact worse in the countryside than in industry.[66] Nearing also replenished his spirits and met nature anew with the aid of Helen Knothe, who anchored his life upon entering it at midpassage.

Born in 1904, she was the product of a bourgeois home made comfortable through the sale of men's belts and accessories. Her parents were active theosophists and vegetarians in New Jersey who encouraged her desire to become a professional musician. After graduation from high school and studies and concerts in Europe, she returned home, where she met Nearing, the invited speaker at her father's men's club. She later spent time at the Manumit School and also gave violin lessons to Nearing's elder son; and after another stint in Europe and a bout with factory work, Helen Knothe agreed to live with Nearing on an abandoned homestead in Vermont.[67] The land cost $300 down, with an $800 mortgage, and there they moved into a decrepit house in 1932.

With America sunk into the pit of the Depression, Nearing disengaged himself from the mass suffering that he had predicted and tried to alleviate. Yet others continued the struggle, like Governor Franklin D. Roosevelt, who early favored unemployment insurance and confessed that he stole much of the Socialist program. Norman Thomas lamented the "very poor use of it," but the invisible hand was soon to be amputated and planning substituted, as radicals had long advocated. Running against Roosevelt in 1932, Thomas and his running mate Maurer polled a respectable 884,781 votes.[68] Meanwhile adults and children scoured city dumps and scrambled over the garbage rotting outside restaurants. Farmers jabbed pitchforks into the tires of milk trucks and faced foreclosure agents in the desolate spirit of lynch mobs. In Donora, Pennsylvania, only 277 residents held jobs in 1932, of a population of 13,900. In the state's coalfields the previous summer, three miners had been killed and over two thousand gassed, injured, or wounded during the campaigns of the National Miners' Union. During the Piedmont textile wars, no one was ever convicted for the deaths of seven strikers. Deputies shot two dozen strikers in the back in Marion, North Carolina, where the work week was sixty hours and the pay five cents an hour and anyone asking for ten cents was a Red. A Brookings Institution study in 1929 showed that 0.1 percent of the wealthiest American families earned as much as 42 percent of the poorest combined.[69]

As the grass grew and withered in the wintry streets of Hoovervilles, Nearing constructed a storm cellar within the heartbreak house of capitalism, as the bitter desperation stalking the cities and towns he left behind receded into the night.

CHAPTER EIGHT

ON
TOTALITARIANISM

M ILLENNIALISM COMES WITH THE TERRI-
tory in Vermont. There, in 1790, lived the Dorrilites,
practicing communism and vegetarianism until an unbe-
liever struck down their leader, who had boasted, "No arm
can hurt my flesh." There, a decade later, lived a sect called
the Wood Scrape, whose totem was a divining rod said to
uncover buried treasure; but inaccurate prophecies of the
end of the world caused the group to fade. There, after
1815, lived the Pilgrims, who added theocracy to communism, refused to wash or shave, and wore only bearskin
tunics; they eventually headed west. From Vermont came
William Miller, whose prediction that Christ would return
in 1843 triggered the Adventist movement. Even when the
date was prudently switched to 1844, popular feeling in the
area was so intense that the continuation of the world
caused insanity in some Millerites. There, too, John
Humphrey Noyes elaborated the creed of Perfectionism,
which freed his followers from the burden of sin, until the
reports of "complex marriage" within communism drove
the sect out of the state. There too, almost a century later,

came Scott Nearing to live on sixty-five acres in the Pikes
Falls valley between Jamaica and Bondville, up past the Millerites' first church, far away from the blasting area of history.

A dozen families lived along the ten-mile dirt road leading to the property. The barn supported a leaky roof, the
kitchen contained a pump and a black iron sink, the shed
culminated in an outhouse, and the land included a swamp
as well as a meadow and spring. "I didn't know what end of
a saw to pick up," his companion in the enterprise recalled;
but Nearing's boyhood in rural Pennsylvania helped. To
achieve economic independence, they raised as much food
as they could, especially because of their fear of "food pro-
cessing and poisoning." They also made as many of their
implements as possible, renting or trading for the heavy
equipment and machinery that they needed. Ownership of
a pickup truck was justified as "indispensable," a "mechani-
cal wheelbarrow." Machine tools, they asserted, demolished
"many of the most ancient, most fascinating, and most creative human skills," and were rarely used. With the aid of
friends and neighbors, they built a stone house, and for fuel
used wood that they cut themselves. They were therefore
successful in avoiding many of the ravages of the Depression and also "as much as possible, the cruder forms of
exploitation." [1]

The secret of their economic resilience was modesty: "We
paid no rent. Taxes were reasonable. We bought no candy,
pastries, meats, soft drinks, alcohol, tea, coffee, or tobacco.
. . . We spent little on clothes and knickknacks. We lighted
for fifteen years with kerosene and candles. We never had a
telephone or radio. Most of our furniture was built in and
handmade." Neither loaning nor borrowing money, they
earned money through Nearing's lectures and the sale of
maple sugar and syrup. "We kept careful cost figures, but
we never used them to determine whether we should or

should not make syrup. . . . We tried to foresee the money required to meet our cash obligations. When we had the estimated needs, we raised no more crops and made no more money for that period." Sometimes they bartered their crops with producers of citrus fruits and raisins as far away as Florida and California. Sometimes they entered the open market and into cooperative agreements with several families to produce and then divide proportionately the maple syrup. Like most of their neighbors, they shared the bounty of their garden with others, especially the needy.[2]

Such prudence enabled them to work half the year in order to devote the other half to leisure and research, lecturing, and writing; Helen Knothe was, after all, introduced to Vermonters as Nearing's secretary. The day was divided into two four-hour blocks, with the weather determining the application of either "bread labor" or "personally determined activities." At the end of a given period, the blocks were supposed to balance. Their work was usually "significant, self-directed, constructive, and therefore interesting"; and they loved it. They were rarely rushed; they labored carefully and tried to foresee emergencies. Although they tried to turn meals into social occasions with guests and neighbors, they did not interrupt their plan or alter their principles to accommodate visitors. Their idea of conviviality was to discuss politics or vegetarianism while serving sunflower seeds to guests, and if "by some we were thought uncordial . . . we did not aim to entertain." Only on Sundays did they cease bread labor to play music, read aloud, and engage in group discussions. Nearing boasted to Sinclair that he had never been "so economically independent as I have been up here, and never have I been able to see the inadequacies of life in the big ant heaps. Also I have got a perspective on our relations with the universe which is easier to get here than in town." [3]

Nearing's claim to hear the music of the spheres distinguished him from orthodox Socialists, who had tin ears; but he was sufficiently nonconformist to alienate his neighbors. A carefully husbanded trust fund, life insurance annuities, social security, and lecture fees helped make the homestead an economic success, especially if defined more modestly than "salvaging what was still usable from the wreckage of the decaying social order in North America and western Europe." Socially, however, the experiment was disastrous for these adherents of pacifism, collectivism, and vegetarianism. By refusing to adapt to the tastes and behavior of Vermonters, Nearing violated a standard rule for winning over the masses. "We never baked a pie, we seldom ate cake or cookies and almost never doughnuts. In a community which serves pie, cake, and doughnuts for two if not three meals a day, conduct such as ours was not only unbelievable but reprehensible." Helen Knothe, who had never tasted meat, and Nearing censured "the revolting practice of consuming dead animal carcasses," the consumption of white bread, and even "eating strawberries and green peas in a cold climate, every month of the year," which they considered "extravagant and irresponsible." When the sociologist Werner Sombart speculated in 1906 that American socialism could not make headway against the abundance of roast beef and apple pie, he clearly had something else in mind. The dances held in the community center they regarded as a needless expenditure of energy, and the introduction of liquor provoked their withdrawal from the center.[4] Excoriation of the hedonism of Vermonters must be virtually unique in the history of moralist literature.

Nor was their collectivism emulated. Nearing exuded the supreme self-confidence useful to leaders of many intentional communities, but he could not retain followers, who were disillusioned by the austerity of the work and the imperious asceticism of the prophet. A form letter therefore warned potential visitors that the farm was not "an inn or a sanatarium or a vacation center. We work at bread labor at least four hours a day . . . and expect those who happen to stay here to fit in. Meat, tobacco, and alcohol are taboo on the place. . . . We are always glad to see people of our way of thinking and living, and to share with them whatever we have, do, feel, and think." They themselves had no children, and young couples did not tarry on Nearing's property. Rarely did more than four or five adults linger, of whom a high proportion were pacifists like Richard Gregg, the foremost American exponent of the philosophy of Gandhi. Sidney Hook, the foremost American exponent of the philosophy of Marx, lived nearby, but here the rub was dialectics, not dietetics: he found Nearing too simplistic for extensive discourse.[5]

Nor could the advocate of mutual aid enlist local residents to follow his advice and his example, for they were "trained to private enterprise and, for the most part, [were] rejects from private enterprise economy." [6] He also blamed the abortion of communitarianism upon the anomie of rural life and upon the individualism that he himself so obviously epitomized. Whether in a metropolis or in a remote valley, he suffered the fate that Tocqueville ascribed to the American heretic: "reduced to impotence not because he is conquered but because he is alone."

Nearing lived in comparative isolation in order to practice his credo in a secure and stable atmosphere; the last thing he wanted was a jacquerie. Simultaneously, in Washington, the "Roosevelt Revolution" sought to stem the flow of farmers to the white lights and to refurbish the ideal of homesteading with an innovative resettlement program of subsistence and cooperative farms. In charge was Nearing's former student and teaching assistant Rex Tugwell, who had become, in one journalist's estimate, "the prophet of the Roosevelt Revolution, as well as one of its boldest practitioners," and an advocate of planning in a technologically complex economy. But Tugwell as chief of the Resettlement Administration was, like Thurman Arnold as head of the Anti-Trust Division, almost a contradiction in terms, for he considered homestead farming anachronistic and did not mourn the passing of a rural economy.[7]

Yet, beginning in 1935, Undersecretary of Agriculture Tugwell inaugurated over a hundred resettlement projects, a third of which were communitarian and an experimental alternative to the family farm. And unlike his teacher, Tugwell wanted to revitalize agriculture through mechanization. Yet both men were conscious of failure, which they attributed to the American impulse toward individual aggrandizement and private pecuniary gain. Tugwell was forced to resign after the 1936 Presidential campaign because of the hostility of conservative farm groups, and the next year the Resettlement Administration was abolished, having failed to mobilize its constituency among the rural poor. In the next decade almost half of all farms were still mortgaged, a tenth produced half the nation's agricultural commodities, and the rural malnutrition rate was double the urban rate.[8]

The New Deal did not transform the countryside; and only Nearing's rigorous self-discipline exempted him from the generalization of Harold Ware, shortly before his death in an automobile accident, that subsistence farming was no antidote to poverty, that agriculture was inextricably bound to industry.[9] Migration to towns and cities continued, and even Nearing did not become an eremite. He frequently descended from the Green Mountains to engage in oratory, travel, and fellow-traveling.

BLAZING WITH THE ASSURANCE OF AN ADVENTIST, HE continued to predict imminent collapse for capitalist society, with the dictatorship of the proletariat inaugurating the secular equivalent of the Second Coming. "We need stern discipline and a strong hand to pull us out," he told Sinclair. The Russians "have made their mistakes, but they certainly go about their work with a zest." After the Weimar Republic perished in the flames of the Reichstag Fire, Nearing was ready with a pamphlet entitled *Fascism* to explain the German dictatorship. Although fairly sound in his account of Nazi impulses, he erred badly in predicting that "Fascists are following a path which has only one possible outlet—village economy, localism, and the annihilation of modern science and technique." Nearing also indulged in wish-fulfillment in arguing that the West faced exactly two choices: Fascism or Communism.[10]

The irrepressible Münzenberg had already organized a World Congress Against War in Amsterdam in the summer of 1932, with Henri Barbusse and Romain Rolland issuing an appeal to pacifists and liberals to help defend the beleaguered Socialist motherland. An international committee included Maxim Gorki, Heinrich Mann, and Bertrand Russell as well as Einstein and Madame Sun Yat-sen. The American delegation included Nearing; his son John, an organizer for the Electrical Workers' Union; and Sherwood Anderson. Over two thousand delegates promised to struggle against armaments, war preparations, colonialism, imperialism, and "slander aimed at the Soviet Union." The next year Münzenberg fled Germany, converted the permanent residue of the Congress into the World Committee Against War and Fascism, organized a Committee for the Relief of the Victims of German Fascism, and virtually created his own Comintern.[11]

After the Amsterdam Congress John Scott went to Russia, where he worked in blast furnace construction and in a chemical plant, studied engineering, and married a Russian. Nearing returned home to add his name to the roster of the American Committee for Struggle Against War, whose honorary chairman was Dreiser. The Committee also included Anderson, Baldwin, Barnes, Bloor, John Dos Passos, DuBois, Freeman, Gold, Hook, Corliss Lamont, Lovett, Sinclair, Steffens, Wald, and Thornton Wilder. Nearing also served on the national committee of the Friends of the Soviet Union, whose propaganda was directed by Harold Ware's wife, Jessica Smith. Despite his expulsion from the American Communist party, Nearing was a reliable lecturer on behalf of the front organization. He acknowledged Russia's "leadership for world peace" immediately after German Stalinists—following the self-inflicted logic of the Third Period—helped Hitler attain power, praised the "Soviet handling of the agrarian crisis" while perhaps two million kulaks were being slaughtered, and favored the Communists' "methods of handling tools [*sic*] of production" while the labor camps were gathering in between two and five million prisoners.[12] In order to achieve socialism in one country, Nearing proposed no limitations, in effect, upon that people's mortgage of misery.

With the Depression paralyzing the political nerve of the West, the incursions of Germany, Italy, and Japan turned the peace of Versailles into what Churchill called a Second Thirty Years War. Many pacifist and liberal illuminati therefore viewed the Soviet Union, benign in its foreign policy and impervious to the cycle of economic boom and bust, expanding its proletariat and educating its peasantry, building not just power plants but Socialism, as consequently leaping from the realm of necessity to the realm of freedom. Communists appeared to be reformers without sanctimoniousness, liberals without *Sitzfleisch;* and the Fabian Socialists Sidney and Beatrice Webb punctuated their admiration by dropping the question mark from the 1937 edition of *Soviet Communism: A New Civilization?*. Reverend Lyman P. Powell, who had befriended Nearing before the Great War, sensed so much "real human brotherhood" there "that we Christian nations may one day find ourselves obliged to learn anew at Russia's feet the deeper meaning of the social teachings of Jesus." One historian has characterized fellow-traveling as "a return to the eighteenth-century vision of a rational, educated, and scientific society based on the maximization of resources and the steady improvement (if not perfection) of human nature as visualized by objective, unprejudiced brains." [13]

Nearing, a prophet in one country, could not restrain his enthusiasm for the priests of another. At Cornell University he debated the Socialist Paul Blanshard on the economic crisis before the presentation of "Storm Over Asia," which one of Münzenberg's film companies had produced. At the University of Pennsylvania in 1936, Nearing was prevented at the last minute from speaking in the Christian Association Hall. So he collected a crowd of about fifty undergraduates, led them across the street, and painted a picture *en plein air* of universal amity without capitalism. In a *World Tomorrow* symposium with editors Reinhold Niebuhr and Douglas, he celebrated the fiftieth anniversary of Marx's death by foreseeing the imminent collapse of capitalism and proletarian seizure of power. Nearing envisioned the epiphany of a classless society stamped with "the mark of creative effort, of joyous service . . . the mark of responsible social action and of the individual desire to share, to work, and to dream." [14]

No wonder he tried to rejoin the Communist party. He was rejected, according to Browder, not for deviancy on the question of imperialism but for race chauvinism, which meant that Nearing sympathized with the argument of Oswald Spengler's *Decline of the West*. Mike Gold explained that "Scott Nearing preferred the false bourgeois picture, the chauvinist picture that ignored the class struggle, and turned the upsurge of the Eastern masses into a new race war." Although Gold doubted whether Nearing "was con-

scious of the logic of his conclusions, or that he is a Speng-
lerite or chauvinist," this aberrant communist was better off
in front organizations, which proliferated with the hasty
burial of the Third Period and the birth of the Popular
Front in 1935.[15] Hillquit had died in 1933 of the tuberculosis he had contracted in the sweatshops, so that the Communists found it easier to welcome even the Socialists in the
common struggle against fascism and war.

One tiny revolutionary sect was excluded from the Popular Front, however; and even Nearing, who scorned the
left's penchant for fighting at close quarters, carefully disso-
ciated himself from Trotskyism. In 1933 he complained to
Calverton that *Modern Monthly* suffered from "an overdose
of Trotsky," which in Russia could be fatal but in America
led mostly to hypertension. When a Socialist newspaper in
British Columbia reported Nearing's support of the heresy,
the *Daily Worker* repeated the charge, which he quickly denied: "The Communist party is the only serious new party
in the U.S.A. today. As such, it deserves the support of all
serious workers." The *Daily Worker* then apologized for having fallen for a "reformist provocation" and expressed its
gratitude for Nearing's "loyal support . . . to the general
activities of the revolutionary movement, and especially to
the Soviet Union." [16]

After another Canadian newspaper assaulted Nearing,
H. L. Mencken gibed that the not-so-reclusive Socialist
"spends half his time roving Europe in search of horrors
and the other half roving America to tell about them. He
has been predicting the advent of Communism in this
country since the war, and I suppose he'll keep on doing it
until the last galoot's ashore." Once he even found horrors
in the Soviet Union, while visiting his son behind the Urals
in 1935. Not only was Nearing "shocked at the backward-
ness of the living conditions and the regimentation by the
Party over the whole community," but the Great Purge ren-

dered problematic whether Communism had extirpated tsarism, "with its secret police, its little father, its red-tape-ridden bureaucracy; and its huge military establishment as a facade behind which individuals plot and scheme in secret—because there is no legally recognized way to oppose." Given Russia's "drastic regimentation with a bureaucratic military set-up," Nearing wondered whether socialism required the violation of "all our freedoms," which might then constitute "an excessive price." Edging tantalizingly close to sympathy for bourgeois civil liberties, he nonetheless refused to publicize his doubts, and continued to give directions to the splendid Moscow subway rather than to the torture cellars of the NKVD. He retained his Progressive faith in social control and in efficiency, like Anna Louise Strong, who observed that Stalin's "method of running a committee reminded me somewhat of Jane Addams . . . or Lillian D. Wald. . . . They had the same kind of democratically efficient technique, but they used more high pressure than Stalin did." [17] Unlike the Moscow correspondent of the Federated Press, however, Nearing remained in the Diaspora.

The Nazi-Soviet pact in August 1939 meant the dismemberment of Poland, the invasion of the Baltic States and Finland, economic cooperation between the new neighbors, an exchange of political and racial prisoners between the Gestapo and the NKVD, and the phony war in the West. For many believers the Soviet Union became "the god that failed," but Nearing was addicted to theodicy and took the pact in stride. "The next move inside Germany evidently will be to the left," he assured Calverton's readers, because the Nazis could attack the West only after making "concessions to the peace, bread, and freedom which the German masses are seeking." And the Western powers could defeat the Third Reich only by scuttling "free enterprise, competition, and the other phases of profit economy, [which] are as

helpless before economic and social planning and coordina-
tion as are hordes of sturdy savages against modern military
formations." [18] First it was the Fascists, then it was the capitalists who could not conduct modern warfare. Perhaps
those who predict the future of civilization should not be
expected to get the details right, though Nearing might
have realized that an economy, because privately controlled,
no more makes a nation weak than an economy, because
collectivized, makes a society just.

In the spring of 1940 Russia's ally made *Blitzkrieg* a common noun; and Münzenberg, condemned to death by the
Gestapo in 1935 for antifascism, was hanged while fleeing
south, probably by Russian agents. Then the German army
massed 150 divisions in the East. John Scott, who had become an anti-Communist and a correspondent for the London *News Chronicle,* left Russia in April 1941 with his family
and other Americans, in exchange for a Soviet espionage
agent arrested in San Diego.[19] On June 21, Communists
were still picketing the White House appealing for peace
and disarmament. The next day they disappeared.

Six months later Pearl Harbor dissipated most of the pacifism that remained in America. In denouncing labor agitation and a projected march of Negroes on Washington,
Communists breathed life into Talleyrand's criterion of
treason as a matter of timing. The united front became so
elastic that Browder offered to shake hands with J. P.
Morgan, Jr., only to be informed that the banker had died
nine months earlier. In testimony to Soviet-American
friendship, the Communist Party of America obligingly destroyed itself, leaving only the "Communist Political Association" and the disconcerting grin of the Cheshire Cat.[20]
Also anti-Axis were antimilitarists from the First World
War, like Douglas, who joined the Marines. Neither Baldwin nor Thomas nor Lochner, who returned from Berlin in
1942, ardently opposed the use of military force against the

Third Reich. Bertrand Russell, who was prevented from teaching mathematics and logic at City College of New York in 1940, believed the survival of civilization to require Nazi defeat: "Ever since the war began [,] I have felt that I could not go on being a pacifist. . . . If I were young enough to fight myself I should do so, but it is more difficult to urge others." Sinclair and Wise had been pacifists before the Great War, pro-war during it, and remorseful pacifists again thereafter. They too supported the Second World War.[21]

Nearing, however, could no more be a pacifist between wars than he could be a vegetarian between meals; and in the conflict between pro-Communist politics and a credo of nonviolence, between Stalin and Tolstoy, he chose the latter. Memories of the First World War undoubtedly remained fresh but, given the character of the Second World War, his position was neither sensible nor even fully consistent. His pacifism did not connect theory to practice; it was not a program but an alternative to one. He never urged, with all the eloquence at his command, the defenders of Stalingrad to turn the other cheek or the besieged inhabitants of Leningrad to renounce force as a method of settling disputes. As Slavs they could not exercise the option of the Aryans in Denmark to resist Nazism nonviolently. Nearing presumably wanted the Third Reich to be defeated but, as one Socialist leader had argued a couple of years earlier, "It was not our job to say so." He did, however, wish to record his dissent from the American war effort. Because the Fellowship of Reconciliation was "not only Christian but offensively so," Nearing had resigned from the organization two decades earlier. Immediately after Pearl Harbor, however, he asked its secretary, A. J. Muste, to reenroll him.[22]

Nearing's opposition to the war reflected his conviction that in the past decade America had been "falling a prey to fascism" anyway. This exotic description of the New Deal must have baffled such vitriolic Roosevelt haters as William Dudley Pelley and Father Coughlin and Gerald Winrod and Ezra Pound, or the unit of the Christian Front that used a likeness of the President as target practice. More specifically, Nearing condemned "the plutocratic military oligarchy . . . sweeping into power in North America," as though the activities of the American Liberty League and its fabulously wealthy backers had escaped his attention, as though the overwhelmingly Republican big businessmen of the period came to Washington with the self-confidence of insiders. After the blitzkrieg this "military oligarchy" could brandish only 350 usable infantry tanks, 2,806 mostly outmoded aircraft, and about half a million soldiers including the National Guard. In understanding how America might fall "prey to fascism," Nearing ought to have attended the largest peacetime maneuvers in the Army's history, held in August 1940, as described by one historian: "Pieces of stovepipe served as antitank guns, beer cans as ammunition, rainpipes as mortars, and broomsticks as machine guns. . . . No combat planes were available; and . . . men maneuvered trucks bearing placards with the word 'TANK.' " [23]

No echo of the People's Council resounded in the Second World War, so that Nearing expressed his antiwar convictions primarily in the columns of the Federated Press. But the labor unions that subscribed to the service were as patriotic as the Communists and other radicals who operated it. Alexander L. Crosby, the chief of the New York bureau, was fired in 1942 for considering strike news inherently important rather than detrimental to the struggle against fascism.[24] Early the next year the New York bureau, where Nearing sent copy, voted to discontinue his column, not only because only three newspapers subscribed to it, but because "Nearing's recent columns were disruptive of national unity and the war effort." [25]

Haessler, the political objector to the First World War, quickly repudiated the statement of the New York bureau. But he reconsidered when sources close to the FBI warned that a declaration of loyalty might be prudent, and he severely edited a passage in which Nearing "called upon American workers to rise in revolt." Branding his columnist's attitude "childish," Haessler asked Nearing to call upon workers under Nazi rule to throw off their chains. After having "exchanged some super-heated words," Nearing either quit or was fired—depending upon who tells the story. Friendship between Nearing and Haessler remained intact, however. The Federated Press itself was abolished in 1956.[26]

The circle of his influence was narrowing when Nearing decided to become an editorial staff of one and to produce his own journal. *World Events* was a newsletter that appeared quarterly after an erratic start in 1943 and which cost subscribers $1 per year. Since business details distracted from the tasks of punditry, Frederick A. Blossom became the publisher and subscription manager of *World Events*. American radicals have generally been, like Lord Macaulay's Irishmen, interesting rather than successful; and Blossom had led at least an interesting life. After his graduation from Amherst in 1898, where he engaged in a campus protest against anti-Negro discrimination, Blossom got a doctorate in Romance languages and joined the Wobblies, helping to organize the silk workers of Paterson. In 1916 he became president of the New York State Birth Control League and helped edit Margaret Sanger's *Birth Control Review*, but they quarreled after American intervention in Europe. Blossom, a scholar of Flaubert, was a Francophile; Sanger was a pacifist, arguing that "the primary cause of this war lay in the terrific pressure of population in Germany." A month after the declaration of war, she found her office stripped of all furniture and records; Blossom had left the League with only a telephone. Sanger appealed to the district attorney and shocked radicals by her recourse to capitalist justice; without their support she decided to work for birth control through the techniques of middle-class reform. Blossom went on to raise funds for the Hillquit mayoralty campaign and to organize lectures for Nearing at the Rand School. They lost contact for two decades until Blossom, then editor of publications for the Library of Congress, offered to publish a newsletter if Nearing would become a regular contributor.[27]

On August 6, 1945, a B-29 dropped a bomb on the city of Hiroshima. Sixty-two years old that day, Nearing wrote President Truman: "Your government is no longer mine. From this day onward our paths diverge: you to continue on your suicide course, blasting and cursing the world. I turn my hand to the task of helping to build a human society based on cooperation, social justice, and human welfare." [28] The war was over.

FROM THIS PERIOD ON, NEARING'S WRITINGS CONVEY A sensation akin to riding a dodge'em car in an amusement park, careening jerkily and haphazardly, alternately colliding against and evading blurred forms without apparent direction or purpose, finally grinding to a halt at the end of the allotted minutes or pages, and achieving no sense of change or development or even significance. His 1945 volume, *Democracy Is Not Enough,* for example, displays the meandering discourse, the want of proportion, the imprecision, and the inconsistency of someone who has talked too long to himself. The picture of "democracy" is ruined by double exposure: sometimes it is meant to distinguish the Soviet Union from the Western powers, which are plutocratic; sometimes it is used to derogate the American political system, which is too unscientific, too undisciplined, too free. The decline of popular government is blamed not only upon the propaganda of the oligarchs but also upon the "abundance of mild and cheap narcotics in the form of tea, coffee, tobacco, and alcoholic liquors. . . . Entire generations passed through life with their senses habitually drugged." The result has been the New Deal, a version of "national socialism, with its one-party government, its subordination of private interests to the needs of the state, its ruthless suppression of all forms of dissidence, and its leader principle." Nearing believed that he was already living in "a totalitarian society which denounced freedom in principle and strangled it in practice. . . . There is good reason to suppose that President Roosevelt's insistence upon a third term marked the end of the Republic." [29]

Despite such gloom Nearing also proposed solutions, although the level of argumentation remained subterranean, or perhaps extraterrestrial. He recommended "contact with the magnetic circuits of the earth" and, without elaborating, asserted that "the connection between planetary law and order and popular government is plain enough." Socialism necessitated centralization, so he advocated it; his own pariah status caused him to value decentralization, so he wanted that too; his book makes no attempt to reconcile the two ideas. Consistency is not the only touchstone of truth, but inconsistency hardly enhances an argument. Nor did his failure to persuade a half dozen others to share cooperative farming prevent him from concocting a scheme of universal majority rule, a world federation of people's republics.[30]

In the meantime he supported the imposition of the people's republics in Eastern Europe, and he showed that subtlety was not wholly outside his range: the Soviet Union was called "expansive rather than imperialist." His pacifism was again in phase with his pro-Communism, and at Drake University in 1946 Nearing bit the bullet: "If the world will be united, it will be by totalitarianism. The postwar epoch is in the hands of the totalitarians. You can hate Russia all you like. . . . But when you're through there is the future." When another symposiast, Bertram Wolfe, denounced the Russians' massacre of the Polish officer corps at Katyn and the execution of Bundist leaders, Nearing rebutted that the elimination of an elite constituted "a great social service." But when the former director of the Workers School told him, "You know, Scott, that if the Communists took control in this country, you would be one of the first to be executed," Nearing replied, "Yes, I know that." [31] Wolfe's attempt to reason with a man who welcomed his own executioners was honorable, if futile. An alternative might have been simply to note the prescience of Kafka's exposure of the totalitarian mind, "The Penal Colony," in which the officer demonstrates the efficiency of his infernal torture machine by executing himself.

What a man would purportedly die for may differ from what he lives for; and Nearing continued not only to farm his private plot but to write and lecture as a free lance on behalf of an internationalism that was compatible with Soviet foreign policy and devalued Polish nationalism, American nationalism, and Zionism. Rabbi Wise thereupon asked his former friend: "Can one not serve one's people and, in addition, all who are oppressed? . . . It is not hard to lecture throughout the country in behalf of a new social and economic order, forgetting the urgency of people suffering now." And Wise added, "Is one required to forget one's family to become a servant of the world?" [32]

It was a poignant question. Four years earlier Nearing was embarking on a lecture tour when his mother was dying in New Jersey and his brothers and sisters went to her side. Nearing sent a telegram asking that he be kept informed, but she died in his absence at the age of seventy-eight. In 1947 Louis Nearing died at the age of eighty-six, a

month after the passing of Nellie Seeds, who had recently re-
tired as director of adult education for the War Labor
Board. Her death enabled Helen Knothe to become Mrs.
Scott Nearing before a registrar in Los Angeles in 1947. She
was, according to her stepson, virtually the only person in
the family with whom Nearing developed a relationship of
genuine affection.[33]

"How Should the U.S.A. Meet the Challenge of the
U.S.S.R.?" was a more important subject for Nearing than
his family and was the topic of his debate with Evan
Thomas, the chairman of the War Resisters League, in
1947. Nearing asserted that the challenge should be met by
imitation: "If the U.S.S.R. represents the attempt of a segment of the human race to set up a new social pattern to
replace an outmoded one, it is folly to uphold the disin-
tegrating pattern." What was needed, he added, was not liberty but "individual and social discipline. We need social
control." In reply Norman Thomas's brother criticized
Communism for spurning "morals, and . . . it adopts the
power politics idea." He proposed disarmament as a
prerequisite for ending war and eroding Communism.[34]

But the Cold War that, for different reasons, both
Thomas and Nearing opposed had already stiffened the
erstwhile allies into postures of rigid hostility. Soon Greece,
Turkey, Prague, Berlin, and the 38th Parallel marked the
fault lines of the postwar world; and A and H became the
most ominous letters in the alphabet. Chambers, who had
become a colleague of John Scott's at *Time* magazine,
charged the head of the Carnegie Endowment for International Peace with espionage; and soon thereafter another
Red Scare infected American ideals and institutions. Gitlow
delivered stirring speeches on behalf of the American
Legion, Mandel joined the staff of the House Un-American
Activities Committee, and Nearing's old nemesis Creel actively defended the acetylene anti-Communism of Joseph

McCarthy and Richard Nixon. Appellate Judge Learned Hand weakened Holmes' already weak "clear and present danger" test, which had sent Socialists to prison after the First World War, with a new formulation that four Supreme Court Justices adopted in *Dennis* v. *U.S.*, jailing Communists for the exercise of speech.[35] In an atmosphere of suspicion and intolerance, the radical cry for justice was virtually stilled. The last year a Socialist ran for President was in 1956, when even the Prohibitionist candidate outpolled one Darlington Hoopes. That year, after half a century's dissemination of the Socialist vision, the Rand School closed.

Yet, paradoxically, the rights that Nearing had been denied in 1915 were strengthened at the very time both he and conservative fanatics showed such contempt for liberty. "The problem of academic freedom had been lying dormant in my mind for a very long time," explained Louis Rabinowitz, a businessman who had heard Nearing's debate with Seligman after the expulsion. "From my point of view, Scott Nearing got the best [*sic*] of the argument at that time. He showed to my satisfaction that unless one toed the line set by the administration and the board of trustees, an academic position was not secure." [36] Rabinowitz therefore provided funds to establish a project to define and champion *Lehrfreiheit*, and in 1951 the Academic Freedom Committee was created at Columbia University under the chairmanship of political scientist Robert MacIver.

The following year, in *Adler* v. *Board of Education,* the Supreme Court mentioned for the first time the right of academic freedom, although in a dissenting opinion; later that year the right was affirmed in a concurring opinion. In 1957 a former Harvard economist and member of the Progressive party, Paul M. Sweezy, elicited from six Justices the Constitutional protection of academic freedom, after he had refused to divulge to a state legislative investigator his political beliefs or the nature of his lectures at the University of New Hampshire. Chief Justice Earl Warren proclaimed that "scholarship cannot flourish in an atmosphere of suspicion and distrust. Teachers and students must always remain free to inquire, to study, and to evaluate. . . . Otherwise our civilization will stagnate and die."

Sweezy v. *New Hampshire* implanted the First Amendment on the campus, but the Supreme Court has not yet articulated the procedural safeguards that the AAUP had erected for nontenured teachers like Nearing. Fifteen years after Sweezy was vindicated, the Supreme Court addressed itself to a pair of cases that at least faintly resembled Nearing's dismissal. David F. Roth was an assistant professor at Wisconsin State University at Oshkosh who was not rehired upon the completion of a one-year contract. Robert Sindermann had taught in the state college system of Texas for ten years before his series of one-year contracts expired. Both political scientists were nontenured; both claimed that criticisms of their respective university administrations had provoked their dismissals; both demanded the right to a hearing and to an explanation for the nonrenewal of their contracts. But in 1972 a majority of the Court, speaking through Justice Potter Stewart, denied that the Fourteenth Amendment's protections of "liberty" and "property" had been infringed. Stewart assumed that the freedom of both Roth and Sindermann to seek employment elsewhere, inside and outside academe, remained intact. Nor could any violation of their property interests be found, since their contracts ran for only one year anyway.

The two cases could nevertheless be distinguished. Sindermann was granted the right to a hearing because, as a former co-chairman of his department at Odessa Junior College, he could reasonably expect reemployment. He worked within a system of de facto tenure, unlike the less-experienced Roth, who on due process grounds was not entitled to a hearing. Justice William O. Douglas, one of the two dissenters in both cases, protested the majority's refusal to examine the alleged circumstances of Roth's dismissal: "No more direct assault on academic freedom can be imagined than for the school authorities to be allowed to discharge a teacher because of his or her philosophical, political, or ideological beliefs." Nor did Douglas regard the issue of tenure as relevant, since Sweezy's rights as a guest lecturer had earlier been upheld.[37]

A writer as well as teacher, Sweezy founded the "anti-imperialist and pro-socialist" *Monthly Review* in 1949 with Leo Huberman, whose own introduction to such principles had been yet another Nearing-Seligman debate. According to Huberman, Nearing was a "profound scholar" and a "saint with brains" who, already in the second issue of the magazine, was explicating collectivism, pacifism, and proper diet. When Frederick Blossom moved to East Palatka, Florida, he had difficulty not only building socialism there but also printing and distributing *World Events*, so he arranged for Nearing to become a columnist for *Monthly Review* instead. The unexpired subscriptions to the newsletter were filled; and, beginning in April 1953, Nearing was endowed with six unrestricted pages in all but special issues of the Marxist monthly.[38] His own columns were only quasi-Marxist. They were also non-Weberian, pre-Keynesian, and predictable. Rarely illuminating world events with subtle or sophisticated insights, Nearing usually contented himself with statistics, as though there were safety in numbers. Altogether he contributed two hundred such columns.

By then the Nearings had also moved away, for the "competitive, acquisitive, exploitive, coercive social order" was "rigged" against them. Besides, a ski lodge was to be built in the neighborhood. Their house was eventually sold to Pearl S. Buck, and in 1952 they purchased a farm off a dirt road near Harborside, Maine.[39] Except for the solid house into which they moved, the Nearings started their homesteading project all over again, an exacting two decades later. Yet they demonstrated their characteristic fortitude and gritty dedication, upheld the same regimen and principles, and made the land bloom.

In Maine, Nearing also devised a nonprofit educational corporation, the Social Science Institute, publishing to date only the books he and his wife have written. Afraid of "some future frame-up" designed to silence him, Nearing reasoned on the basis of his 1919 trial that a corporation would provide limited liability in case of prosecution. Actually, since the jury convicted the corporation and acquitted Nearing, the experience should have suggested something else. Nevertheless a board of directors was established, including Blossom and two ministers from the Boston area, Donald Lothrop and Everett Gendler; and when cash reserves from the sale of previous books and pamphlets permitted another work was published.[40] The Institute's favorite author thus continued to demonstrate a capacity to move readily between the abstract and the concrete, to expatiate on the course of human history and yet still pay his bills.

After resettlement on the shores of Cape Rosier, Scott and Helen Nearing spent their first three winters touring the United States in order "to shed what light we can before the darkness becomes superficially complete." [41] One consequence was *U.S.A. Today,* the Baedeker of the paranoid style in American politics. It also showed the authors' desire to oppose McCarthyism without necessarily opposing repression. Nearing's political ethics had become not Tolstoy's but Lenin's—*kto kovo:* what mattered was simply who acted upon whom.

Each summer the Nearings also attended a camp in Conway, New Hampshire, whose founder had spent ten days fasting and praying atop White Face Mountain in 1940, and then descended "as if guided to a 300-acre property . . .

which was for sale." Lola Maverick Lloyd, granddaughter of the author of *Wealth Against Commonwealth,* daughter of an erstwhile millionaire Communist, contributed to the down payment; and Willard Uphaus, the co-chairman of the American Peace Crusade, became the director of the World Fellowship Camp. While Helen Nearing usually sold books, trinkets, fruit, and vegetables to the guests, her husband delivered lectures for several evenings during the week of their visit. Nearing conveyed "a directness, a decisiveness that comes from a disciplined mind," Uphaus recalled. "Sometimes he was considered inflexible in his answering of questions, but his arguments were hard to meet." The attorney general of New Hampshire also submitted queries regarding the camp's speakers and guests, but the Methodist layman refused to submit his guest list and correspondence. Charged with contempt, Uphaus lost his case before the Supreme Court, which decided in 1959 that the state's substantial interest in the names of possible subversives outweighed the right to privacy and the potential damage to the right of dissent. The attorney general went to Congress; and Uphaus, at the age of sixty-nine, went to jail for a year.[42]

When the Subversive Activities Control Board required the registration of the Communist party, Nearing was among those who supported an amicus curia brief that proposed the abolition of the Board instead. An outraged chairman, Francis E. Walter of the House Un-American Activities Committee, thereupon included Nearing among those "identified in sworn testimony as members of the Communist party," which he had not been for over two decades. It was confusing, however, when the editor of the *Daily Worker,* John Gates, quit the Party after the suppression of the Hungarian Revolution of 1956; while Nearing, who often left his home in Maine in November rather than watch hunters kill deer, defended Soviet tanks in Budapest. "Hungarian white guardists, exiled for a decade from their motherland," he explained, "were joining the rebels to fight for the restoration of their property, prestige, and power." Unmentioned was his favorite passage from the Declaration of Independence; the right of revolution was apparently not applicable from Stettin in the Baltic to Trieste in the Adriatic. While welcoming the Russians back into Hungary, he also urged "a graceful acceptance by Secretary Dulles" of the Soviet request to leave Europe.[43]

So long as there had been a Soviet Union, Nearing had publicly justified its domestic and foreign policies, and such reliability deserved to be rewarded. At the Communists' fortieth birthday celebration in 1959, he was given star billing. After Elizabeth Gurley Flynn, the former Wobbly spitfire who had been jailed under the Smith Act, urged the recruitment of American youth, Nearing told the Carnegie Hall audience what it wanted to hear: "The United States tonight is the greatest threat in the world to the peace and happiness . . . of mankind." [44] In charge of the American arsenal was Secretary of Defense Thomas Gates, Jr., whose father had spearheaded the alumni campaign to drive Nearing from the Wharton School more than half a century earlier. In 1959's best-selling novel, *Advise and Consent,* a substantial political movement openly proclaims, "We would rather crawl to Moscow on our knees than perish under a bomb," a slogan representing the author's feverish imagination more than the impact of the Communist Party itself. For by then it had been devastated by the prosecution and imprisonment of its leaders and by postwar internal purges, and it was generally discredited not only by its advocacy of collective ownership but by its defense of a bleak and ominous tyranny. Its battered cadres thus preferred to suffer for an idea rather than to pursue a better one, to condemn the inexcusable restriction upon their freedom of expression rather than to exercise what remained inviolable: freedom of thought.

After a visit to Hungary, the Soviet Union, and China, the Nearings praised the social discipline and economic advances they had observed. In writing *The Brave New World* they hoped to bring "glad tidings . . . to the peoples of a bored, disillusioned, demoralized, pessimistic, capitalist West. How rejoiced we thought our fellow citizens would be to hear the good news of peace, friendship, progress, and co-existence." Yet their boosterism went unnoticed in the capitalist press; and instead of the governmental suppression they feared, in 1958 the Nearings' passports were revoked.[45]

Just as Secretary of State Robert Lansing refused recognition to Soviet Russia in 1918 in the hope of speeding its collapse, so his nephew, Secretary of State John Foster Dulles, continued to block recognition of the Communist government of China. The Nearings' two previous passport applications each time had taken a mysterious fifteen months to process, while they were interrogated after some of Nearing's speeches had been monitored. When the Passport Office asked for their passports, they refused to surrender them and invoked the sanctity of contracts: "We paid the required fee. . . . Our passports are the record of a contract entered into by the government of the United States. . . . A contract may not be repudiated at will." [46]

In the spring of 1959 a hearing was arranged in Washington in which Nearing scorned "legalisms" but argued for the basic right to travel freely. Placing loyalty to social science and to his "constituency" above allegiance to the American government, he identified himself as an "outspoken and vigorous" critic of its foreign policy. When representatives of the Passport Office asked if he would return to China, Nearing replied: "I have the opportunity to do that at any time. . . . Where you call 'beyond the iron curtain,' people are happy to do anything for Americans who are not in harmony with the policy of the United States government. So that, in a sense, when you are in China you are more among friends than . . . when you are in the United States. . . . We do not accept the limitation of nationalism." [47]

The Passport Office was unimpressed with such an argument. In May its director, Frances G. Knight, formally canceled their passport facilities because "travel to and in Communist China would be prejudicial . . . to the interests of the United States" and to the "orderly conduct" of its foreign policy. Citing the "unresolved conflict" over Korea and the Straits of Taiwan, accusing the Chinese regime of "lawless acts," ignoring the Nearings' own sense of personal security there, she warned that the American government would be unable to protect them. Although the Nearings cited poverty as the reason for their failure to attack the ruling in the courts, the restriction upon their right to travel coincided with the passport difficulties of other leftists like Corliss Lamont, Paul Robeson, and, later, Herbert Aptheker. Their litigiousness converted the passport from a badge of political conformity to nothing more than an identity card. In the most important decision, *Kent* v. *Dulles,* the Supreme Court in 1958 defined the right of travel as "part of the 'liberty' of which the citizen cannot be deprived without due process of law. . . . Freedom of movement is basic in our scheme of values." [48] Afterwards passports were issued to the Nearings without further hearings or delays.

Nearing visited East Germany, for example, and reported that the National Front that governed there "is wholly voluntary. It has no means of forcing anyone to do anything." Further south he found citizens who "looked rested, secure, hopeful, cheerful," in a land without poverty, where "they are building solidly and fundamentally for a better future." [49] This El Dorado was none other than the People's Republic of Albania. Nearing also visited Cuba shortly before the CIA's Bay of Pigs invasion and British Guyana before CIA-financed strikes helped overthrow Prime Minister Cheddi Jagan, whom Nearing praised for his "efforts to replace colonialism with Fabian principles." [50]

The economist also visited capitalist nations, such as Venezuela, where he lectured to students in 1960 on "The Expanding American Empire." His oratory could still raise the room temperature. After denouncing the Monroe Doctrine, the lecturer was asked for his solution and calmly replied, "Social revolution." Instead of thoughtful nods, "pandemonium broke loose. The students stamped, applauded, screamed, and yelled. . . . The students dispersed soon after in a greatly excited mood." Two years later Nearing returned to Caracas while heading for the Continental Congress for Solidarity with Cuba in Rio de Janeiro. But when airport police searched Nearing and found that his lecture notes on "The Socialist Century" had been jotted down on envelopes bearing the return address of the Soviet embassy in Washington, they then rifled through his magazines, took his passport and ticket, and impounded a penknife from the slender, seventy-nine-year-old scholar. Taken to Caracas police headquarters in a car with a Sten gun on the floor, Nearing surrendered his shoe polish and flashlight batteries to the scrutiny of these Fearless Fosdicks. An inspector informed him that he could remain in Venezuela only overnight; the other bed in his hotel room was occupied by a guard.

His shoe polish, batteries, and penknife returned, Nearing arrived in Baranquila, Colombia, passed customs, secured a hotel room, and then was hauled to police headquarters. Searched all over again, he was detained, although not arrested, for days in a barred room at police headquarters, and then was deported at his own expense to the

United States. Legal costs prevented Nearing from pressing charges, so he flew directly to Rio to help arrange the Congress, whose ranks were depleted when visas were denied Mrs. Janet Jagan and J. D. Bernal, of the World Peace Council. As in Minnesota in 1917, the hall that the delegates had hired was canceled at the last moment, so they used the hall of naval yard workers across the bay from Rio in Niterio in March 1963. Nearing was pleased with the militancy that the Congress conveyed, and his report of its proceedings resembled a medieval morality play in which fiendish imps must ultimately scurry to the exits: "The imperialists, in their insatiable greed, have battered each other to pieces, leaving only one great power still intact, but trembling and tottering on its crumbling colonial foundations in Latin America." [51]

Five months later Nearing became an octogenarian, but a gala party in his honor was postponed three months to coincide with the anniversary of the Bolshevik Revolution. Jessica Smith, editor of *Soviet Russia Today* and, later, *New World Review*, chaired the New York affair; Malvina Reynolds sang folk songs; Helen Nearing, Muste, and Uphaus were among the speakers; and a bronze bust was presented to Nearing, who predicted the doom of "capitalist imperialism" to the applause of a great many of the approximately 800 guests. Testimonials poured in from Janet Jagan and Rockwell Kent; from Dorothy Day of the *Catholic Worker* and R. Palme Dutt of Britain's *Labour Monthly;* from Harry Laidler of the League for Industrial Democracy and A. Philip Randolph of the Brotherhood of Sleeping Car Porters; from Gus Hall, the secretary of the American Communist party, and from Herbert Aptheker, whose American Institute for Marxist Studies Nearing helped to found the following year; from Roger Baldwin and Norman Thomas; from Rex Tugwell and Harry Elmer Barnes; from Anna Louise Strong of Peking and John Howard Lawson of the

Hollywood Ten; from Leo Huberman and Carl Haessler.[52] That evening the flow of his life seemed to congeal.

Nearing himself had not mellowed or relaxed or become reconciled to what he had fought during half a century. Such fidelity to ideals was uncommon, but—more importantly—were these ideals valid? Had the vagaries of history, to which Nearing appeared so immune, transmuted the worth of his principles? His totalitarian apologetics drastically curtailed his credibility and his influence and were the consequence of an embittered and defiant inflexibility. The united front that paid him personal tribute that evening only temporarily disguised his isolation, even within the left. Nor could affectionate testimonials stifle Tugwell's later reflection and "strange wonder that such enormous abilities should have been largely wasted." [53] Indeed Nearing's very strength of character, his don't-tread-on-me mien, imprisoned him not only in his own idiosyncratic idealism but in a political stance that was finally neither pertinent nor trustworthy.

CHAPTER NINE
OF MIND
AND CHARACTER

NEARING SOUGHT TO EDUCATE OTHERS BY his example, to demonstrate that principles need not be abandoned in an unjust society, that integrity could be realized despite its apparent disrepute. He aimed to convert his fellow citizens with ideals against which their calculations and rationalizations might ultimately be judged. He asserted that reach had to exceed grasp if grasp were to be attained; that compromise implicated its practitioners in defects that had to be surmounted rather than sanctioned; that only a perspective detached from a party or a nation could transcend myopia and make possible social advance. Nearing cherished the freedom to pursue ideas to their conclusions, the right to proclaim the common good against particular interests, and the obligation his conscience dictated to uphold individual inviolability against the pressure of conformity. He wanted to devise programs and strategies of change without asking the assent of their beneficiaries, to condemn or defend without the limitations imposed by representation. He avoided whenever possible the organizational commitments that he feared would detract from the pursuit of righteousness.

In this sense, the quarter-century he worked within the organized left was not wholly different from the withdrawal that followed. Even as chairman of the People's Council, or as president of the Garland Fund, he preferred to adorn groups rather than shape them. He adopted a posture that sometimes made an impression, but he did little actively to alter anyone's position. He announced ideas but was often inattentive to their implementation. Too aloof to practice successfully the manipulative arts, yet too self-possessed to accede for long to the will of a majority, Nearing could neither effectuate his aims nor fully disengage himself from political concern. Too activist for boards of trustees, he was too purist for radical organizations thereafter. Yet frustrated by the failures of the 1920s, he did not, in the next four decades of seclusion, achieve the kind of sublime vision or philosophic plenitude that could resonate in minds comfortable with complexity. As the immediacy of other lives no longer permeated his own, his grip upon issues loosened and his ideas ceased to be relevant. A price may be exacted even for integrity, and Nearing was among those who paid it.

For isolation did not release untapped creative energies or deepen his reflective powers. He did not freshly perceive the work of man, or develop or amplify the ideas with which he began. By the end of the 1920s, at the very latest, all of his publications in politics and economics are the products of a one-tract mind, the titles no more distinguishing them than the dates of issue. "Never in the course of a piece of social research have I changed my assumptions so fundamentally and so often," he wrote in a 1961 volume, yet the pages that followed the preface were interchangeable with whatever he had written earlier and later.[1] Esteeming simplicity of thought as highly as simplicity of life, Nearing substituted attitudinizing for argumentation and emotion for thought, like the silent film actors who must exaggerate their gesticulation because they have so little to say.

His conversation was often oracular, as he disengaged himself from more acute minds and gained little insight from introspection. Rarely acknowledging intellectual debts to others, unreceptive to ideas that challenged his own, he generally kept only admirers within his circle, as intellectual satellites within his own orbit. Not, in Dr. Johnson's phrase, "a clubbable man," Nearing loved Humanity but could only intermittently abide the company of most other people. The consequence of always speaking *ex cathedra,* especially because his profession was not pontifical, was not felicitous for social science.

One index of his intellectual sterilization was the deterioration of his prose, which was once spare, clean, and effective. Early in his career as a pamphleteer, he could string out sentences like barbed wire. But, as he exhausted his stock of new ideas, his diction began to falter and his taste became unsure. He concocted new words, like "worldism," "rubbleize," and "policemanized ghettos." He called the two categories of human experience "I-ness and We-ness." He used odd modifiers, like "lower culture nomads," " 'Destroy Germany' advocates," and "wage working masses"—not to be confused with the redundant "popular masses" or with the awkward "super-normally equipped men and women." Survival, he wrote, depended "not upon rights-freedoms, but upon duties-disciplines." Sometimes the effect could be numbing: "Freedom in the power age is in part the consequence of a cycle of development leading up to the efflorescence of freedom discussion, freedom theories and freedom practices in the West. . . ." Coolidge's flash of understanding that "when people are out of work, unemployment results" could be matched by Nearing's incisive sentence:

"Acquisition becomes the chief end of life in a community dedicated to the accumulation of possessions." [2] Wielding a pen like a hacksaw, Nearing performed open-heart surgery on the English language.

He drew up blueprints for a united world for presentation to a pragmatic, nationalistic people, warned a country barely endowed with class consciousness of the menace of plutocracy, stood in an almost trillion-dollar marketplace to inveigh against the corruption of consumption, proclaimed himself an idealist while others were fond of inquiries like "How much is he worth?", and called upon the American citizen to "soak the rich" when all he wanted was—"deal me in!" [3] In a society in which one demagogue promised to make "every man a king," in which a Cadillac was supposed to be both exclusive and accessible, in which a status race that no one could quite win was preferable to a class struggle that some would necessarily lose, Nearing attempted to puncture the faith that conflicts were resolvable, that the consequences of greed and ignorance might be avoided, that even the defeated might still keep their horses for the spring plowing. The dismissals and resignations that marked his career had scarcely equipped him to understand—much less educate—such a placable and resilient nation.

A connoisseur of capitalist decay, Nearing dismissed Lord Keynes as "crazy" and compared the unbalanced Federal budget to a mismanaged household, when even village newspaper editorial writers eventually recognized the invalidity of the analogy.[4] His own lifetime coincided with the creation of both the welfare state and the warfare state, yet he took little theoretical notice of these transformations. What he had studied and described at the University of Pennsylvania was no longer the same capitalism, although it was hardly socialism either. In the projected budget for the fiscal year 1974, for example, it is hard to choose from among its huge figures the most awesome: the $81.1 billion spent for national defense, or (counting Social Security) the $125.5 billion spent for "human resources." The system had duplicated, adapted, and mutilated a remarkable number of ideas first articulated in his adolescence by Populists and Socialists. This absorptive power does not mean that the economic order is just, only that predictions of its eclipse should be viewed through the smoked glass of skepticism.

Another sign of Nearing's limitations as a political economist was his lack of interest in social democracy, in nations with both extensive public ownership and private enterprise. Since the Depression, Scandinavia has been to the liberal and democratic Socialist mind what Pennsylvania was to Voltaire. "Why should anyone want to go to Russia when one can go to Denmark?" Justice Brandeis once asked; but Nearing continued to see in Communism the only genuine alternative to the boom-and-bust cycle of capitalism and its maldistribution of wealth.

The key to his Manichean economics, to his division of the world into "capitalism" and "socialism," indeed to his entire social philosophy, was his fear of the power of the very wealthy. Against the plutocracy he devoted a shelf full of pamphlets and a lifetime of polemic, which now smack quaintly of the antique, almost like phrenology. More importantly, Nearing's works did not make a strong case even for the existence of a wealthy coterie defined as virtually synonymous with the American government. Its extraordinarily tenacious and pervasive control was assumed rather than proved. Nearing's anatomy of power in America was ectomorphic; and his argument, when abstracted from his writings, was tautological: whatever elected representatives do is at the behest of the very rich, whose malign influence is demonstrated by the decisions and policies of the government. Such an argument is difficult to controvert. He did not delineate in detail the composition of this oligarchy, its history, its special character. Nor did he ever explain whether any democratic or institutional constraints operate upon the plutocracy; or whether its control permeates all sectors of American society with equal force; or how accurately it defines its own interests; or whether major disagreements erupt within its ranks and how they are resolved; or whether its interests ever coincide with the interests of other classes and groups. In Nearing's writings, words like "plutocracy" and "oligarchy" had little substantive meaning. They merely signaled the immediate arrival of other, incantatory words, like "revolution" and "collectivism."

Against the oligarchs he pitted not so much the masses as the "super-normally equipped men and women," the social engineers. "The success of the revolution," he wrote in 1920, "depends upon the intelligence, the courage, the foresight, the idealism, and the scientific knowledge of those upon whom the responsibility falls for directing the change." This vanguard would do just about everything for the masses except leave them alone, and over four decades later his identification with this elite was intact: "We social engineers must scan history for its lessons, pool our knowledge and experiences . . . and utilize our individual and collective energies to help build a life that will bring the greatest degree of wealth and well-being to the greatest possible number of our fellows. . . . Our consciences should continue to bother us until we have set matters to rights." [5]

Unlike many radicals, Nearing indulged infrequently in romantic exaltation of the masses, nor did he idolize the worker. Little genuine feeling for the texture of lower-class life can be detected in his books, except, ironically enough, those written under the banner of liberal reform. His real interest was directed elsewhere, in the ideals of control and efficiency, in the harnessing of social forces, and in the development of political and technical mastery, which is why he so admired Communism and kicked its leaders, like the "opportunistic" Khruschchev, only when they were down. Such an interest explains his denigration of the value of freedom, his indifference to democratic procedures and philosophy, and his dislike of Vermont town meetings, which he considered "boring" and "obstructive." [6]

Nearing's discomfiture in the face of human diversity and weakness, his limited capacity for friendship, may be the obverse of his unusually strong love of animals. He owned no pets because "domesticated (enslaved) animals have no rights that their human masters are bound to respect," and he excoriated "the enslavement, torturing, imprisonment and killing of animal, bird and insect fellow creatures to satisfy human fancy, whim, habit or assumed need." Even the cutworms which invaded his garden were picked up and placed in a box. When asked about the fate of the cutworms, Nearing replied, according to his son, that "he preferred not to be associated with the liquidation of any living thing. What he really did was accumulate the cutworms until some hapless guest like myself came along, and the guests were then entrusted with the execution of the miscreant cutworms. . . . This was perhaps a step above Leo Tolstoy, who is reputed to have collected cutworms in the same fashion but have then thrown them over the fence into the neighbors' garden." [7]

Whatever Nearing's superior behavior in this situation, he deeply admired the Russian novelist, taught his philosophy, anthologized his pacifist essays, and applied his ideas. Indeed Nearing's affinity for Tolstoy was so genuine that a perceptive essay like George Orwell's "Lear, Tolstoy, and the Fool" can be appropriated to evaluate his American disciple. The sage of Yasnaya Polyana "was capable of abjuring physical violence and of seeing what this implies," Orwell wrote, "but he was not capable of tolerance or humility." Despite the renunciation of privilege, Tolstoy still occasionally regressed "to the attitudes of an aristocrat, in spite of his peasant's blouse." Despite his quest for sainthood and his attempt to be different in kind and not just in degree from other human beings, he had not "abjured the principle of coercion, or at least the *desire* to coerce others." Orwell suspected that pacifists may be especially vulnerable to "spiritual bullying" precisely because the apparent repudiation of base motives facilitates the claim "that everyone else should be bullied into thinking likewise." [8]

The pathos of such a fate, of exchanging one kind of egoism for another, may well account for Nearing's lack of serenity and proportion, for his suspiciousness and crankiness. Despising the pleasures of others, he had not achieved his own aim to help interrupt the process of militarism and imperialism, and the sloth and self-indulgence that capitalism engendered. The ambiguity of his legacy lies in the very strength and independence of character that hurled him against the dominant forces of his age and also doomed Nearing to extended frustration, isolation, and impotence. The personal force and will that so often commanded the respect of others overwhelmed his capacity to tolerate their rights and opinions, without which the humane visions that had once nourished him could not be fully realized. Politicians cannot be expected to see the light, but Nearing's insular absolutism could barely make them feel the heat. In refusing to adapt himself to others, he acted imprudently; yet in so doing, he helped, however inadvertently, to enlarge the circumference of freedom. His deficiencies seemed inextricably intertwined with his virtues, for both the sterility and the dignity of his alienation from American life were equally authentic manifestations of his moral intelligence.

ONE WAY TO ASSESS THE MEANING OF NEARING'S LIFE IS to counterpoint the careers of two radicals who were once his close friends and associates. Roger Baldwin was "one of a very dangerous class of persons," according to Attorney General Gregory, and his telephone was tapped as early as the Great War. Norman Thomas was "worse than Debs," according to Postmaster General Burleson, who once vowed to imprison him "for life." Yet, unlike Nearing, both of these dissenters chose to fight authorities with the weapons of organization, working for reforms without—they hoped—abandoning transcendent dreams of a more just society. Like Nearing, they wanted to stir up trouble; unlike him, they were willing to negotiate and compromise, to wrest consensus out of the conflict they promoted. Both born within a year of Nearing, they took the risks inherent in a position on the periphery, but not fundamentally outside, of conventional American politics. For the sake of concrete and immediate improvement, they cajoled, hectored, and negotiated, thus hazarding the erosion of their ideals, the deflection of their objectives, the recognition of other sorts of legitimacy.

During the Second World War and immediately thereafter, Baldwin behaved in a puzzling fashion for an emeritus draft resister and an admirer of Emma Goldman. He was loath to condemn the confinement of Japanese-Americans to concentration camps in the West, and some conscientious objectors doubted the fervor of the ACLU's commitment to the defense of their rights. Afterwards he became a civil rights adviser in Japan to General Douglas MacArthur, whose proconsulship Baldwin hailed as "the greatest social revolution of our time." But against such lapses from the libertarianism and pacifism he professed must be weighed an extraordinary and unique contribution toward a democratic society: the creation of an agency exclusively committed to the Bill of Rights. Unlike the obscure Free Speech League of the Progressive era, the ACLU was professional, activist, and litigious. Unlike the Wobblies' gallant struggle

for the rights of speech and assembly, the ACLU was ostensibly disinterested, committed on principle to the extension
of freedom, even, as Baldwin put it, "for s.o.b.'s." With the
steadfast concentration and confidence readily ascribed to
the New England crusader and the engaging shrewdness of
a snake oil peddler, Baldwin helped make the Bill of Rights
the Constitutional centerpiece in the struggle for justice.[9]

Yet he never voted for his best friend, despite frequent
opportunities to do so, because he surmised that Norman
Thomas had no chance of election. Baldwin was also
amazed at his comrade's capacity for instant indignation
whenever a case of victimization came to his attention.
Thomas was indeed quick to attack the incarceration of the
Nisei. In the succeeding decades, however, he also know-
ingly became enmeshed in the operations of the Central Intelligence Agency, using its funds primarily to combat Communism in foreign trade unions. Lacking the apparatus of
the Socialist party, he supported Lyndon Johnson in 1964
and backed Hubert Humphrey in the final weeks of the
1968 campaign. If Thomas was perhaps less a Socialist
than—like Roosevelt—"a Christian and a democrat," he
thus incarnated the conscience of the left. With exemplary
exuberance he assisted tenant farmers in Arkansas, resisted
martial law in Indiana, battled the Ku Klux Klan in Florida,
exposed municipal corruption and comforted disillusioned
ex-Communists in New York, and castigated the American
intervention in Vietnam. He also did much to organize and
enrich the ACLU, the League for Industrial Democracy,
the Workers Defense League, the American Committee on
Africa, Spanish Refugee Aid, and the Committee for a Sane
Nuclear Policy.[10] While Thomas and Baldwin were thrown
in jail in Jersey City in 1938 for helping the CIO to organize, Nearing was concerning himself with the sale of maple
sugar.

Homesteading, therefore, was not, as Nearing claimed, a

In the Early 1970s

prerequisite "for those who propose to live satisfying, productive lives." Nor were intellectuals who failed to become subsistence farmers necessarily "conformists, sybarites, the comfortably gregarious, the irresponsibles, the congenitally parasitic, the ne'er-do-wells." [11] The career of Paul Goodman refutes such a charge. At City College in the 1920s, Nearing impressed him "by the way he handled the question period" after one speech. "He gave reasons, he answered objections with more specific reasons, he did not resort to slogans . . . I took his position seriously, although I didn't become a Marxist." Instead anarchist principles guided Goodman's thought and life, as a teacher at Manumit School and elsewhere, as a demonstrator against war, as a lay therapist, as the writer of well over a score of books, plus innumerable petitions and letters to editors and officials. "Unlike most 'social critics,'" he asserted, "I am rather scrupulous about not attacking unless I can think up an alternative or two." [12]

Goodman's unabashed utopianism never interfered with his inventiveness and resourcefulness as an author of "practical proposals" to make life, especially city life, tolerable. Because he was so versatile, so observant, so systematically ingenious, and so consistently useful, he ought to be considered the most talented radical American intellectual of this century, not excepting DuBois. Like Nearing, he was loyal to pacifist principles during the Second World War; unlike him, Goodman consistently opposed thereafter both Communism and the American celebration. Both lived with simplicity, often barely above subsistence. [13] But while Nearing unsystematically advised others to imitate his disengagement from an urban and industrial society, Goodman suggested policies to achieve a different equilibrium between town and country and explored the consequences of migration. Poised thus between what Weber called the ethic of responsibility and the ethic of ultimate ends, Goodman made virtually every other radical intellectual, including Nearing, seem in need of vocational therapy.

Yet, finally, this appraisal of Nearing's career and character is not reduced to the accusation that he was not Goodman, or Baldwin, or Thomas, or other comrades like Hillquit and Muste and Sinclair. It rests upon the sense that Nearing was not quite the man a half-century later that he was before the Great War embittered him. The difference may have been marginal, but it was precious. The precise biographical moment, before something valuable within him dissolved, may not be discernible. But perhaps the loss of equipoise came only after he was driven from Toledo, only after his statement of resignation elegantly proclaimed his opposition to all forms of "tyranny, despotism, and irresponsive power . . . I believe in democracy and in the brotherhood of all men. No community can endure which ignores the . . . basic law of social life—'Each for all, and all for each.' " Sometime thereafter his outlook became suffused with *Schadenfreude,* as his apocalyptic vision was pickled and preserved against additional and possibly challenging evidence. He had thus forsaken our most honorable form of patriotism, which is to "be a critic of one's country without being an enemy of its promise." [14]

A Hasidic fable is appropriate here. In the world to come, Rabbi Zusya feared, God would not ask, "Why were you not Moses?" Instead the question would be more specific: "Why were you not Zusya?"

CHAPTER TEN

NEARING REDIVIVUS

"**W**ITH A FEW MORE YEARS OF POWER FAIL-
ures, transit strikes, epidemics of heroin overdose, water
shortage, unacceptable levels of air pollution" and other
commonplaces of the urban condition, Goodman once speculated, "hundreds of thousands of New Yorkers will
regard Scott and Helen as uncanny prophets." Because the
catalogue of city terrors could be so easily extended, a cultural tradition hostile to the artificiality, squalor, and decadence of the American metropolis has recently been revital-
ized, and Nearing has become one of its totemic figures. By
the ninth decade of his life, his retreat to nature bespoke
prescience, wisdom, and grandeur to a far wider circle of
admirers than the aging liberals and radicals who attended
the 1963 birthday party. Almost a decade later the *New
Republic* considered him "a hero, a figure of genuine importance in the political history of twentieth century America.
. . . If ten men like Nearing had been found in them, even
Sodom and Gomorrah would have been spared." [1]

One apparent sign of grace, or at least of immunization
against oblivion, has been the increased receptivity to *Living
the Good Life,* the account of the Vermont experiment that
he wrote in collaboration with his wife. It was virtually ig-

nored when privately published in 1954, and even gloriously eccentric journals like the *Catholic Worker* blended
praise for the book's "vitality and sense of growth" with dismay at "a certain aloofness, a dogmatism which will not take
into account the weaknesses and foibles of mankind, an
unreality which expects cool reasons to determine men's actions, a lack of warmth and humor." In the next sixteen
years, 10,000 copies of *Living the Good Life* were sold.[2]

Since September 1970, however, 100,000 more copies
have been purchased in hardcover and in paperback, often
with a companion volume on maple sugar and pioneering.
The New York *Times Book Review* included both works on its
Christmas 1971 shopping list, classifying them as "bibles of
the present back-to-the-land counter-culture." *Time* magazine called *Living the Good Life* "bracing" and "an authentic
long-term survival tool," *Newsweek* called it "crisp" and
"lucid," and *Harper's* described it as "strong and cranky and
absorbing." Not only did it receive the imprimatur of the
Whole Earth Catalogue, but a symposiast in the magazine of
the War Resisters League judged it one of the three books
most likely to be meaningful for the 1970s: "It's unequalled
for relating principles to practice, the individual to the
whole, etc.; practical and inspiring, like its authors." [3]

In 1971 the Maine State Commission on the Arts and
Humanities selected Nearing to receive one of the five annual awards for "life and work [which] have brought special
distinction to our state." Governor Kenneth M. Curtis
added that Nearing "has made an art of his life, but it is
most especially to the problems of the natural man that he
has addressed himself. . . . He spoke out against child
labor, against war; he predicted the decay of great cities, the
pollution of air and waters, the decline of personal independence." At a faculty club dinner two years later, Nearing
became an honorary emeritus professor of economics at the
University of Pennsylvania. In promoting him from the

rank of assistant professor after an interval of fifty-eight years, President Martin Meyerson praised him "for adhering to a belief that to seek out and to teach the truth is life's highest aim." [4] And the historical dimension has rarely been so abruptly short-circuited as when this almost sole surviving ex-Progressive, born a year after Emerson died, joined the other guests on the David Frost Show.

But the most conspicuous shock of recognition has come from the young, who read not only *Living the Good Life* but *Howl,* in which Allen Ginsberg remembered Nearing as "a grand old man a real mensch." The trickle of young visitors and campers in the 1950s has become a flood of thousands in the 1970s. The erstwhile champion of the working-class child has become a prophet for a segment of middle-class youth. Nearing's politics have helped, for he has opposed every American war, major and minor, from Vera Cruz to Vietnam. But what is intriguing is his fusion of the two strongest motifs in the heritage of American dissent, the agrarian and the socialist. In him the two antibodies most resistant to industrial capitalism have been injected, and those who have lived in communes or who otherwise sought rural redemption were bound to imbue Nearing with prophetic qualities.

Yet differences of generational style and temperament have not been fully transcended. "The issue of making a living," Goodman observed, "does not have the same psychological and moral force as it did in the Thirties." [5] The question of abundance, which Patten detonated at the turn of the century, had finally exploded the work ethic itself, as the economic value of asceticism ceased to be compelling. For middle-class youth at least, the distinction between the reality principle and the pleasure principle has been blurred; and the desire for subsistence, which preoccupied the authors of *Living the Good Life,* has rarely been felt. The

Nearings' simplicity and repudiation of the bounty of technology was almost instinctive and, except for a jeep and a phonograph, consistently practiced. In contrast, the frequent strictures of young radicals against technology often could not be heard above the din of amplified rock music blasted in stereophonic sound and preserved on wide-screen documentaries of concerts so blocked off by buses and automobiles that helicopters had to be summoned for medicine and food.

Nor have many shared Nearing's fervent opposition to "dope," which has embraced coffee, tobacco, and some forms of tea. Imagine his chagrin at the review of *Living the Good Life* in the *New Republic,* in which a communard praised not only the book but "acid, [which] has given us the insight to look inward and not to be afraid of what we find." [6] Moreover Nearing's individualist proclivities have seemingly resembled the "ego-tripping" that became one of the most pejorative terms in the argot of the young. And when the word "shit" appeared in the magazine of the War Resisters League, Nearing performed the *beau geste* of resigning in protest from the League's advisory board. Obviously his own morals have been closer, say, to Carry Nation than to Woodstock Nation.

Nearing has lived in his own way, inimitably, and with extraordinary zest and conviction. Although longevity is a family trait, his own energy is particularly astonishing, whether shaping haystacks, sawing wood, building with stone, or skating on the pond in the winter. Suspicious of physicians, he has not needed their services in four decades; and he once bewildered a friend confined to a sanatorium with the advice to avoid doctors.[7] He embodies something more than a sinewy, agile, particularized argument against carnivorous indulgence. He seems rather to exemplify the tenacity of life itself, fragile wings beating against the awesome silence and the immeasurable darkness, borne aloft only with the vision of human sympathy and the resources of apprehension and art to console us.

"After a certain age," Camus' protagonist asserts in *The Fall*, "every man is responsible for his face"; and Nearing's is, in the coda of his life, craggily beatific. Ruddy and weather-beaten, with tributaries of wrinkles setting off his somber eyes, thatched with thin white hair, speaking with force and clarity inside the spare gray clapboard house, he is surrounded not only by magazines and newspapers and books but by the corn and herbs that dry as they hang from the ceiling. The aroma of the kitchen offers a lingering clue that the garden brims with raspberries and strawberries and blueberries, with lettuce and potatoes and turnips and carrots and other vegetables. Beyond the garden bloom rose bushes, and past the trees dangling with pears and apples hovers the wilderness, almost as still as Lyell found it. At the edge of the farm, across a sinuous, pockmarked road, lies a cove, a gentle, shaded refuge where the salt water licks the land.

NOTES

CHAPTER ONE. THE MAKING OF A PROGRESSIVE

1. Lyell, *Travels in North America*, I, 61–64.

2. Steffens, *Autobiography*, p. 392; Lloyd, "The Story of a Great Monopoly," *Atlantic*, XLVII (March, 1881), 322.

3. Sexton, *Outline History*, pp. 4, 34, 35, 177.

4. *Ibid.*, pp. 54, 57; Whitford, *Canal System*, II, 1160–61; New York *Herald*, May 7, 1905, p. 65; Toledo *News-Bee*, March 10, 1917, p. 2; Gutman, "Two Lockouts in Pennsylvania, 1873–1874," *Pennsylvania Magazine of History and Biography*, LXXXIII (July, 1959), 324–26.

5. Interview with Guy Nearing, Ramsey, New Jersey, November 30, 1970; New York *Herald*, May 7, 1905, p. 65; interview with Beatrice N. Pierce, Towson, Maryland, October 20, 1971.

6. Nearing, *Radical*, p. 16; New York *Herald*, May 7, 1905, p. 65.

7. New York *Herald*, May 7, 1905, p. 65.

8. Interview with Guy Nearing; Nearing, *Radical*, pp. 12–13.

9. Nearing, *Radical*, p. 8; interview with Guy Nearing; interview with Beatrice N. Pierce; Zabriskie, *Zabriskie Family*, p. 1002.

10. Interview with Guy Nearing; Max Nearing to author, October 24, 1971; interview with John Scott, New York City, November 5, 1970; interview with Scott Nearing, Harborside, Maine, July 15, 1970; Nearing, *Radical*, pp. 10, 17, 19, 30.

11. Interview with Scott Nearing, July 15, 1970.

12. Nearing, *Radical*, pp. 31–32; interview with Scott Nearing, Harborside, Maine, June 27, 1971.

13. Veysey, *American University*, p. 339n; Slosson, *Great American Universities*, pp. 362–63; Rudolph, *American College*, pp. 378–80.

14. Tugwell, "Notes on the Life and Work of Simon Nelson Patten," *Journal of Political Economy*, XXXI (April, 1923), 181.

15. Fox, *Discovery of Abundance*, pp. 68, 96, 148; Curti and Nash, *Philanthropy*, pp. 73–75; Nearing, *Radical*, p. 53.

16. Tugwell, "Notes on the Life and Work of Simon Nelson Patten," *Journal of Political Economy*, XXXI (April, 1923), 194; Reminiscences of William Harvey Allen, Oral History Research Office of Columbia University, I, 28, 30.

17. Interview with Margaret Mead, Cambridge, Massachusetts, February 25, 1971.

18. *Ibid.;* Nearing, *Educational Frontiers,* p. ix; Fox, *Discovery of Abundance,* pp. 70, 95–96, 112, 115–16, 144.

19. Disbrow, "Progressive Movement in Philadelphia," pp. 12–13.

20. *Ibid.,* p. 250; Burr, *Russell H. Conwell,* pp. 313–14; interview with Scott Nearing, June 27, 1971; Nearing, *Radical,* p. 32.

21. Interviews with Scott Nearing, July 15, 1970, and June 27, 1971; Nearing, *Radical,* p. 34.

22. Trattner, *Crusade for the Children,* pp. 36, 41, 48, 50, 65, 72; minutes of general meeting, April 15, 1904, National Child Labor Committee Papers; Box 1, Charles L. Chute Papers; Graham, *Encore for Reform,* p. 189.

23. McAhren, "Making the Nation Safe," pp. 28, 31, 37; Trattner, *Crusade for the Children,* pp. 61, 70–71.

24. Nearing, "The Child Labor Situation in Pennsylvania," in Charles L. Chute Papers; Trattner, *Crusade for the Children,* p. 71; Marot, "Progress in Philadelphia," *Charities,* XIV (June 10, 1905), 836.

25. Jones, *Autobiography,* pp. 128–29; Bloor, *We Are Many,* p. 75.

26. Trattner, *Crusade for the Children,* pp. 71, 74, 77; Nearing, "The Child Labor Situation in Pennsylvania," in Charles L. Chute Papers.

27. Marot, "Progress in Philadelphia," *Charities,* XIV (June 10, 1905), 834–35; Trattner, *Crusade for the Children,* p. 75; treasurer's reports in Box 6, National Child Labor Committee Papers; interview with Scott Nearing, June 27, 1971; *An Illustrated Handbook of the Industrial Exhibit* (December, 1906), pp. 4, 9–11, 16–18, in Charles L. Chute Papers.

28. Secretary's report, October 1, 1907, in Box 6, National Child Labor Committee Papers.

29. Wike, *Pennsylvania Manufacturers' Association,* p. 17; Disbrow, "Progressive Movement in Philadelphia," p. 23; Trattner, *Crusade for the Children,* pp. 74, 107; Bloor, *We Are Many,* pp. 74–75.

30. Trattner, *Crusade for the Children,* pp. 75, 79; Nearing, *Child Labor Problem,* pp. v, 94, 96.

31. Philadelphia *Inquirer,* June 21, 1908, p. 4; Nearing, *Radical,* p. 53; interview with Scott Nearing, June 27, 1971.

32. Interview with Guy Nearing; Reminiscences of Upton Sinclair, Oral History Research Office, Columbia University, p. 96; interview with Scott Nearing, July 15, 1970; Bloor, *We Are Many,* p. 66.

33. Sinclair, *American Outpost,* p. 243; interview with Scott Nearing, July 15, 1970; Scott Nearing to Upton Sinclair, January 27, 1911, in Upton Sinclair Papers.

34. Interview with Scott Nearing, July 15, 1970; Bloor, *We Are Many,* p. 67; Ervin, *Homegrown Liberal,* pp. 36–37.

35. Hillquit, *History of Socialism,* p. 253; interview with Guy Nearing; "Monopoly," *Fortune,* XII (December, 1935), 40.

36. Nearing, *Radical,* pp. 40–41; interview with Scott Nearing, July 15, 1970; Graham, *Encore for Reform,* p. 143n; Bloor, *We Are Many,* p. 71.

37. Fisher, "Last Muckraker," p. 19; Ezra Pound to Upton Sinclair, January 30, 1935, in Sinclair, *My Lifetime in Letters,* p. 373; Sinclair, *American Outpost,* p. 232.

38. Nearing, *Radical,* p. 53; *curriculum vita* in Box 730 of University of Pennsylvania Alumni Records.

39. Nearing, *Radical*, p. 54; interview with Scott Nearing, July 15, 1970; interview with Harry Reinstine, Jacksonville, Florida, April 13, 1972; Simon N. Patten quoted in Smith, "Dismissing the Professor," *Survey*, XXXV (November 6, 1915), 131; Rexford G. Tugwell to Scott Nearing 80th Birthday Committee, October 10, 1963, scrapbook in possession of Scott Nearing.

40. Sternsher, *Tugwell*, pp. 4–5.

41. Nearing, *Wages*, pp. 10, 14–15, 208–209; Douglas, *Real Wages*, p. 76.

42. Nearing, *Wages*, pp. 50–51, 120, 172–73, 197, 208.

43. Rees, *Real Wages in Manufacturing*, p. 3; Scott Nearing to Upton Sinclair, August 15, 1914, Upton Sinclair Papers; New York *Times*, June 23, 1914, p. 5; "Wages in the United States," *International Socialist Review*, XII (December, 1911), 355.

44. Nearing, *Social Adjustment*, pp. 5, 91, 151, 189; Nearing, *Social Sanity*, pp. 83, 155, 253.

45. Nearing, *Women and Social Progress*, pp. 4, 71–72, 75, 85, 255; Nearing, *Social Adjustment*, p. 91.

46. Nearing, *Social Sanity*, pp. 70–71.

47. *Ibid.*, pp. 83, 103, 181, 230; Nearing, *Social Adjustment*, pp. 16, 40–42, 45, 126–27, 307, 320–21, 330; Haber, *Efficiency and Uplift*, pp. ix–x.

48. Smith, "Dismissing the Professor," *Survey*, XXXV (November 6, 1915), 132–33; Sinclair, *Goose-Step*, pp. 101–102.

49. Interview with Scott Nearing, July 15, 1970; Rudolph, *American College*, p. 363.

50. Philadelphia *North American*, November 30, 1910, p. 1, and November 13, 1911, pp. 1, 5.

51. Disbrow, "Progressive Movement in Philadelphia," p. 286; Nearing, *Radical*, pp. 58–61, 72.

52. Interview with Scott Nearing, July 15, 1970.

53. New York *Times*, October 6, 1915, p. 5; Nearing, *Radical*, p. 84.

54. Disbrow, "Progressive Movement in Philadelphia," pp. 74, 85, 96, 105–106, 340.

55. *Ibid.*, pp. 122–23, 174, 178, 185, 220.

56. Scott Nearing to Joel E. Spingarn, February 9, 1914, in Joel E. Spingarn Papers.

CHAPTER TWO. REPORT FROM THE ACADEMY

1. Witmer, *Nearing Case*, p. ix; interview with Scott Nearing, July 15, 1970.

2. Baltzell, *Philadelphia Gentlemen*, pp. 32, 40, 57, 131, 132, 139; Burt, *Perennial Philadelphians*, pp. 15, 32, 35, 40, 219–20.

3. Burt, *Perennial Philadelphians*, p. 87.

4. *Ibid.*, p. 85; New York *Times*, October, 5, 1915, p. 12.

5. Slosson, *Great American Universities*, p. 369.

6. Nearing, *Educational Frontiers*, pp. 47–48; Curti and Nash, *Philanthropy*, p. 193; Cheyney, *University of Pennsylvania*, p. 376.

7. Hutton, *Grundy*, pp. 54, 133–34, 137, 146; Wike, *Pennsylvania Manufacturers' Association*, pp. 18, 86; Disbrow, "Progressive Movement in Philadelphia," p. 70.

8. Wike, *Pennsylvania Manufacturers' Association*, p. 19; Philadelphia *North American*, April 8, 1913, p. 10; Witmer, *Nearing Case*, pp. 117–19.

9. Witmer, *Nearing Case,* pp. 3–4; interview with Scott Nearing, July 15, 1970; Sinclair, *Goose-Step,* p. 106.

10. "Light on the Nearing Case," *Literary Digest,* LI (August 7, 1915), 248; New York *Times,* September 1, 1915, p. 17; Witmer, *Nearing Case,* pp. 94, 116.

11. Memorandum by George Wharton Pepper, 1915, in Book 5, George Wharton Pepper Papers; New York *Times,* July 18, 1915, IV, 1; Philadelphia *Public Ledger,* May 19, 1915, p. 15.

12. Philadelphia *Evening Bulletin,* January 1, 1911, in Box 730, University of Pennsylvania Alumni Records.

13. New York *Morning Telegraph,* February 16, 1911, in *ibid.*

14. Philadelphia *Evening Times,* December 6, 1912, in *ibid.*

15. Philadelphia *Public Ledger,* July 12, 1907, p. 8.

16. Witmer, *Nearing Case,* p. 31; interview with Margaret Mead.

17. McLoughlin, *Billy Sunday,* pp. 237–38, 240; Reed, "Back of Billy Sunday," *Metropolitan,* XLII (May, 1915), 10; Witmer, *Nearing Case,* p. 54.

18. Witmer, *Nearing Case,* p. 76; Sinclair, *Goose-Step,* p. 105; "Light on the Nearing Case," *Literary Digest,* LI (August 7, 1915), 248; New York *Times,* July 18, 1915, IV, 1.

19. Boorstin, *Image,* p. 57.

20. Smith, "Dismissing the Professor," *Survey,* XXXV (November 6, 1915), 154; George Wharton Pepper to Edith Hilles, July 6, 1915, in Book 5, George Wharton Pepper Papers.

21. Bloom, "Philadelphia *North American,*" p. 517n; Pennypacker, *Autobiography,* p. 297; interview with Scott Nearing, July 15, 1970; Ervin, *Homegrown Liberal,* p. 62.

22. White, "A Letter on the Nearing Case," *Old Penn Weekly Review,* XIV (October 2, 1915), 13; "Report on the Dismissal of Dr. Scott Nearing from the University of Pennsylvania," AAUP *Bulletin,* II (May, 1916), 31; "Light on the Nearing Case," *Literary Digest,* LI (August 7, 1915), 248.

23. "Report on the Dismissal of Dr. Scott Nearing from the University of Pennsylvania," AAUP *Bulletin,* II (May, 1916), 15, 17.

24. *Ibid.,* p. 18.

25. Witmer, *Nearing Case,* pp. 84–85.

26. "Report on the Dismissal of Dr. Scott Nearing from the University of Pennsylvania," AAUP *Bulletin,* II (May, 1916), 37, 54–55.

27. *Ibid.,* pp. 54–55; minutes of the Board of Trustees, June 14, 1915, in Volume 17, Box 7, Archives of the University of Pennsylvania; Wharton Barker to Bolton Hall, June 23, 1915, in Box 12, General Correspondence, Wharton Barker Papers.

28. Witmer, *Nearing Case,* pp. 4–5; Kellogg, "Case of Scott Nearing," *Survey,* XXXIV (June 26, 1915), 289; Roswell C. McCrea to Edgar F. Smith, June 22, 1915, Wharton School Files.

29. Nearing, *Radical,* pp. 84–85; interview with Margaret Mead; Cheyney, "Trustees and Faculties," *School and Society,* II (December 4, 1915), 798.

30. Clyde L. King to Samuel McCune Lindsay, July 15, 1915, in Box 18, Samuel McCune Lindsay Papers; Nearing, *Radical,* p. 87; "University of Pennsylvania and Professor Nearing," *School and Society,* II (July 10, 1915), 20–21, 65–66.

31. Witmer, *Nearing Case,* pp. 1–2; New York *Times,* June 22, 1915, p. 5.

32. Simon N. Patten to Samuel McCune Lindsay, June 24, 1915; Samuel Mc-

Cune Lindsay to Simon N. Patten, July 3, 1915; Samuel McCune Lindsay to Lyman P. Powell, August 5, 1915, in Box 18, Samuel McCune Lindsay Papers.

33. Clyde L. King to Samuel McCune Lindsay, July 15, 1915, Lightner Witmer to Edmund J. James, August 5, 1915, in Box 18, Samuel McCune Lindsay Papers; Edgar Cope, Jr., to Edgar F. Smith and Trustees, October 1, 1915, in Wharton School Files; New York *Times*, June 23, 1915, p. 6 and October 10, 1915, II, 16.

34. Memorandum by George Wharton Pepper, 1915, in Book 5, George Wharton Pepper Papers.

35. "The Freedom of University Teaching," *New Statesman*, V (August 21, 1915), 463; Philadelphia *North American*, June 24, 1915, p. 10; Philadelphia *Bulletin*, June 28, 1915, p. 3; Rolnick, "Academic Freedom and Tenure," pp. 168–69.

36. New York *Times*, June 22, 1915, p. 5; Philadelphia *North American*, June 23, 1915, p. 10; New York *Call*, October 9, 1915, p. 1; Gompers, *Seventy Years*, I, 441; Disbrow, "Progressive Movement in Philadelphia," p. 206.

37. Ralph M. Easley to John C. Bell, July 2, 1915, John C. Bell to Ralph M. Easley, July 3, 1915, in General Correspondence (1915), Box 52, National Civic Federation Papers.

38. Marcy, "The Reward of Truth Telling," *International Socialist Review*, XVI (August, 1915), 95; New York *People*, June 26, 1915; New York *Times*, July 2, 1915, p. 10.

39. Barnard, "Education: A Community Masque," *Masses*, VIII (September, 1916), 14–15.

40. Witmer, *Nearing Case*, p. 76; "Who Owns the Universities?", *New Republic*, III (July 17, 1915), 270.

41. New York *Evening Sun*, October 4, 1915, p. 6; Philadelphia *North American*, June 23, 1915, p. 10; New York *Times*, June 20, 1915, II, 14.

42. Smith, "Dismissing the Professor," *Survey*, XXXV (November 6, 1915), p. 131; New York *Times*, July 18, 1915, IV, 2, October 10, 1915, p. 16, and January 21, 1916, p. 8.

43. Metzger, *Academic Freedom*, pp. 89–92, 112–15, 122–23; Hook, *Academic Freedom*, pp. 34–35.

44. Metzger, *Academic Freedom*, pp. 147, 164–65, 191–92; Pearson, "Decisions of Committee A," pp. 17, 18.

45. Metzger, *Academic Freedom*, pp. 149–53, 171–74.

46. Faulkner, *Quest for Social Justice*, p. 200; Witmer, *Nearing Case*, p. 21.

47. Smith, "Dismissing the Professor," *Survey*, XXXV (November 6, 1915), 134; Metzger, *Academic Freedom*, pp. 135–36, 184–85; Cheyney, "Trustees and Faculties," *School and Society*, II (December 4, 1915), 795; Tyler and Cheyney, "Academic Freedom," American Academy of Political and Social Science *Annals*, CC (November, 1938), 113.

48. Tyler and Cheyney, "Academic Freedom," American Academy of Political and Social Science *Annals*, CC (November, 1938), 106; Cheyney, "Trustees and Faculties," *School and Society*, II (December 4, 1915), 803; Smith, "Dismissing the Professor," *Survey*, XXXV (November 6, 1915), 133; Rolnick, "Academic Freedom and Tenure," p. 302.

49. Thilly, "The American Association of University Professors," *American Review*, III (March, 1925), 200; Dewey, "Presidential Address." AAUP *Bulletin*, I (December, 1915), 11–12.

50. Pearson, "Decisions of Committee A," p. 37; Nearing, *Radical*, p. 62; Rol-

nick, "Academic Freedom and Tenure," pp. 229–31; interview with Scott Nearing, June 27, 1971; E. R. A. Seligman to Joel E. Spingarn, December 28, 1916, in Box 31, E. R. A. Seligman Papers.

51. Arthur O. Lovejoy to Richard T. Ely, June 29, 1915, in Box 98, Richard T. Ely Papers.

52. Clyde L. King to Samuel McCune Lindsay, July 15, 1915, in Box 18, Samuel McCune Lindsay Papers.

53. "Report on the Dismissal of Dr. Scott Nearing from the University of Pennsylvania," AAUP Bulletin, II (May, 1916), 22–24, 28–29.

54. Ibid., p. 29; Effingham B. Morris to Edgar F. Smith, November 29, 1915, Wharton School Files; Pepper, Philadelphia Lawyer, p. 109.

55. "Report on the Dismissal of Dr. Scott Nearing from the University of Pennsylvania," AAUP Bulletin, II (May, 1916), 29–30.

56. Ibid., pp. 11, 12, 13, 37–40, 52–53.

57. Ibid., pp. 42–43; Rolnick, "Academic Freedom and Tenure," p. 313; Cheyney, University of Pennsylvania, p. 371; Marcus, "Scott Nearing Case," p. 12.

58. "The University of Pennsylvania and Academic Freedom," Outlook, CXI (December 29, 1915), 1017; Villard, "Academic Freedom," Nation, CI (December 23, 1915), 745–46; Lovejoy, "The American Association of University Professors," Nation, CII (February 10, 1916), 170.

59. "Report on the Dismissal of Dr. Scott Nearing from the University of Pennsylvania," AAUP Bulletin, II (May, 1916), 44–49.

60. Charles A. Beard to Henry W. Tyler, June 16, 1917, in Box 78, E. R. A. Seligman Papers; Metzger, Academic Freedom, p. 211.

61. Pearson, "Decisions of Committee A," pp. 89, 93; Rolnick, "Academic Freedom and Tenure," pp. 165, 297; Metzger, Academic Freedom, pp. 204, 217, 220.

62. "Light on the Nearing Case," Literary Digest, LI (August 7, 1915), 248.

63. Scott Nearing to Rose Pastor Stokes, June 23, 1915, in Box 2, Series I of Rose Pastor Stokes Papers; Scott Nearing to Joel E. Spingarn, June 30, 1915, in Joel E. Spingarn Papers; Baltimore Sun, October 16, 1915, p. 7.

64. Interview with Scott Nearing, July 15, 1970; Scott Nearing to Samuel McCune Lindsay, October 6, 1915, in Box 18, Samuel McCune Lindsay Papers.

65. Interview with Scott Nearing, Harborside, Maine, September 8, 1970; Simon N. Patten to Samuel McCune Lindsay, July 6, 1915, in Box 18, Samuel McCune Lindsay Papers.

66. Samuel McCune Lindsay to Lyman P. Powell, August 5, 1915; Simon N. Patten to Samuel McCune Lindsay, September 10, 1915; Scott Nearing to Samuel McCune Lindsay, October 6, 1915, in Box 18, Samuel McCune Lindsay Papers.

67. Disbrow, "Progressive Movement in Philadelphia," pp. 224, 226; Philadelphia North American, January 3, 1916, p. 10.

CHAPTER THREE. THE MAKING OF A RADICAL

1. Nearing, Radical, pp. 82–83; interview with Scott Nearing, September 8, 1970.

2. New York Sun, October 22, 1915, p. 4; New York Tribune, October 22, 1915, p. 14; Philadelphia North American, November 15, 1915, p. 5.

3. Hickerson, "University of Toledo," pp. 3, 302, 329, 495; Scott Nearing to

Samuel McCune Lindsay, October 6, 1915, in Box 18, Samuel McCune Lindsay Papers; Elliot J. Anderson, "The Scott Nearing Controversy in Toledo, 1916–1917 (Part I)," *Northwest Ohio Quarterly,* XXIX (Spring, 1957), 78.

4. Interview with Scott Nearing, September 8, 1970.

5. Toledo *Blade,* September 11, 1916, p. 4 and September 14, 1916, p. 4, quoted in Elliot J. Anderson, "The Scott Nearing Controversy in Toledo, 1916–1917 (Part I)," *Northwest Ohio Quarterly,* XXIX (Spring, 1957), 80.

6. Toledo *Blade,* May 9, 1916, p. 4 and June 3, 1916, quoted in Elliot J. Anderson, "The Scott Nearing Controversy in Toledo, 1916–1917 (Part II)," *Northwest Ohio Quarterly,* XXIX (Summer, 1957), 162–64; Hickerson, "University of Toledo," p. 315.

7. New York *Times,* July 6, 1916, p. 24 and July 8, 1916, p. 8; Elliot J. Anderson, "The Scott Nearing Controversy in Toledo, 1916–1917 (Part II)," *Northwest Ohio Quarterly,* XXIX (Summer, 1957), 164–65; Toledo *Blade,* January 31, 1916, quoted in Hickerson, "University of Toledo," p. 315.

8. Toledo *Blade,* March 8, 1916, p. 9, and Toledo *Union-Leader,* June 9, 1916, p. 1, quoted in Elliot J. Anderson, "The Scott Nearing Controversy in Toledo, 1916–1917 (Part I)," *Northwest Ohio Quarterly,* XXIX (Spring, 1957), 83, 86; Toledo *News-Bee,* June 2, 1916, p. 9, and June 3, 1916, p. 12.

9. Toledo *News-Bee,* February 14, 1917, p. 5.

10. *Ibid.,* March 5, 1917, p. 6.

11. *Ibid.,* March 9, 1917, pp. 1, 4.

12. *Ibid.,* March 10, 1917, pp. 1, 2, March 14, 1917, p. 7, and April 11, 1917, p. 3; Elliot J. Anderson, "The Scott Nearing Controversy in Toledo, 1916–1917 (Part III)," *Northwest Ohio Quarterly,* XXIX (Autumn, 1957), 211–13, 215–16.

13. Hickerson, "University of Toledo," pp. 318–19; Toledo *News-Bee,* April 18, 1917, p. 3; Toledo *Blade,* March 20, 1965, p. 13.

14. Nearing, "Who's Who among College Trustees," *School and Society,* VI (September 8, 1917), 297–98; Beck, *Men Who Control Our Universities,* pp. 8–9, 12.

15. New York *Times,* April 21, 1917, p. 72; statement of resignation by Scott Nearing, March 10, 1917, copy in possession of author.

16. "The Latest Publicity Features of the Anti-'Preparedness' Committee," *Survey,* XXXVI (April 1, 1916), 37; "Swinging around the Circle against Militarism," *Survey,* XXXVI (April 22, 1916), 95–96; Maurer, *It Can Be Done,* p. 218; Wald, *Windows,* p. 302; Cook, "Woodrow Wilson," pp. 19, 61.

17. Interview with Roger N. Baldwin, New York City, October 26, 1970.

18. Reminiscences of Roger N. Baldwin, Oral History Research Office, Columbia University, I, 53; Cook, "Woodrow Wilson," pp. 18, 201; William Jennings Bryan to Lillian D. Wald, February 9, 1917, in Lillian D. Wald Papers.

19. Hillquit, *Loose Leaves,* p. 171; Florence, "Ford Peace Ship," in Julian Bell, ed., *We Did Not Fight,* pp. 101, 123; Lasch, *American Liberals,* p. 40.

20. Grubbs, *Struggle for Labor Loyalty,* pp. 22, 24–26; Maurer, *It Can Be Done,* p. 223; Hillquit, *Loose Leaves,* p. 171; Florence, "Ford Peace Ship," in Julian Bell, ed., *We Did Not Fight,* p. 121.

21. *Report of the First American Conference for Democracy and Terms of Peace,* pp. 9, 86, in People's Council of America Papers.

22. Lovett, *All Our Years,* pp. 140–41; Toledo *News-Bee,* May 30, 1917, pp. 1, 3; Grubbs, *Struggle for Labor Loyalty,* pp. 23, 34.

23. Heaton, *Cobb of "The World"*, p. 270; Perry, "Americanism," *Yale Review*, VII (April, 1918), 670; Hajo Holborn, Introduction to Fritz Fischer, *Germany's Aims in the First World War*, p. ix.

24. Peterson and Fite, *Opponents of War*, pp. 185–86, 199.

25. Bean, "George Creel and His Critics," p. 114.

26. Franklin and Starr, ed., *The Negro in 20th Century America*, pp. 462–64.

27. Peterson and Fite, *Opponents of War*, pp. 118–19, 134.

28. *Milwaukee Social Democratic Publishing Company* v. *Burleson*, 255 Fed. 407, 436 (1921); Chafee, *Free Speech*, p. 99; Adrian N. Anderson, "Albert Sidney Burleson," pp. 227, 231.

29. Cook, "Woodrow Wilson," p. 234; interview with Scott Nearing, September 8, 1970.

30. Toledo *News-Bee*, September 13, 1917, p. 1; New York *Times*, September 13, 1917, p. 3, and September 14, 1917, p. 5; Rolnick, "Academic Freedom and Tenure," p. 286n.

31. Oliver Wendell Holmes, Jr., "Law and the Court," in Lerner, ed., *Mind and Faith of Justice Holmes*, p. 390; Bierce, *Devil's Dictionary*, p. 65; *Appeal to Reason* (Girard, Kansas), May 3, 1902, quoted in Shannon, *Socialist Party*, p. 4.

32. Shannon, *Socialist Party*, pp. 55–56; Weinstein, *Decline of Socialism*, pp. 36, 75, 78, 84–85; Kipnis, *American Socialist Movement*, p. 5; Theodore Roosevelt to Rómulo Sebastian Naón, January 6, 1915, in Morison, ed., *Letters of Theodore Roosevelt*, VIII, 872.

33. Shannon, *Socialist Party*, p. 61; Daniel Bell, *Marxian Socialism*, p. 61; Dunne, *Mr. Dooley*, p. 252.

34. Hillquit, *Loose Leaves*, pp. 62–65.

35. Daniel Bell, "The Tamiment Library," Bibliographical Series No. 6, New York University Libraries (1969), 10–11, 15.

36. New York *Call*, November 7, 1915, p. 1, June 8, 1916, p. 4, and October 8, 1917, p. 2; interview with Louis Waldman, New York City, November 25, 1970; Cornell, "History of the Rand School."

37. Metzger, *Academic Freedom*, p. 230; Gruber, "Mars and Minerva," pp. 97, 109n, 207; Lovejoy, "A Communication: To Conscientious Objectors," *New Republic*, XI (June 16, 1917), 187–88; Lovejoy, "Academic Freedom in War Time," *Nation*, CVI (April 4, 1918), 402.

38. New York *Times*, December 19, 1916, p. 10; Brooklyn *Times*, March 17, 1917, in Box 730 of University of Pennsylvania Alumni Records.

39. Kolbe, *Colleges in War Time*, p. 223; Patten, *Discovery of Abundance*, p. 126.

40. New York *Times*, April 7, 1917, p. 13; Gruber, "Mars and Minerva," pp. 207n–208n; Cook, "Democracy in Wartime," in Chatfield, ed., *Peace Movements*, p. 46.

41. George D. Herron to Morris Hillquit, April 5, 1915, in Correspondence Reel 2, Morris Hillquit Papers; Currie, "Allan L. Benson, Salesman of Socialism, 1902–1916," *Journal of Labor History*, XI (Summer, 1970), 287, 290, 300–302.

42. Weinstein, *Decline of Socialism*, p. 126; Shannon, *Socialist Party*, pp. 94–98; Fine, *Labor and Farmer Parties*, pp. 310–14.

43. Daniel Bell, *Marxian Socialism*, pp. 100–101; George D. Herron to Morris Hillquit, August 7, 1917, in Correspondence Reel 2, Morris Hillquit Papers.

44. Transcript of Record, *American Socialist Society* v. *United States*, 266 Fed. 214

(1920), p. 83, in Tamiment Institute Library, New York University; Nearing, *Radical*, p. 111.

45. Reminiscences of John Lord O'Brian, Oral History Research Office of Columbia University, p. 299; Rhoads, "Election of 1920," p. 13.

CHAPTER FOUR. FOR DEMOCRACY AND PEACE

1. A. W. Ricker to Judah L. Magnes, June 6, 1917, P3/F16–L169, Judah L. Magnes Papers.

2. Chatfield, "World War I and the Liberal Pacifist in the United States," *American Historical Review*, LVI (December, 1970), 1920; Grubbs, *Struggle for Labor Loyalty*, p. 37.

3. Chatfield, *For Peace and Justice*, p. 10; Curti, *Peace or War*, pp. 249, 255; Voss, *Rabbi and Minister*, p. 143; New York *Times*, September 24, 1917, p. 13; David Starr Jordan to Judah L. Magnes, September 19, 1917, P3/F16–L130, Judah L. Magnes Papers; Jordan, *Days of a Man*, I, 739–40; Randall, *Improper Bostonian*, pp. 221, 246; Jane Addams to David Starr Jordan, October 2, 1917, in Volume CIV, War and Peace Correspondence, David Starr Jordan Papers; Cook, "Woodrow Wilson," p. 13.

4. Fleischman, *Norman Thomas*, p. 69; Duffus, *Lillian Wald*, p. 193; Reminiscences of Roger N. Baldwin, Oral History Research Office of Columbia University, I, 54.

5. Reminiscences of Roger N. Baldwin, Oral History Research Office of Columbia University, I, 54–55; Fleischman, *Norman Thomas*, pp. 71–78; Lillian D. Wald to Jane Addams, August 14, 1917, in Lillian D. Wald Papers.

6. Grubbs, *Struggle for Labor Loyalty*, p. 57; Lillian D. Wald to Crystal Eastman, August 28, 1917, American Union against Militarism Papers; Wald, *Windows*, p. 305; Duffus, *Lillian Wald*, pp. 193–94.

7. Strong, *I Change Worlds*, p. 57; Scott Nearing to Judah L. Magnes, June 4, 1917, P3/F16–L155, Judah L. Magnes Papers.

8. Minutes of the organizing committee, June 8, 1917, p. 4, People's Council of America Papers; New York *Call*, July 22, 1917, p. 1; Fola LaFollette, *Robert M. LaFollette*, II, 752.

9. Woodrow Wilson quoted in Johnson, *Challenge to American Freedoms*, p. 22n; New York *Times*, August 13, 1917, p. 8.

10. Louis P. Lochner to executive committee, August 19, 1917, People's Council of America Papers; New York *Times*, August 29, 1917, p. 1.

11. Rebecca Shelley to executive committee, August 28, 1917, People's Council of America Papers; Hillquit, *Loose Leaves*, pp. 174–75.

12. Eastman, *Love and Revolution*, p. 53; Hillquit, *Loose Leaves*, p. 175.

13. Lochner, *Always the Unexpected*, p. 70; New York *Times*, September 2, 1917, p. 4, and September 3, 1917, p. 6.

14. Louis P. Lochner to executive committee, September 10, 1917, People's Council of America Papers; New York *Call*, September 1, 1917, p. 1.

15. Joseph Freeman, *American Testament*, p. 102; New York *Sun*, August 31, 1917, pp. 1, 4.

16. Hillquit, *Loose Leaves*, p. 177; "The Pacifist Pilgrims," *Literary Digest*, LV (September 15, 1917), 16.

17. New York *Times,* September 2, 1917, p. 4, and September 3, 1917, p. 1; Hutchinson, *Lowden,* I, p. 379; Ickes, *Curmudgeon,* pp. 189–91; McDonald, *Insull,* p. 168.

18. New York *Times,* September 3, 1917, p. 3; Joseph Freeman, *American Testament,* p. 103; Peterson and Fite, *Opponents of War,* p. 77; New York *Call,* September 2, 1917, p. 1; statement of the executive committee, September 2, 1917, pp. 1–2, People's Council of America Papers.

19. Hillquit, *Loose Leaves,* pp. 178–79; interview with Scott Nearing, September 8, 1970; Lochner, *Always the Unexpected,* p. 71,

20. Hutchinson, *Lowden,* pp. 379–80; New York *Times,* September 5, 1917, pp. 1, 3.

21. Rolnick, "Academic Freedom and Tenure," p. 319; Charles A. Beard to Nicholas Murray Butler, October 8, 1917, and New York *Times,* October 10, 1917, p. 10.

22. Statement of the executive committee, September 2, 1917, pp. 1–2, People's Council of America Papers.

23. Interview with Scott Nearing, September 8, 1970; Eastman, *Love and Revolution,* p. 49; Reminiscences of Roger N. Baldwin, Oral History Research Office of Columbia University, I, 56; Judah L. Magnes to Louis P. Lochner, April 5, 1918, P3/F14–L56, Judah L. Magnes Papers; Lochner, *Always the Unexpected,* p. 76; Joseph Freeman, *American Testament,* pp. 332, 334; Paul H. Douglas to author, October 29, 1969; A. J. Muste to Scott Nearing 80th Birthday Committee, November 4, 1963.

24. Interview with Margaret Mead; New York *Times,* May 24, 1932, p. 3.

25. Interview with Scott Nearing, September 8, 1970; interview with Louis P. Lochner, Red Bank, New Jersey, March 21, 1970; Scott Nearing to Judah L. Magnes, October 12, 1917, P3/F16–L155, Judah L. Magnes Papers.

26. Louis P. Lochner to executive committee, September 10, 1917, and minutes of executive committee, September 21, 1917, and October 16, 1917, People's Council of America Papers.

27. People's Council of America *Bulletin,* I (August 1, 1918), p. 3, and I (September–October 1918), p. 3.

28. Nearing, *Radical,* p. 110; memorandum by Elizabeth Freeman, December 20, 1917, People's Council of America Papers; New York *Times,·* September 18, 1917, p. 4; George MacAdam, "Ebb of Pacifism in America," New York *Times Magazine,* December 23, 1917, p. 5.

29. Gompers, *Seventy Years,* II, 323, 332, 343, 378; Mandel, *Samuel Gompers,* pp. 388–89.

30. Reminiscences of John Spargo, Oral History Research Office of Columbia University, pp. 264, 267; Grubbs, *Struggle for Labor Loyalty,* p. 43; Mandel, *Samuel Gompers,* p. 391; Weinstein, *Corporate Ideal,* pp. 241–42; Gompers, *Seventy Years,* II, 380–82; Maurer, *It Can Be Done,* p. 228; Radosh, *American Labor,* p. 59.

31. Hendrickson, "The Pro-War Socialists, the Social Democratic League, and the Ill-Fated Drive for Industrial Democracy in America, 1917–1920," *Journal of Labor History,* XI (Summer, 1970), 312–13; Weinstein, *Corporate Ideal,* p. 242; Radosh, *American Labor,* p. 60; George Creel to Frank P. Walsh, September 1, 1917, in Box 17, Frank P. Walsh Papers; Algie Martin Simons to May Simons, September 5, 1917, Algie Martin Simons Papers.

32. Frank P. Walsh to George Creel, September 10, 1917, and Scott Nearing to Frank P. Walsh, September 6, 1917, in Frank P. Walsh Papers.

33. People's Council of America *Bulletin,* II (April, 1919), p. 5; Gompers, *Seventy Years,* II, 385; New York *Times,* November 13, 1917, pp. 1, 3; Kreuter, *American Dissenter,* p. 174.

34. New York *Times,* September 23, 1917, I, 8; statement by People's Council of America, September 25, 1917, P3/F16–L128, Judah L. Magnes Papers; minutes of the executive committee, September 21, 1917, People's Council of America Papers.

35. Nearing, *Open Letter to Profiteers,* p. 1; Mock, *Censorship,* pp. 159–61, 164–68.

36. Memorandum by Scott Nearing, October 8, 1917, People's Council of America Papers; New York *Times,* September 22, 1917, p. 9; Grubbs, *Struggle for Labor Loyalty,* p. 82; Hillquit, *Loose Leaves,* pp. 205–206, 214–15, 234; New York *Call,* October 15, 1917, pp. 1–2.

37. Minutes of the executive committee, November 8, 1917, and Scott Nearing to the executive committee, October 31, 1917, People's Council of America Papers; Scott Nearing to Henry Wadsworth Longfellow Dana, October 18, 1917, and November 7, 1917, in Box 1, Henry Wadsworth Longfellow Dana Papers.

38. Louis Marshall to Judah L. Magnes, June 1, 1917, in Reznikoff, ed., *Louis Marshall,* II, 972–73; Scott Nearing to Judah L. Magnes, November 9, 1917, P3/F16–L155, Judah L. Magnes Papers.

39. Chicago *Tribune,* November 11, 1917, p. 7.

40. New York *Times,* November 13, 1917, p. 22, and November 14, 1917, p. 15; New York *Call,* November 13, 1917, p. 3.

41. Scott Nearing, "Chairman's Report of Western Trip," People's Council of America *Bulletin,* I (December 18, 1917), 3; Peterson and Fite, *Opponents of War,* p. 76.

42. Scott Nearing, "Chairman's Report of Western Trip," People's Council of America *Bulletin,* I (December 28, 1917), 3; Roosevelt, *Foes,* pp. 287–88; Roosevelt, *Great Adventure,* p. 122.

43. S. Stanwood Menken to Elihu Root, September 13, 1917, quoted in Keller, *Defense of Yesterday,* p. 122; Ralph M. Easley to Thomas W. Gregory, May 6, 1918, in Box 55, National Civic Federation Papers.

44. New York *Call,* April 2, 1918, p. 6; George Creel quoted in Peterson and Fite, *Opponents of War,* p. 76.

45. Thomas D. McCarthy to Thomas W. Gregory, January 18, 1918, Mail and Files Division, File No. 919, Sub 1758, Record Group 60, General Records of the Department of Justice.

46. New York *Sun,* January 10, 1918, p. 2.

47. *Ibid.;* New York *Times,* November 21, 1917, p. 3; People's Council of America *Bulletin,* I (February 15, 1918), p. 3; New York *Tribune,* January 10, 1918, p. 7; Chafee, *Free Speech,* p. 40.

48. Scott Nearing to Judah L. Magnes, January 23, 1918; Judah L. Magnes to Scott Nearing, January 24, 1918; and Scott Nearing to Judah L. Magnes, February 14, 1918, P3/F16–L155, Judah L. Magnes Papers.

49. Telegram from American Defense Society to Thomas W. Gregory, February 13, 1918, Mail and Files Division, File No. 919, Sub 1758, Record Group 60, General Records of the Department of Justice; New York *Times,* February 17,

1918, I, 14; People's Council of America *Bulletin*, I (March 1, 1918), pp. 1–2, 4, 5, 7.

50. New York *Times*, February 18, 1918, p. 5.

51. Weinstein, *Decline of Socialism*, pp. 162–63; Shannon, *Socialist Party*, pp. 119–20; Norman Thomas to Lillian D. Wald, March 1, 1918, in Box 4, Norman Thomas Papers.

52. Grubbs, *Struggle for Labor Loyalty*, pp. 125, 127–28; memorandum by Louis P. Lochner, August 27, 1918, People's Council of America Papers; People's Council of America *Bulletin*, I (August 1, 1918), p. 3, and I (September–October, 1918), p. 3; Thomas W. Gregory quoted in Scheiber, *Wilson Administration*, p. 49.

53. Lincoln Steffens to Allen H. Suggett, October 20, 1917, in Winter and Hicks, ed., *Letters of Lincoln Steffens*, I, 409–10.

54. A. W. Ricker to Edward M. House, April 30, 1918, and Scott Nearing to A. W. Ricker, April 30, 1918, in Drawer 16, Edward M. House Papers.

55. Ginger, *Eugene V. Debs*, pp. 364–65, 373–78; Transcript of Record, *Debs v. United States*, 249 U.S. 211 (1919), p. 8.

56. Nearing, *Debs Decision*, pp. 14–15; Elizabeth Freeman to Henry Wadsworth Longfellow Dana, October 15, 1918 and October 20, 1918, in Box 1, Henry Wadsworth Longfellow Dana Papers; Louis P. Lochner to the executive committee, November 21, 1918, People's Council of America Papers.

57. Grubbs, *Struggle for Labor Loyalty*, pp. 139, 141, 143–44; New York *Call*, June 9, 1919, pp. 1–2; New York *Times*, September 6, 1919, p. 2.

58. Weinstein, *Decline of Socialism*, p. 161; Hendrickson, "The Pro-War Socialists, the Social Democratic League, and the Ill-Fated Drive for Industrial Democracy in America, 1917–1920," *Journal of Labor History*, XI (Summer, 1970), 315, 321; Kreuter, *American Dissenter*, pp. 175, 177, 204, 214; Radosh, *American Labor*, pp. 49–53; John Spargo to H. M. Hyndman, June 30, 1920, in John Spargo Papers.

CHAPTER FIVE. ON TRIAL

1. Norman Thomas to Billy ?, March 26, 1918, in Box 4, Norman Thomas Papers; New York *Times*, March 22, 1918, p. 4.

2. New York *Times*, March 22, 1918, p. 4.

3. Statement in Mail and Files Division, File No. 919, Sub 1758, Record Group 60, General Records of the Department of Justice.

4. Ralph M. Easley to Thomas W. Gregory, February 12, 1918, in *ibid.;* New York *Tribune*, February 11, 1918, p. 1.

5. New York *Tribune*, February 18, 1918, p. 14; Reminiscences of John Lord O'Brian, Oral History Research Office of Columbia University, pp. 230, 235; John Lord O'Brian to author, July 19, 1970.

6. Thomas W. Gregory to John Lord O'Brian, February 19, 1918, and Alfred Bettman to John Lord O'Brian, February 18 and February 21, 1918, Mail and Files Division, File No. 919, Sub 1758, Record Group 60, General Records of the Department of Justice.

7. Reminiscences of John Lord O'Brian, Oral History Research Office of Columbia University, p. 271; Caffey, *National Unity*, pp. 3, 4, 6.

8. Francis G. Caffey to Thomas W. Gregory, February 26, 1918; Scott Nearing to Thomas W. Gregory, January 10, 1918; Francis G. Caffey to Thomas W.

Gregory, March 2, 1918; and John Lord O'Brian to Francis G. Caffey, February 28, 1918, Mail and Files Division, File No. 919, Sub 1758, Record Group 60, General Records of the Department of Justice.

9. New York *Times,* March 22, 1918, p. 4.

10. Philadelphia *Bulletin,* April 3, 1918, p. 3; New York *Times,* April 11, 1918, p. 2.

11. Open letter from Louis P. Lochner, April 2, 1918, People's Council of America *Bulletin,* I (April 15, 1918), 1.

12. People's Council of America Bulletin, I (August 1, 1918), p. 4; financial statement of Nearing Defense Fund, P3/F14–L72, Judah L. Magnes Papers.

13. New York *Times,* April 3, 1918, p. 3; *United States* v. *Nearing,* 252 Fed. 224 (1919).

14. Transcript of Record, *American Socialist Society* v. *United States,* 266 Fed. 214 (1920), pp. 3, 31; *United States* v. *Nearing,* 252 Fed. 224–25 (1919).

15. *United States* v. *Nearing,* 252 Fed. 227–28 (1919); *Masses Publishing Company* v. *Patten* 246 Fed. 38 (1917); Chafee, *Free Speech,* p. 50; O'Brian, *Civil Liberty,* p. 16.

16. Interview with Scott Nearing, September 8, 1970; Jones, *Autobiography,* p. 203; Hillquit, *Socialism Summed Up,* pp. 45–47; Claessens, *Didn't We Have Fun,* pp. 101, 148.

17. New York *Times,* June 27, 1918, p. 4; Hillquit, *Loose Leaves,* p. 70; leaflet, 1918, Socialist Party of New York State Papers.

18. Mann, *LaGuardia,* pp. 94–95; New York *Call,* September 23, 1918, p. 1.

19. Fiorello H. LaGuardia to Isaac Siegel, March 23, 1918, quoted in Mann, *LaGuardia,* p. 94; LaGuardia, *Making of an Insurgent,* p. 151.

20. Waldman, *Labor Lawyer,* p. 83; New York *Call,* September 12, 1918, p. 2, and September 21, 1918, p. 3; New York *Times,* September 13, 1918, pp. 10, 15.

21. Mann, *LaGuardia,* pp. 95–96; LaGuardia, *Making of an Insurgent,* p. 199.

22. New York *Call,* October 3, 1918, p. 3.

23. Waldman, *Labor Lawyer,* p. 43; New York *Call,* September 22, 1918, p. 3 and October 18, 1918, p. 3.

24. New York *Evening World,* October 30, 1918, p. 17; New York *Globe,* November 1, 1918, p. 5; New York *American,* October 30, 1918, p. 5; Mann, *LaGuardia,* p. 97; Zinn, *LaGuardia in Congress,* pp. 31–32.

25. New York *Call,* October 7, 1918, p. 2, October 10, 1918, pp. 4, 6, October 11, 1918, p. 6, and October 23, 1918, p. 4; Boffel, ed., *Art Young,* p. 411.

26. New York *American,* November 2, 1918, p. 5; LaGuardia, *Making of an Insurgent,* p. 199; Mann, *LaGuardia,* pp. 95, 97.

27. Scott Nearing to John Reed, October 11, 1918, in John Reed Papers; Mann, *LaGuardia,* p. 98; New York *Call,* November 3, 1918, p. 3; New York *Times,* November 2, 1918, p. 7.

28. Interview with Scott Nearing, June 27, 1971; LaGuardia, *Making of an Insurgent,* p. 200.

29. Waldman, *Labor Lawyer,* pp. 79–80.

30. New York *Times,* November 6, 1918, p. 1; New York *Call,* September 30, 1918, p. 3, and November 6, 1918, p. 1; Algernon Lee to Morris Hillquit, November 17, 1918, Correspondence Reel 2, Morris Hillquit Papers.

31. New York *Times,* December 1, 1925, pp. 1, 18; Mayer, *Law of Free Speech,* pp. 6, 10, 15, 19; Nearing, *Great Madness,* pp. 41–42.

32. New York *Call,* February 12, 1919, p. 1.

33. *Trial of Scott Nearing,* pp. 17–21.

34. Interview with Scott Nearing, June 27, 1971; New York *Call,* February 14, 1919, p. 1; Giovannitti, "Scott Nearing Reprieves Democracy," *Liberator,* II (April, 1919), 6.

35. New York *Call,* February 11, 1919, p. 1; *Trial of Scott Nearing,* pp. 37–39, 57, 62–65; Ervin, *Homegrown Liberal,* p. 63.

36. *Trial of Scott Nearing,* pp. 123, 125, 137–38; Nearing, *Great Madness,* p. 22.

37. *Trial of Scott Nearing,* pp. 130, 157–61.

38. *Ibid.,* p. 169; statement on conscientious objection, 1917, American Union against Militarism Papers; New York *Times,* February 14, 1919, p. 24.

39. *Trial of Scott Nearing,* pp. 183–85, 191, 194, 204–205.

40. New York *Times,* December 1, 1925, p. 18; *United States v. American Socialist Society,* 260 Fed. 892 (1919); Mayer, *Law of Free Speech,* p. 15.

41. New York *Call,* February 19, 1919, p. 1, and February 20, 1919, p. 2; Scott Nearing to Robert M. LaFollette, February 17, 1919, in Box 84, Series B, Robert M. LaFollette Papers.

42. Chafee, *Free Speech,* p. 25.

43. *United States v. American Socialist Society,* 260 Fed. 888 (1919); Hillquit, *Loose Leaves,* p. 245; Walter Nelles, "The Prosecution of Scott Nearing and the American Socialist Society," *American Labor Year Book,* III (1920), 109; interview with Scott Nearing, June 27, 1971.

44. Hillquit, *Loose Leaves,* pp. 228, 230; O'Brian, *Civil Liberty,* p. 20.

45. Reminiscences of Norman Thomas, Oral History Research Office of Columbia University, p. 124; Walter Nelles, "The Nearing Case," People's Council of America *Bulletin,* II (March, 1919), 2; Transcript of Record, *Debs v. United States,* 249 U.S. 239, 247 (1919).

46. Eastman, *Trial of Eugene Debs,* p. 13; New York *Times,* February 20, 1919, p. 1; Francis G. Caffey to Thomas W. Gregory, February 20, 1919, Mail and Files Division, File No. 919, Sub 1758, Record Group 60, General Records Division of the Department of Justice.

47. *United States v. American Socialist Society,* 260 Fed. 888–91 (1919).

48. *American Socialist Society v. United States,* 266 Fed. 214 (1920).

49. *United States v. American Socialist Society,* 260 Fed. 885–86, 892 (1919); Nelles, *Liberal in Wartime,* p. 139.

50. New York *Call,* February 20, 1919, p. 8, and March 5, 1919, p. 1; "Scott Nearing," *Messenger,* II (March, 1919), pp. 23–24; Giovannitti, "Scott Nearing Reprieves Democracy," *Liberator,* II (April, 1919), 6; Walter Nelles to Morris Hillquit, March 15, 1919, Correspondence Reel 2, Morris Hillquit Papers.

51. New York *Call,* October 19, 1921, p. 1; interview with Louis Waldman.

CHAPTER SIX. ON REVOLUTION

1. Fisher, "Last Muckraker," pp. 45–46; Sinclair, *Jimmie Higgins,* pp. 280–82.

2. Foner, ed., *Bolshevik Revolution,* pp. 32, 50; Kennan, *Decision to Intervene,* pp. 338, 382; Unterberger, *America's Siberian Expedition,* pp. 230–32.

3. Eugene V. Debs quoted in Foner, ed., *Bolshevik Revolution,* pp. 50–51.

4. New York *Call,* November 8, 1918, p. 4.

5. Lusk Committee, *Revolutionary Radicalism,* I, i, 536; New York *Times,* November 18, 1918, p. 9; Hicks, *John Reed,* p. 324; Draper, *Roots of American Communism,* pp. 109–10, 131–33; Weinstein, *Decline of Socialism,* p. 327.

6. New York *Times,* April 28, 1919, p. 10, and April 29, 1919, p. 14.

7. Louis P. Lochner to William I. Hull, April 9, 1919, People's Council of America Papers; Nearing, *One Big Union,* p. 32.

8. New York *Times,* January 25, 1919, pp. 1, 4.

9. Murray, *Red Scare,* pp. 101–102; Wingo, "Clayton R. Lusk," p. 115.

10. Chamberlain, *Loyalty and Legislative Action,* pp. 15–16, 21; Wingo, "Clayton R. Lusk," p. 156; Lusk Committee, *Revolutionary Radicalism,* I, i, 953, and II, i, 1462–63.

11. Scott Nearing to Upton Sinclair, July 11, 1919, in Upton Sinclair Papers.

12. New York *Times,* May 6, 1919, p. 10; New York *Call,* November 28, 1919, p. 1.

13. Flynn, *My Own Piece,* pp. 233–34; Roger N. Baldwin to Henry Wadsworth Longfellow Dana, March 7, 1918, in Henry Wadsworth Longfellow Dana Papers; Rhoads, "Election of 1920," p. 133; New York *Times,* February 23, 1922, p. 18; interview with Scott Nearing, June 27, 1971.

14. Hicks, *John Reed,* p. 324; Macdonald, "The Defense of Everybody (Part I)," *New Yorker,* XXIX (July 11, 1953), 50; Reminiscences of Roger N. Baldwin, Oral History Research Office of Columbia University, I, 71, 97–102.

15. Unpublished autobiographical manuscript, in possession of Roger N. Baldwin; interview with Roger N. Baldwin, New York City, December 1, 1970; interview with John Scott.

16. Milner, *Education of an American Liberal,* p. 92; interview with Scott Nearing, September 8, 1970.

17. Interview with Scott Nearing, June 27, 1971; general letter from Scott Nearing, April 2, 1922, in Upton Sinclair Papers; Chaplin, *Bars and Shadows,* pp. 10–11; Chaplin, *Wobbly,* pp. 254, 282, 321–22.

18. *Miami Valley Socialist* (Dayton, Ohio), March 12, 1920, in Volume X, Eugene V. Debs Scrapbook #1; Rhoads, "Election of 1920," pp. 45, 113, 136–37, 139, 216; Ginger, *Eugene V. Debs,* p. 421; Maurer, *It Can Be Done,* pp. 228–30.

19. Scott Nearing to Eugene V. Debs, May 4, 1920, Debs Prisoner File, RG 129, R4FRC, quoted in Rhoads, "Election of 1920," p. 135; Shannon, *Socialist Party,* pp. 157–58.

20. Scott Nearing to Judah L. Magnes, n.d., P3/F43–L101, Judah L. Magnes Papers; interview with Louis P. Lochner; Haessler, Letter to the Editor, *Journal of Labor History,* XI (Summer, 1970), 396; Lusk Committee, *Revolutionary Radicalism,* I, ii, 1997; Federated Press *Monthly,* No. 1 (September, 1922), 1, 4, and No. 17 (March–July, 1924), 4.

21. Carl Haessler to author, March 7, 1971; Carl Haessler quoted in Thomas, *Conscientious Objector,* pp. 24–25; Lovett, *All Our Years,* p. 146.

22. Federated Press *Monthly,* No. 4 (December, 1922), 1; Lochner, *Always the Unexpected,* p. 114; Lusk Committee, *Revolutionary Radicalism,* I, ii, 1997.

23. Scott Nearing to Upton Sinclair, May 8, 1920, in Upton Sinclair Papers; Federated Press *Monthly,* No. 14 (October, 1923), 1 and No. 18 (December, 1924), 4.

24. McKay, *A Long Way from Home,* p. 79; interview with Scott Nearing, June 27, 1971; Federated Press *Labor Letter,* IX (August 12, 1925), 4; Lansbury, *My Life,* p. 104; Nearing, *Radical,* pp. 163–64.

25. *American Labor Year Book,* VI (1925), 202, VIII (1927), 155, XI (1930), 178; Fisher, "Last Muckraker," p. 52; Murphy, *Freedom of Speech,* pp. 175, 325n, 327n.

26. Curti and Carstensen, *University of Wisconsin,* II, 141, 145; Madison *Capital-*

Times, November 1, 1921, p. 1; Madison *Wisconsin State Journal,* November 3, 1921, p. 3.

27. Madison *Capital-Times,* October 31, 1921, p. 1, and November 1, 1921, pp. 1, 3; Curti and Carstensen, *University of Wisconsin,* pp. 146–47, 150; Madison *Wisconsin State Journal,* December 4, 1921, p. 3.

28. Worcester *Telegram,* March 15, 1922, and Worcester *Post,* March 15, 1922, in Clark University Scrapbook (1922); Clark College *Monthly,* X (March, 1922), 206; "The Free Speech Controversy at Clark University," *School and Society,* XV (April 15, 1922), 420; Dorfman, *Thorsten Veblen,* p. 463.

29. Worcester *Telegram,* March 15, 1922, and Worcester *Post,* March 15, 1922, in Clark University Scrapbook (1922).

30. Clark College *Monthly,* X (March, 1922), 216; New York *Times,* March 17, 1922, p. 31; Worcester *Telegram,* March 16, 1922, in Clark University Scrapbook (1922).

31. Worcester *Telegram,* March 16 and March 21; Worcester *Gazette,* March 16, in Clark University Scrapbook (1922); "The Free Speech Controversy at Clark University," *School and Society,* XV (April 15, 1922), 420; "Report of the Committee of Inquiry Concerning Clark University," AAUP *Bulletin,* X (October, 1924), 73; Sinclair, *Goose-Step,* p. 298.

32. New York *Times,* March 21, 1922, p. 4; Worcester *Gazette,* March 23, 1922, and Worcester *Post,* March 16, 1922, in Clark University Scrapbook (1922).

33. Bunting, *Liberty and Learning,* p. 91; Bliven, "Free Speech, But—!", *New Republic,* XXX (April 5, 1922), 162; "Report of the Committee of Inquiry Concerning Clark University," AAUP *Bulletin,* X (October, 1924), 41, 71, 74–76, 94, 100; Stewart M. Pratt to author, November 13, 1970.

34. Federated Press *Labor Letter,* VIII (March 11, 1925), 2, and XII (December 8, 1926), 6; Algernon Lee to Morris Hillquit, December 17, 1918, Correspondence Reel 2, Morris Hillquit Papers.

35. *American Labor Year Book,* V (1923–1924), 226; New York *Call,* September 26, 1918, p. 2, October 25, 1918, p. 7, and November 2, 1918, p. 5; interview with Scott Nearing, July 15, 1970.

36. *American Labor Year Book,* III (1919–1920), 207, and V (1923–1924), 212; Fox, *Discovery of Abundance,* pp. 130, 142.

37. Trotsky, *My Life,* p. 274; Draper, *Roots of American Communism,* pp. 110, 262–63; Ruth Fischer, *Stalin,* pp. 141–43.

38. Interview with Louis Waldman; Rhoads, "Election of 1920," p. 153; interview with Scott Nearing, July 15, 1970.

39. Interview with Scott Nearing, September 8, 1970.

40. Nearing and Russell, *Soviet Form of Government,* pp. 19, 22–25, 27.

41. Louis P. Lochner, "Our Provincialism," People's Council of America *Bulletin,* I (July 1, 1918), 2; Russell, *Autobiography,* pp. 137–39.

42. Nearing and Russell, *Soviet Form of Government,* pp. 33–34, 36–39, 41, 43–44, 53–54, 68.

43. Nearing, *Radical,* p. 146; *American Labor Year Book,* VIII (1927), iv.

44. Scott Nearing to Algernon Lee, November 1, 1925, in Algernon Lee Papers; New York *Times,* October 6, 1924, p. 3.

45. Nearing, *Radical,* pp. 6–7; interview with John Scott; interview with Robert Nearing, Troy, Pennsylvania, November 28, 1970; interview with Guy Nearing.

46. Guest book of Ridgewood, New Jersey, in possession of Robert Nearing; interview with Margaret Mead.

47. Interview with Robert Nearing; interview with John Scott; memorandum by John Scott, October, 1970.

48. Interview with Margaret Mead.

49. Cremin, *Transformation of the School*, p. 278; *American Labor Year Book*, VIII (1927), 170–71; Lovett, *All Our Years*, p. 209.

50. Cremin, *Transformation of the School*, pp. 226, 260–64; Elizabeth Gurley Flynn to Scott Nearing, November 14, 1925, Correspondence of the Board of Directors (1923–1933), American Fund for Public Service Papers; interview with Robert Nearing.

51. Scott Nearing to Lincoln Steffens, January 11, 1927, in Lincoln Steffens Papers; interview with Scott Nearing, July 15, 1970; Nearing, ed., *Law of Social Revolution*, pp. v–vii, ix–x, 6.

52. Louis Silverstein, "The American Revolution of 1776," in Nearing, ed., *Law of Social Revolution*, pp. 51, 56.

53. Chambers, *Witness*, pp. 211–13.

CHAPTER SEVEN. "THE ONLY HUSKY PATIENT"

1. James Weldon Johnson, *Along This Way*, p. 386; Reminiscences of Roger N. Baldwin, Oral History Research Office of Columbia University, II, 325–26; minutes of the Board of Directors, July 27, 1922, American Fund for Public Service Papers.

2. Charles Garland to Roger N. Baldwin, July 15, 1922, Miscellaneous Correspondence (1923–1933), American Fund for Public Service Papers.

3. Curti, "Subsidizing Radicalism: The American Fund for Public Service, 1921–1941," *Social Service Review*, XXXIII (September, 1959), 276.

4. *Ibid.*, pp. 280–81.

5. Interview with Morris L. Ernst, New York City, October 4, 1971; Ernst, *Best is Yet*, pp. 243–45; Reminiscences of Roger N. Baldwin, Oral History Research Office of Columbia University, II, 327; interview with Scott Nearing, July 15, 1970.

6. Roger N. Baldwin to Scott Nearing, May 17, 1926, Miscellaneous Correspondence (1923–1933), American Fund for Public Service Papers.

7. Roger N. Baldwin to Morris L. Ernst, December 20, 1926, in *ibid.*

8. Minutes of the Board of Directors, July 22, 1925, American Fund for Public Service Papers; Roger N. Baldwin to Lewis Gannett and Scott Nearing, March 26, 1923, and Scott Nearing to Roger N. Baldwin, October 15, 1923, Correspondence of the Board of Directors (1923–1933), American Fund for Public Service Papers.

9. Roger N. Baldwin to Judah L. Magnes, February 19, 1925, Correspondence of the Board of Directors (1923–1933), American Fund for Public Service Papers.

10. Scott Nearing to Norman Thomas, December 4, 1924, and Scott Nearing to Roger N. Baldwin, December 17, 1925, in *ibid.*; interview with Roger N. Baldwin, November 26, 1970.

11. Interview with Roger N. Baldwin, November 26, 1970; memorandum by Scott Nearing, April 3, 1924, Miscellaneous Correspondence (1923–1933), American Fund for Public Service Papers.

12. Curti, "Subsidizing Radicalism: The American Fund for Public Service, 1921–1941," *Social Service Review*, XXXIII (September, 1959), 282; memorandum by Scott Nearing *et al.*, September 8, 1924, Miscellaneous Correspondence, and minutes of the Board of Directors, May 6, 1925, American Fund for Public Service Papers.

13. Minutes of the Board of Directors, March 25, 1925, American Fund for Public Service Papers; interview with Scott Nearing, September 8, 1970.

14. Scott Nearing to Roger N. Baldwin, October 15, 1923; Norman Thomas to Roger N. Baldwin; memorandum by Roger N. Baldwin, April 23, 1926, Correspondence of the Board of Directors (1923–1933), American Fund for Public Service Papers; Curti, "Subsidizing Radicalism: The American Fund for Public Service, 1921–1941," *Social Service Review*, XXXIII (September, 1959), 282–83.

15. Joseph Freeman, *American Testament*, pp. 335–36. Nearing and Freeman, *Dollar Diplomacy*, pp. xiii, 172.

16. Memorandum by Scott Nearing, April 3, 1924, Miscellaneous Correspondence (1923–1933) and minutes of the Board of Directors, April 22, 1925, American Fund for Public Service Papers.

17. New York *Times*, March 29, 1926, p. 1; Joseph Freeman, *American Testament*, p. 339; Nearing, "Return of the Native," *New Masses*, I (May, 1926), 18.

18. Joseph Freeman, *American Testament*, 337; Scott Nearing, Letter to the Editor, *New Masses*, IV (July, 1928), 2; George Goetz (V. F. Calverton) to Scott Nearing, May 3, 1924, and Scott Nearing to George Goetz, December 23, 1924, February 14, 1926, and December 4, 1926, in V. F. Calverton Papers.

19. Paul H. Douglas, Letter to the Editor, *Masses*, IX (November, 1916), 22; Max Eastman to Norman Thomas, May 28, 1917, in Box 2, Norman Thomas Papers; Margaret Anderson, *My Thirty Years War*, p. 128; Debs, "Socialist Ideals," *Arena*, XL (November, 1908), 433–34.

20. Minutes of the Board of Directors, March 21, 1923, and Scott Nearing to Roger N. Baldwin, November 1, 1925, Correspondence of the Board of Directors (1923–1933), American Fund for Public Service Papers; Nearing, "The Control of Labor Education," *Modern Quarterly*, I (March, 1923), 37.

21. Hentoff, *Peace Agitator*, pp. 58–60, 70–71; Reminiscences of Roger N. Baldwin, Oral History Research Office of Columbia University, II, 328; interview with Morris L. Ernst.

22. Scott Nearing to Roger N. Baldwin, September 21, 1928, and September 26, 1928, Correspondence of the Board of Directors (1923–1933), American Fund for Public Service Papers; Morris, *Conflict within the AFL*, pp. 124–25.

23. Report of Committee on Labor Education, October 17, 1929, Miscellaneous Reports (1922–1941), I, 142–43, and minutes of the Board of·Directors, July 9, 1924, and June 12, 1925, American Fund for Public Service Papers.

24. Tom Tippett, "Labor Education at Taylorville," Federated Press *Bulletin*, VIII (November 15, 1924), 3; Federated Press *Labor Letter*, IX (June 24, 1925), 1.

25. Art Shields, "Fourth W. E. B. Convention," and Nearing, "Impressions," Federated Press *Labor Letter*, IX (April 29, 1925), 4; Philadelphia *Evening Bulletin*, April 20, 1925, 3.

26. Iversen, *Communists and the Schools*, pp. 13, 20–22.

27. New York *Times*, May 26, 1925, p. 2.

28. *Ibid.*, May 29, 1925, p. 18; *Daily Worker* (New York), May 29, 1925, p. 3; Iversen, *Communists and the Schools*, p. 22.

29. Iversen, *Communists and the Schools*, pp. 23, 32; Nearing, "Education and the Open Mind," *Modern Quarterly*, II, No. 4 (1925), 289.

30. Scott Nearing to Elizabeth Gurley Flynn, October 10, 1925, and October 22, 1925, Miscellaneous Correspondence (1923–1933), American Fund for Public Service Papers.

31. Scott Nearing to Roger N. Baldwin, November 1, 1925, and Scott Nearing to Elizabeth Gurley Flynn, December 1, 1925, in *ibid.*

32. Scott Nearing to George Goetz, October 16, 1927, in V. F. Calverton Papers; *American Labor Year Book,* X (1929), 154; interview with Scott Nearing, September 8, 1970; Nearing, *Radical,* pp. 146–47.

33. Sinclair, "Communists in the Making," Institute of Social Studies *Bulletin,* I (Spring, 1952), 56; Bloor, *We Are Many,* pp. 266, 268–71.

34. V. I. Lenin to the Society of Friends of Soviet Russia, October 20, 1922, in *Collected Works,* XXXIII, 380; Curti, "Subsidizing Radicalism: The American Fund for Public Service, 1921–1941," *Social Service Review,* XXXIII (September, 1959), 281–82.

35. Nearing, *Radical,* p. 147; Chambers, *Witness,* pp. 332–34.

36. Nearing, *Radical,* p. 147; Joseph Freeman, *American Testament,* pp. 342–46; *Daily Worker* (New York), January 21, 1935, p. 5; Chambers, *Witness,* p. 208.

37. Reminiscences of Max Shachtman, Oral History Research Office of Columbia University, I, 65; interview with Scott Nearing, September 8, 1970; *American Labor Year Book,* X (1929), 216, and XI (1930), 189.

38. Iversen, *Communists and the Schools,* p. 80; *American Labor Year Book,* VIII (1927), 163–64; Joseph Freeman, *American Testmament,* p. 257; Federated Press *Labor Letter,* X (January 6, 1926), 6.

39. Rodney, *Soldiers of the International,* pp. 130–31; interview with Harry Freeman, New York City, October 5, 1971.

40. Nearing, *Radical,* pp. 141–44; Wilbur, Introduction to Ch'en Kung-po, *Communist Movement in China,* pp. 6, 11–12; Brandt, *Stalin's Failure in China,* pp. 22–24, 42.

41. Margulies, *Pilgrimage to Russia,* pp. 38–40; Joseph Freeman, *American Testament,* p. 626.

42. Kennell, *Dreiser and the Soviet Union,* pp. 22–23, 25, 62; Swanberg, *Dreiser,* pp. 329–30; Dorothy Thompson to Sinclair Lewis, November 8, 1927, quoted in Sheean, *Dorothy and Red,* p. 60.

43. Sam Darcy to Scott Nearing 80th Birthday Committee, November 2, 1963.

44. Schleimann, "The Life and Work of Willi Muenzenberg," *Survey,* No. 55 (April, 1965), 73–74; R. N. Carew Hunt, "Willi Muenzenberg," *St. Antony's Papers,* No. 9 (1960), 73, 76; Manuel Gomez to author, November 11, 1971.

45. *New York Times,* February 20, 1928, p. 6; Manuel Gomez to author, November 11, 1971; "Enlist with Sandino," *New Masses,* III (April, 1928), 3; *American Labor Year Book,* X (1929), 205.

46. Chaplin, *Wobbly,* p. 361; Reminiscences of Max Shachtman, Oral History Research Office of Columbia University, I, 180, 184, 187–88.

47. Interview with Morris L. Ernst; "Civil Liberties in Massachusetts," Federated Press *Labor Letter,* X (March 3, 1926), 4; interview with Scott Nearing, June 27, 1971; *New York Times,* February 22, 1926, p. 3.

48. *Daily Worker* (New York), October 8, 1928, pp. 1, 5, and November 1, 1928, p. 5; interview with Scott Nearing, June 27, 1971.

49. Goldman, *Living My Life,* p. 987; interview with Scott Nearing, June 27, 1971.

50. *New York Times,* March 31, 1928, p. 12; Norman Thomas to Alexander Trachtenberg, October 18, 1918, in Box 4, Norman Thomas Papers.

51. Norman Thomas to Scott Nearing, October 1, 1963, in Scott Nearing 80th

Birthday Committee Scrapbook; interview with Roger N. Baldwin, November 26, 1970; Sinclair, *American Outpost,* p. 161.

52. Draper, *American Communism and Soviet Russia,* pp. 302–305; Chambers, *Witness,* pp. 255–56; Iversen, *Communists and the Schools,* p. 24; *American Labor Year Book,* XI (1930), 142.

53. Interview with Scott Nearing, September 8, 1970.

54. Draper, *American Communism and Soviet Russia,* pp. 191, 239n, 306–307, 422, 429–30, 439; Cannon, *First Ten Years,* pp. 146–47.

55. Interviews with Scott Nearing, September 8, 1970, and June 27, 1971; New York *Times,* August 6, 1928, p. 8; *Daily Worker* (New York), August 6, 1928, p. 1, November 3, 1928, p. 1, and November 6, 1928, p. 1.

56. Scott Nearing to Committee on Research and Publications, October 2, 1929, and committee report, October 21, 1929, Miscellaneous Correspondence (1923–1933), American Fund for Public Service Papers.

57. International Press Correspondence, December 12, 1928, quoted in Draper, *American Communism and Soviet Russia,* p. 349; Nearing, *Black America,* pp. 7, 132, 228, 262; Scott Nearing to V. F. Calverton, February 10, 1929, in V. F. Calverton Papers.

58. Brown, *Negro in American Fiction,* p. 181; Rideout, *Radical Novel,* pp. 194, 317.

59. Nearing, *Twilight of Empire,* pp. v, 179; interview with Scott Nearing, September 8, 1970.

60. *Daily Worker* (New York), January 8, 1930, p. 4.

61. Memorandum by Scott Nearing, December 12, 1929, Correspondence of the Board of Directors (1923–1933), American Fund for Public Service Papers.

62. Freeman, *American Testament,* pp. 332–34; interview with Roger N. Baldwin, October 26, 1970; Baldwin, "A Puritan Revolutionist," in Allen, ed., *Adventurous Americans,* pp. 263–64, 274–75.

63. Iversen, *Communists and the Schools,* pp. 23, 76; Manuel Gomez to author, November 11, 1971; Draper, *American Communism and Soviet Russia,* p. 310.

64. Curti, "Subsidizing Radicalism: The American Fund for Public Service, 1921–1941," *Social Service Review,* XXXIII (September, 1959), 293–95; Reminiscences of Roger N. Baldwin, Oral History Research Office of Columbia University, II, 328, 330–32.

65. Zieger, "Senator George Wharton Pepper and Labor Issues in the 1920's," *Journal of Labor History,* IX (Spring, 1968), 163, 167, 179, 182n; Pepper, *Philadelphia Lawyer,* p. 194; Bernstein, *Lean Years,* pp. 59, 331.

66. New York *Call,* April 4, 1921, p. 2, and November 28, 1921, p. 5; New York *Times,* December 1, 1924, p. 7; Nearing, *Living the Good Life,* pp. xvi–xvii.

67. Interview with Scott and Helen Nearing, Boston, Massachusetts, October 30, 1971; Freedman, "Scott Nearing," p. 82n; memorandum by John Scott, October, 1970.

68. Nearing, *Radical,* p. 212, and *Living the Good Life,* p. xv; Waldman, *Labor Lawyer,* p. 187.

69. Bernstein, *Lean Years,* pp. 41, 63, 297–98, 317, 388, 422.

CHAPTER EIGHT. ON TOTALITARIANISM

1. New York *Times,* April 28, 1971, p. 40; Nearing, *Living the Good Life,* pp. xvii, 9, 23, 39, 125.

2. Nearing, *Living the Good Life,* pp. 24–26, 147.

3. *Ibid.,* pp. 42–45; interview with Basil Rauch, New Haven, Connecticut, February 12, 1972; Scott Nearing to Upton Sinclair, May 18, 1945, in Upton Sinclair Papers.

4. Nearing, *Living the Good Life,* pp. xv–xvi, 97, 118, 134, 159, and *Radical,* p. 50.

5. Nearing, *Living the Good Life,* pp. 167, 188, 190–96; interview with Basil Rauch; interview with Sidney Hook, Waltham, Massachusetts, December 15, 1970.

6. Nearing, *Living the Good Life,* p. 168.

7. Lindley, *Roosevelt Revolution,* p. 304; Kirkendall, *Social Scientists and Farm Politics,* pp. 42–43; Schlesinger, *Coming of the New Deal,* pp. 369–70.

8. Conkin, *Tomorrow a New World,* pp. 153, 168, 176, 185; Schlesinger, *Coming of the New Deal,* pp. 371–73; Kirkendall, *Social Scientists and Farm Politics,* pp. 114, 116, 122; Griswold, *Farming and Democracy,* pp. 5, 137, 178.

9. Ware and Powell, "Planning for Permanent Poverty," *Harper's,* CLXX (April, 1935), 521, 523–24.

10. New York *Times,* February 3, 1930, p. 23; Scott Nearing to Upton Sinclair, September 23, 1931, and March 10, 1933, in Upton Sinclair Papers; Nearing, *Fascism,* pp. 56, 58.

11. *World Congress against War,* pp. 2, 24–27; Carew Hunt, "Willi Muenzenberg," *St. Antony's Papers,* No. 9 (1960), 77–79.

12. Memorandum by John Scott, October, 1970; *World Congress against War,* pp. 30–31; Reading *Eagle,* February 11, 1933, in Box 730, University of Pennsylvania Alumni Records.

13. Powell, "A Clergyman Looks in on Russia," *Review of Reviews,* XC (October, 1934), 68; Caute, *Fellow-Travellers,* p. 250.

14. Newark *Star,* October 19, 1932, in Box 730, University of Pennsylvania Alumni Records; Philadelphia *Record,* May 15, 1936, p. 32; Nearing, "Marx's Contribution to Social Advance," *World Tomorrow,* XVI (March 15, 1933), 252, and *ABC of Communism,* p. 25.

15. Philip J. Jaffe to author, November 18, 1971; *Daily Worker* (New York), January 21, 1935, p. 5.

16. Aaron, *Writers on the Left,* p. 343; *Daily Worker* (New York), March 2, 1935, p. 8.

17. Henry L. Mencken to James H. Gray, January 2, 1935, in Henry L. Mencken Papers; memorandum by John Scott, October, 1970; Scott Nearing to V. F. Calverton, March 13, 1938, in V. F. Calverton Papers; Strong, *Soviets Expected It,* p. 47.

18. Nearing, "Will Germany Go Left?", *Modern Quarterly,* XI (Autumn, 1939), 68, and "The Shifting Center of World Power," *Modern Quarterly,* XI (Autumn, 1940), 80.

19. Memorandum by John Scott, October, 1970.

20. Daniel Bell, *Marxian Socialism,* p. 184; Shannon, *Decline of American Communism,* pp. 5–6.

21. Wittner, *Rebels against War,* pp. 3, 37; Adler, *Isolationist Impulse,* p. 229; interview with Louis P. Lochner; Macdonald, "The Defense of Everybody (Part II)," *New Yorker,* XXIX (July 18, 1953), 54; Bertrand Russell to Kingsley Martin, May 13, 1940, in Russell, *Autobiography,* p. 341.

22. Interview with Scott Nearing, July 15, 1970; Daniel Bell, *Marxian Socialism,* p. 180; A. J. Muste to Scott Nearing 80th Birthday Committee, November 4, 1963.

23. Nearing, *Living the Good Life,* pp. xv–xvi; Leuchtenburg, *Roosevelt and the New Deal,* pp. 277, 300, 306–307.

24. Interview with Alexander L. Crosby, Quakertown, Pennsylvania, October 7, 1971.

25. Note from New York Bureau, February 11, 1943, in 1943/Scott Nearing file, Box 139, Federated Press Papers.

26. Memorandum by Carl Haessler, February 15, 1943, in *ibid.;* Nearing, *Radical,* p. 173; Carl Haessler to author, March 7, 1971, and April 6, 1971.

27. Interview with Scott Nearing, July 15, 1970; "New SCEF Center Has Deep Roots in Struggle," *Southern Patriot,* XXVII (December, 1969), 6; Sanger, *Autobiography,* pp. 210, 253–54; Lader, *Margaret Sanger Story,* pp. 146–48; Kennedy, *Birth Control,* p. 93.

28. Nearing, *Radical,* p. 203.

29. Nearing, *Democracy,* pp. 46, 67, 69, 76, 132.

30. *Ibid.,* pp. 87, 94, 101, 107, 134, 148–50; Hook, *Political Power,* p. 429.

31. Nearing, *Tragedy of Empire,* p. 140; Bertram D. Wolfe to author, July 14, 1971; Des Moines *Tribune,* June 4, 1946, p. 9.

32. Stephen S. Wise to Scott Nearing, January 28, 1946, quoted in Voss, *Wise,* p. 270.

33. Bergen (New Jersey) *Evening News,* February 9, 1942, and Towanda (Pennsylvania) *Review,* January 3, 1947, clippings in possession of Robert Nearing; interview with Beatrice N. Pierce; "Recent Deaths," *School and Society,* LXIV (December 14, 1946), 418; interview with John Scott, November 5, 1970.

34. War Resisters League *News,* No. 17 (June 24, 1947), 1–2; minutes of Eighteenth Annual Conference, June 8, 1947, in Box 12, War Resisters League Papers.

35. Bell, *Marxian Socialism,* p. 133n; Chambers, *Witness,* p. 207; Graham, *Encore for Reform,* p. 91; Mendelson, "Clear and Present Danger: From Schenck to Dennis," *Columbia Law Review,* LII (March, 1952), 330–31.

36. Reminiscences of Louis M. Rabinowitz, Oral History Research Office of Columbia University, p. 37.

37. Konvitz, *Expanding Liberties,* pp. 86–92; *Sweezy v. New Hampshire,* 354 U.S. 234 (1957); *Board of Regents of State Colleges v. Roth,* 408 U.S. 564, 582 (1972); *Perry v. Sindermann,* 408 U.S. 593 (1972).

38. Leo Huberman to Scott Nearing 80th Birthday Committee, January 7, 1963; Nearing, "Why I Believe in Socialism," *Monthly Review,* I (June, 1949), 44–50; Frederick A. Blossom to author, December 16, 1971; "On 'World Events' and Israel," *Monthly Review,* XXII (June, 1970), 38.

39. Nearing, *Living the Good Life,* p. 187; Robert Taylor, "Kings Can Do No More," Boston *Sunday Globe Magazine,* November 1, 1970, p. 9.

40. Interview with Scott and Helen Nearing, October 30, 1971; Nearing, *Radical,* p. 176.

41. Nearing, *U.S.A. Today,* pp. xiii–xiv, 134; Scott Nearing to Upton Sinclair, October 25, 1952, in Upton Sinclair Papers.

42. Willard Uphaus, *Commitment,* pp. 119, 149, 152, 155; interview with Ola Uphaus, New Haven, Connecticut, October 2, 1971; Willard Uphaus to author, January 19, 1972.

43. New York *Times,* June 7, 1956, p. 15, and April 28, 1971, p. 40; Nearing, "World Events," *Monthly Review,* V (April, 1954), 632, and VIII (December, 1956), 299–300; Shannon, *Decline of American Communism,* pp. 314, 352.

44. New York *Times,* September 26, 1959, p. 13.

45. Nearing, *Our Right to Travel,* pp. 8–9, 11.

46. *Ibid.,* pp. 4–6, 10–12, and *Radical,* pp. 249–51.

47. Nearing, *Our Right to Travel,* pp. 13, 17–18.

48. Frances G. Knight to Scott Nearing, May 29, 1959, quoted in *ibid.,* p. 21; interview with Scott Nearing, June 27, 1971; Schwartz, *Open Society,* pp. 67, 78–79; *Kent v. Dulles,* 357 U.S. 116 (1958).

49. Nearing, "World Events," *Monthly Review,* XV (February, 1964), 562, 564, and XX (May, 1968), 38–39.

50. Interview with Scott Nearing, June 27, 1971; Nearing, *Radical,* p. 241; Radosh, *American Labor,* pp. 402–404; New York *Times,* February 22, 1967, pp. 1, 17.

51. Nearing, *Radical,* pp. 241–43, and *Cuba and Latin America,* pp. 14, 34.

52. *Worker* (New York), November 17, 1963, p. 3; Scott Nearing 80th Birthday Committee Scrapbook.

53. Rexford G. Tugwell to author, June 29, 1971.

CHAPTER NINE. OF MIND AND CHARACTER

1. Nearing, *Freedom: Promise and Menace,* p. iii.

2. *Ibid.,* pp. 26, 155, 189; Nearing, *Tragedy of Empire,* pp. 33, 40, 74, 86, 113, 126, *Living the Good Life,* p. 185, and *Democracy,* p. 132.

3. Potter, *People of Plenty,* pp. 99, 102, 119.

4. Interview with Scott Nearing, October 30, 1971; Nearing, "The Dollar on the Rocks," speech in Boston, October 31, 1971.

5. Nearing, *Europe in Revolution,* p. 29, and *Conscience of a Radical,* p. 12.

6. Nearing, "World Events," *Monthly Review,* XV (December, 1964), 517; interviews with Scott Nearing, July 15, 1970, and October 30, 1971.

7. Nearing, *Democracy,* pp. 136–37, and *Conscience of a Radical,* pp. 156–57; interview with John Scott.

8. Orwell, "Lear, Tolstoy, and the Fool," in Sonia Orwell and Angus, ed., *In Front of Your Nose,* pp. 294–302.

9. Macdonald, "The Defense of Everybody (Part II)," *New Yorker,* XXIX (July 18, 1953), 54; Roche, *Quest for the Dream,* pp. 101–102.

10. Reminiscences of Roger N. Baldwin, Oral History Research Office of Columbia University, II, 177; interview with Roger N. Baldwin, October 26, 1970; Lasch, *Agony of the American Left,* pp. 76, 109; Johnpoll, *Pacifist's Progress,* pp. 239–40, 280–81, 284.

11. Nearing, *Man's Search for the Good Life,* pp. 121, 128.

12. Paul Goodman, Introduction to Nearing, *Living the Good Life,* p. vii; Goodman, *New Reformation,* p. 193.

13. Kostelanetz, *Master Minds,* pp. 273–75, 283.

14. Nearing, statement of resignation from the University of Toledo, March 10, 1917, copy in possession of author; Bell, *End of Ideology,* p. 17.

CHAPTER TEN. NEARING REDIVIVUS

1. Paul Goodman, Introduction to Nearing, *Living the Good Life,* p. ix; Morton and Lucia White, *Intellectual versus the City,* pp. 1–3; Caws, "Two Prophets Angry with Their Culture," *New Republic,* CLXVI (February 5, 1972), 25, 27.

2. Hennacy, "Spartan and Servile State," *Catholic Worker*, XXI (March, 1955), 5; *Wall Street Journal* (New York), July 13, 1971, p. 1.

3. Press release by Schocken Books, January 5, 1972; New York *Times Book Review*, December 12, 1971, p. 40; Elliott, "Up on the Farm," *Time*, XCVII (January 18, 1971), 78; "Prophets of the Good Life," *Newsweek*, LXXVI (September 14, 1970), 100; Thompson, "Away from It All," *Harper's*, CCXLI (November, 1970), 120; Gendler, "Read Any Good Books Lately?", *WIN*, VI (June 15, 1970), 25.

4. Leonard M. Nelson to Scott Nearing, November 4, 1971, with citation, copy in possession of author; New York *Times*, April 30, 1972, p. 38.

5. Paul Goodman, Introduction to Nearing, *Living the Good Life*, p. xi.

6. Jezer, "Don't Admire the Turnips," *New Republic*, CLXIII (September 12, 1970), 26, 28.

7. Nearing, *Radical*, p. 10; interview with Robert W. Dunn, New York City, December 31, 1971.

BIBLIOGRAPHY

THE WRITINGS OF SCOTT NEARING

An ABC of Communism. Ridgewood, N.J., the author, 1934?

Black America. New York, Vanguard Press, 1929.

The Brave New World. With Helen K. Nearing. Harborside, Me., Social Science Institute, 1958.

The Conscience of a Radical. Harborside, Me., Social Science Institute, 1965.

"The Control of Labor Education," *Modern Quarterly,* I (1923), 35–37.

Cuba and Latin America. Harborside, Me., Social Science Institute, 1963.

Debate: Resolved: That the Soviet Form of Government is Applicable to Western Civilization. With Bertrand Russell. New York, League for Public Discussion, 1924.

The Debs Decision. New York, Rand School Press, 1919.

Democracy Is Not Enough. New York, Island Workshop Press, 1945.

Dollar Diplomacy: A Study in American Imperialism. With Joseph Freeman. New York, B. W. Huebsch, 1925.

"Education and the Open Mind," *Modern Quarterly,* II (1925), 280–89.

Educational Frontiers: Simon Nelson Patten and Other Teachers. New York, Seltzer, 1925.

Europe in Revolution. New York, Rand School Press, 1920.

Fascism. Ridgewood, N.J., the author, 1933.

Freedom: Promise and Menace. Harborside, Me., Social Science Institute, 1961.

The Great Madness. New York, Rand School Press, 1917.

The Law of Social Revolution: A Cooperative Study by the Labor Research Study Group. New York, Social Science Publishers, 1926.

Living the Good Life: How to Live Sanely and Simply in a Troubled World. With Helen K. Nearing. Harborside, Me., Social Science Institute, 1954.

The Making of a Radical: A Political Autobiography. New York, Harper and Row, 1972.

Man's Search for the Good Life. Harborside, Me., Social Science Institute, 1954.

"Marx's Contribution to Social Advance," *World Tomorrow,* XVI (1933), 250–52.

The One Big Union of Business. New York, Rand School Press, 1920.

An Open Letter to Profiteers. New York, People's Council of America, 1917.

Our Right to Travel. With Helen K. Nearing. Harborside, Me., Social Science Institute, 1959.
"Return of the Native," *New Masses,* I (1926), 18–19.
"The Shifting Center of World Power," *Modern Quarterly,* XI (1940), 77–80.
Social Adjustment. New York, Macmillan, 1911.
Social Sanity. New York, Moffat, Yard, 1913.
The Solution of the Child Labor Problem. New York, Moffat, Yard, 1911.
The Tragedy of Empire. New York, Island, 1945.
The Twilight of Empire. New York, Vanguard Press, 1930.
U.S.A. Today. With Helen K. Nearing. Harborside, Me., Social Science Institute, 1955.
Violence or Solidarity? New York, People's Printer, 1919.
Wages in the United States, 1908–1910. New York, Macmillan, 1914.
"Who's Who among College Trustees," *School and Society,* VI (1917), 297–99.
"Why I Believe in Socialism," *Monthly Review,* I (1949), 44–50.
"Will Germany Go Left?", *Modern Quarterly,* XI (1939), 62–69.
Women and Social Progress. With Nellie S. Nearing. New York, Macmillan, 1912.
"World Events," *Monthly Review.* 1953–1972.
Interviews. July 15 and September 8, 1970, and June 27, 1971, Harborside, Me.; October 30, 1971, Boston.
Scrapbook of Scott Nearing 80th Birthday Committee. In possession of Scott Nearing, Harborside, Me.

PRIMARY SOURCES

Allen, William Harvey. Reminiscences. Oral History Research Office, Columbia University, New York City.
American Fund for Public Service. Correspondence and Reports. New York Public Library, New York City.
American Socialist Society v. United States, 266 Fed. 214 (1920).
American Union against Militarism. Papers. Swarthmore College Peace Collection, Swarthmore, Pa.
Baldwin, Roger N. Personal interviews, October 26 and December 1, 1970, in New York City. The founder and longtime director of the American Civil Liberties Union worked with Nearing in the American Fund for Public Service and other causes.
—— Reminiscences. Oral History Research Office, Columbia University, New York City.
—— Unpublished autobiographical manuscript, in possession of Roger N. Baldwin.
Barker, Wharton. Papers. Library of Congress, Washington.
Blossom, Frederick A. Letter to author, April 19, 1970. Mr. Blossom, in a varied career, helped Nearing to publish the newsletter *World Events.*
Board of Regents of State Colleges v. Roth, 408 U.S. 564 (1972).
Calverton, V. F. Papers. New York Public Library, New York City.
Clark University. Scrapbook (1922). Clark University, Worcester, Mass.
Crosby, Alexander L. Personal interview, October 7, 1971, in Quakertown, Pa. Mr. Crosby, a journalist, once headed the New York Bureau of the Federated Press.

Dana, Henry Wadsworth Longfellow. Papers. Swarthmore College Peace Collection, Swarthmore, Pa.

Debs, Eugene V. Scrapbook. On microfilm at Tamiment Institute Library, New York University, New York City.

Douglas, Paul H. Letter to author, October 29, 1969. The former member of the People's Council and debating foe of Nearing became, of course, United States Senator from Illinois.

Dunn, Robert W. Telephone interview, December 31, 1971, in New York City. Mr. Dunn is the longtime executive secretary of the Labor Research Association.

Ely, Richard T. Papers. State Historical Society of Wisconsin, Madison.

Ernst, Morris L. Personal interview, October 4, 1971, in New York City. A small part of the importance of being Ernst was the attorney's work as treasurer of the American Fund for Public Service.

Federated Press Papers. Columbia University, New York City.

Freeman, Harry. Personal interview, October 5, 1971, in New York City. The editor for the *Worker* and later the Soviet news agency TASS collaborated with Nearing on *Whither China?*

Gomez, Manuel. Letter to author, November 11, 1971. Mr. Gomez served as secretary of the All-America Anti-Imperialist League.

Haessler, Carl. Letters to author, March 7 and April 6, 1971. For virtually its entire life the Federated Press was largely Mr. Haessler's lengthened shadow.

Hillquit, Morris. Papers. State Historical Society of Wisconsin, Madison.

Hook, Sidney. Personal interview, December 15, 1970, in Waltham, Mass. The eminent and embattled philosopher knew Nearing in Vermont.

House, Edward M. Papers. Yale University, New Haven, Conn.

Jaffe, Philip J. Letter to author, November 18, 1971. Mr. Jaffe is an archivist of the American left and was a friend of the late Earl Browder.

Jordan, David Starr. Papers. Hoover Institution on War, Revolution, and Peace, Stanford, Calif.

Kent v. Dulles, 357 U.S. 116 (1958).

LaFollette, Robert M. Papers. Library of Congress, Washington.

Lee, Algernon. Papers. Tamiment Institute Library, New York University, New York City.

Lindsay, Samuel McCune. Papers. Columbia University, New York City.

Lochner, Louis P. Personal interview, March 21, 1970, in Red Bank, N.J. The Pulitzer Prize-winning journalist served as executive secretary of the People's Council while Nearing was chairman.

Magnes, Judah L. Papers. Central archives for the History of the Jewish People, Jerusalem, Israel.

Masses Publishing Company v. Patten, 246 Fed. 38 (1917).

Mead, Margaret. Personal interview, February 25, 1971, in Cambridge, Mass. Margaret Mead is Margaret Mead; her parents were Nearing's colleagues at the University of Pennsylvania.

Mencken, Henry L. Papers. New York Public Library. New York City.

Milwaukee Social Democratic Publishing Company v. Burleson, 255 Fed. 407 (1921).

National Child Labor Committee. Papers. Library of Congress, Washington.

National Civic Federation. Papers. New York Public Library, New York City.

Nearing, Guy. Personal interview, November 30, 1970, in Ramsey, N.J. Scott

Nearing's brother is a horticulturist who has also written poetry and a couple of pamphlets on cosmogony.

Nearing, Max. Letter to author, October 24, 1971. The youngest child of Louis and Minnie Nearing became an engineer for the New York Central Railroad.

Nearing, Robert. Personal interview, November 28, 1970, in Troy, Pa. The younger son of Scott and Nellie Nearing works in a bank in the vicinity of Morris Run.

O'Brian, John Lord. Letter to author, July 19, 1970. Mr. O'Brian served as assistant attorney-general in the administration of Woodrow Wilson.

—— Reminiscences. Oral History Research Office, Columbia University, New York City.

People's Council of America. Papers. Swarthmore College Peace Collection, Swarthmore, Pa.

Pepper, George Wharton. Papers. University of Pennsylvania, Philadelphia.

Perry v. Sindermann, 408 U.S. 593 (1972).

Pierce, Beatrice N. Personal interview, October 20, 1971, in Towson, Md. Scott Nearing's youngest sister became a landscape gardener.

Pratt, Stewart M. Letter to author, November 13, 1970. Mr. Pratt was the student chairman of organizations advocating free speech at Clark College in 1922.

Rabinowitz, Louis M. Reminiscences. Oral History Research Office, Columbia University, New York City.

Rauch, Basil. Personal interview, February 12, 1972, in New Haven, Conn. A professor of history at Barnard College, Mr. Rauch was one of Nearing's neighbors in Vermont.

Reed, John. Papers. Houghton Library, Harvard University, Cambridge, Mass.

Reinstine, Harry. Personal interview, April 13, 1972, in Jacksonville, Fla. An attorney, Mr. Reinstine studied economics under Nearing at Penn.

Scott, John. Personal interview and memorandum, November 5, 1970, in New York City. The elder son of Scott and Nellie Nearing became a journalist and commentator on international affairs for Time, Inc.

Seligman, E. R. A. Papers. Columbia University, New York City.

Shachtman, Max. Reminiscences. Oral History Research Office, Columbia University, New York City.

Simons, Algie Martin. Papers. State Historical Society of Wisconsin, Madison.

Sinclair, Upton. Reminiscences. Oral History Research Office, Columbia University, New York City.

Socialist Party of America, New York State. Papers. Tamiment Institute Library, New York University, New York City.

Spargo, John. Papers. University of Vermont, Burlington, Vt.

—— Reminiscences. Oral History Research Office, Columbia University, New York City.

Spingarn, Joel E. Papers. New York Public Library, New York City.

Steffens, Lincoln. Papers. Columbia University, New York City.

Stokes, Rose Pastor. Papers. Yale University, New Haven, Conn.

Sweezy, Paul M. Letter to author, December 16, 1971. Mr. Sweezy is the co-founder and co-editor of *Monthly Review*.

Sweezy v. New Hampshire, 354 U.S. 234 (1957).

Thomas, Norman. Papers. New York Public Library, New York City.

—— Reminiscences. Oral History Research Office, Columbia University, New York City.

Tugwell, Rexford G. Letter to author, June 29, 1971. Nearing's student and teaching assistant achieved prominence as an economist, historian, and public servant.

United States. Department of Justice. Record Group 60 of General Records. National Archives, Washington.

—— Department of the Treasury. Budget, Fiscal Year 1974. Washington, Government Printing Office, 1973.

United States v. *American Socialist Society*, 260 Fed. 892 (1919).

United States v. *Nearing*, 252 Fed. 224 (1919).

University of Pennsylvania, Alumni Records. Archives of the University of Pennsylvania, Philadelphia.

—— Minutes of the Board of Trustees (1915). Archives of the University of Pennsylvania, Philadelphia.

Uphaus, Ola. Personal interview, October 2, 1971, in New Haven, Conn. Mrs. Uphaus and her husband were directors of the World Fellowship Camp where Nearing frequently lectured.

Uphaus, Willard. Letter to author, January 19, 1972. Mr. Uphaus was a professor of religious education at Yale University.

Wald, Lillian D. Papers. New York Public Library, New York City.

Waldman, Louis. Personal interview, November 25, 1970, in New York City. Mr. Waldman was one of the Albany Five and later Socialist gubernatorial candidate in New York.

Walsh, Frank P. Papers. New York Public Library, New York City.

War Resisters League. Papers. Swarthmore College Peace Collection, Swarthmore, Pa.

Wharton School. Files. Archives of the University of Pennsylvania, Philadelphia.

Wolfe, Bertram D. Letter to author, July 14, 1971. The distinguished historian of Marxism served as Nearing's director at the Workers School in New York.

SECONDARY SOURCES

Aaron, Daniel. *Men of Good Hope: A Story of American Progressives.* New York, Oxford University Press, 1961.

—— *Writers on the Left.* New York, Avon, 1965.

Adler, Selig. *The Isolationist Impulse: Its Twentieth Century Reaction.* New York, Collier, 1961.

Anderson, Adrian Norris. "Albert Sidney Burleson: A Southern Politician in the Progressive Era." Unpublished Ph.D. dissertation, Texas Technological College, 1967.

Anderson, Elliot J. "The Scott Nearing Controversy in Toledo, 1916–1917," *Northwest Ohio Quarterly,* XXIX (1957), 72–88, 161–73, 206–33.

Anderson, Margaret. *My Thirty Years War.* New York, Covici, Friede, 1930.

Baldwin, Roger N. "A Puritan Revolutionist," in *Adventurous Americans.* Edited by Devere Allen. New York, Farrar and Rinehart, 1932.

Baltzell, E. Digby. *Philadelphia Gentlemen: The Making of a National Upper Class.* Glencoe, Ill., Free Press, 1958.

Bean, Walton E. "George Creel and His Critics: A Study of the Attacks on the Committee on Public Information, 1917–1919." Unpublished Ph. D. dissertation, University of California at Berkeley, 1941.

Beck, Hubert Park. *Men Who Control Our Universities: The Economic and Social Composition of Governing Boards of Thirty Leading American Universities.* New York, King's Crown Press, 1947.

Bell, Daniel. *The End of Ideology: On the Exhaustion of Political Ideas in the Fifties.* New York, Free Press, 1962.

—— *Marxian Socialism in the United States.* Princeton, N.J., Princeton University Press, 1967.

—— "The Tamiment Library," Bibliographical Series No. 6, New York University Libraries (1969), 1–27.

Bernstein, Irving. *The Lean Years: A History of the American Worker, 1920–1933.* Baltimore, Penguin, 1966.

Bierce, Ambrose. *The Devil's Dictionary.* New York, Hill and Wang, 1957.

Bliven, Bruce. "Free Speech, But—! ", *New Republic*, XXX (1922), 160–62.

Bloom, Robert L. "The Philadelphia *North American:* A History, 1839–1925." Unpublished Ph.D. dissertation, Columbia University, 1952.

Bloor, Ella Reeve. *We Are Many.* New York, International Publishers, 1940.

Boorstin, Daniel J. *The Image: A Guide to Pseudo-Events in America.* New York, Harper and Row, 1964.

Brandt, Conrad. *Stalin's Failure in China, 1924–1927.* New York, W. W. Norton, 1966.

Brown, Sterling. *The Negro in American Fiction.* Port Washington, N.Y., Kennikat Press, 1968.

Bunting, David Edison. *Liberty and Learning: The Activities of the American Civil Liberties Union in Behalf of Freedom of Education.* Washington, American Council on Public Affairs, 1942.

Burr, Agnes Rush. *Russell H. Conwell and His Work.* Philadelphia, John C. Winston, 1917.

Burt, Nathaniel. *The Perennial Philadelphians: The Anatomy of an American Aristocracy.* Boston, Little, Brown, 1963.

Caffey, Francis G. *National Unity: Address before the Alumni of Howard College.* Birmingham, Ala., the author, 1919.

Cannon, James P. *The First Ten Years of American Communism: Report of a Participant.* New York, Pioneer, 1962.

Carew Hunt, R. N. "Willi Muenzenberg," *St. Antony's Papers,* No. 9 (1960), 72–87.

Caute, David. *The Fellow-Travellers: A Postscript to the Enlightenment.* New York, Macmillan, 1973.

Caws, Peter. "Two Prophets Angry with Their Culture," *New Republic,* CLXVI (1972), 25–27.

Chafee, Zechariah, Jr. *Free Speech in the United States.* New York, Atheneum, 1969.

Chamberlain, Lawrence H. *Loyalty and Legislative Action: A Survey of Activity by the New York State Legislature.* Ithaca, N.Y., Cornell University Press, 1951.

Chambers, Whittaker. *Witness.* Chicago, Henry Regnery, 1952.

Chaplin, Ralph. *Bars and Shadows.* New York, Leonard Press, 1922.

—— *Wobbly: The Rough-and-Tumble Story of an American Radical.* Chicago, University of Chicago Press, 1948.

Chatfield, Charles. *For Peace and Justice: Pacifism in America, 1914–1941.* Boston, Beacon, 1973.

—— "World War I and the Liberal Pacifist in the United States," *American Historical Review,* LVI (1970), 1920–37.

Ch'en Kung-po. *The Communist Movement in China.* Edited by C. Martin Wilbur. New York, East Asian Institute of Columbia University, 1960.

Cheyney, Edward P. *History of the University of Pennsylvania, 1740–1940.* Philadelphia, University of Pennsylvania Press, 1940.

—— "Trustees and Faculties," *School and Society,* II (1915), 793–806.

Chute, Charles L. Papers. Columbia University, New York City.

Claessens, August. *Didn't We Have Fun!* New York, Rand School Press, 1953.

Clark College Monthly, X (1922), 200–219.

Cohen, Warren I. *The American Revisionists: The Lessons of Intervention in World War I.* Chicago, University of Chicago Press, 1967.

Conkin, Paul R. *Tomorrow a New World: The New Deal Community Program.* Ithaca, N.Y., Cornell University Press, 1959.

Conquest, Robert. *The Great Terror: Stalin's Purge of the Thirties.* New York, Macmillan, 1968.

Cook, Blanche Wiesen. "Democracy in Wartime: Antimilitarism in England and the United States, 1914–1918," in Charles Chatfield, ed., *Peace Movements in America.* New York, Schocken, 1973.

—— "Woodrow Wilson and the Antimilitarists, 1914–1917." Unpublished Ph.D. dissertation, Johns Hopkins University, 1970.

Cornell, Frederic. "History of the Rand School." Ed.D. dissertation, Teachers' College, Columbia University, in progress.

Cremin, Lawrence A. *The Transformation of the School: Progressivism in American Education, 1876–1957.* New York, Random House, 1961.

Currie, Harold W. "Allan L. Benson, Salesman of Socialism, 1902–1916," *Journal of Labor History,* XI (1970), 285–303.

Curti, Merle E. *Peace or War: The American Struggle, 1636–1936.* New York, W. W. Norton, 1936.

Curti, Merle E. and Vernon Carstensen. *The University of Wisconsin: A History, 1848–1925.* Madison, University of Wisconsin Press, 1949.

Curti, Merle E. and Roderick Nash. *Philanthropy in the Shaping of American Higher Education.* New Brunswick, N.J., Rutgers University Press, 1965.

—— "Subsidizing Radicalism: The American Fund for Public Service, 1921–1941," *Social Service Review,* XXXIII (1959), 274–95.

Cywar, Alan S. "An Inquiry into American Thought and the Determinate Influence of Political, Economic, and Social Factors in the Early Twentieth Century: Bourne, Dewey, DuBois, Nearing, Veblen, and Weyl." Unpublished Ph.D. dissertation, University of Rochester, 1972.

Debs, Eugene V. "Socialist Ideals," *Arena,* XL (1908), 432–34.

Debs v. United States, 249 U.S. 211 (1919).

Dewey, John. "Presidential Address," American Association of University Professors *Bulletin,* I (1915), 9–13.

Disbrow, Donald W. "The Progressive Movement in Philadelphia, 1910–1916." Unpublished Ph.D. dissertation, University of Rochester, 1956.

Dorfman, Joseph. *Thorstein Veblen and His America.* New York, Viking, 1947.

Douglas, Paul H. *Real Wages in the United States, 1890–1926.* Boston, Houghton Mifflin, 1930.

Draper, Theodore. *American Communism and Soviet Russia.* New York, Viking, 1960.

—— *The Roots of American Communism.* New York, Viking, 1963.

Dubofsky, Melvyn. *We Shall Be All: A History of the International Workers of the World.* Chicago, Quadrangle, 1969.

Duffus, Robert L. *Lillian Wald: Neighbor and Crusader.* New York, Macmillan, 1938.

Dunne, Finley Peter. *Mr. Dooley: Now and Forever.* Stanford, Calif., Academic Reprints, 1954.

Eastman, Max. *Love and Revolution: My Journey through an Epoch.* New York, Random House, 1964.

—— *The Trial of Eugene Debs.* New York, Liberator, 1918.

Elliott, Charles. "Up on the Farm," *Time,* XCVII (1971), 78.

"Enlist with Sandino," *New Masses,* III (1928), 3.

Ernst, Morris L. *The Best is Yet . . .* New York, Harper and Row, 1945.

Ervin, Charles W. *Homegrown Liberal.* New York, Dodd, Mead, 1954.

Faulkner, Harold U. *The Quest for Social Justice, 1898–1914.* New York, Macmillan, 1931.

Fine, Nathan. *Labor and Farmer Parties in the United States, 1828–1928.* New York, Rand School Press, 1928.

Fischer, Fritz. *Germany's Aims in the First World War.* New York, W. W. Norton, 1967.

Fischer, Ruth. *Stalin and German Communism.* Cambridge, Mass., Harvard University Press, 1948.

Fisher, Richard B. "The Last Muckraker: The Social Orientation of the Thought of Upton Sinclair." Unpublished Ph.D. dissertation, Yale University, 1953.

Fleischman, Harry. *Norman Thomas: A Biography.* New York, W. W. Norton, 1964.

Florence, Lella Secor. "The Ford Peace Ship and After," in *We Did Not Fight: 1914–1918 Experiences of War Resisters.* Edited by Julian Bell. London, Cobden-Sanderson, 1935.

Flynn, Elizabeth Gurley. *I Speak My Own Piece: Autobiography of "The Rebel Girl."* New York, Masses and Mainstream, 1955.

Foner, Philip S., ed. *The Bolshevik Revolution: Its Impact on American Radicals, Liberals, and Labor.* New York, New World, 1967.

Fox, Daniel M. *The Discovery of Abundance: Simon N. Patten and the Transformation of Social Theory.* Ithaca, N.Y., Cornell University Press, 1967.

Franklin, John Hope and Isidore Starr, ed. *The Negro in 20th Century America.* New York, Random House, 1967.

Freedman, Estelle. "Scott Nearing, American Radical Intellectual." Unpublished M.A. thesis, Columbia University, 1971.

"The Freedom of University Teaching," *New Statesman,* V (1915), 463.

Freeman, Joseph. *An American Testament: A Narrative of Rebels and Romantics.* New York, Farrar and Rinehart, 1936.

"The Free Speech Controversy at Clark University," *School and Society,* XV (1922), 419–24.

Gendler, Everett. "Read Any Good Books Lately?" *WIN,* VI (1970), 25.

Ginger, Ray. *Eugene V. Debs: A Biography.* New York, Collier, 1962.

Giovannitti, Arturo. "Scott Nearing Reprieves Democracy," *Liberator,* II (1919), 5–7.

Goldman, Emma. *Living My Life*. New York, Alfred A. Knopf, 1931.

Gompers, Samuel. *Seventy Years of Life and Labor*. New York, E. P. Dutton, 1925.

Goodman, Paul. *New Reformation: Notes of a Neolithic Conservative*. New York, Random House, 1970.

—— *People or Personnel and Like a Conquered Province*. New York, Random House, 1968.

—— *Utopian Essays and Practical Proposals*. New York, Random House, 1962.

Graham, Otis L., Jr. *An Encore for Reform: The Old Progressives and the New Deal*. New York, Oxford University Press, 1967.

Griswold, A. Whitney. *Farming and Democracy*. New York, Harcourt, Brace, 1948.

Grubbs, Frank L., Jr. *The Struggle for Labor Loyalty: Gompers, the A.F. of L., and the Pacifists, 1917–1920*. Durham, N.C., Duke University Press, 1968.

Gruber, Carol S. "Mars and Minerva: World War I and the American Academic Man." Unpublished Ph.D. dissertation, Columbia University, 1968.

Gutman, Herbert G. "Two Lockouts in Pennsylvania, 1873–1874," *Pennsylvania Magazine of History and Biography*, LXXXIII (1959), 307–26.

Haber, Samuel. *Efficiency and Uplift: Scientific Management in the Progressive Era, 1890–1920*. Chicago, University of Chicago Press, 1964.

Haessler, Carl. Letter to the editor. *Journal of Labor History*, XI (1970), 396.

Hartz, Louis. *The Liberal Tradition in America*. New York, Harcourt, Brace, 1955.

Heaton, John L. *Cobb of "The World": A Leader in Liberalism*. New York, E. P. Dutton, 1924.

Heilbroner, Robert L. *The Worldly Philosophers: The Lives, Times, and Ideas of the Great Economic Thinkers*. New York, Simon and Schuster, 1953.

Hendrickson, Kenneth E., Jr. "The Pro-War Socialists, the Social Democratic League, and the Ill-Fated Drive for Industrial Democracy in America, 1917–1920," *Journal of Labor History*, XI (1970), 301–22.

Hennacy, Ammon. "Spartan and Servile State," *Catholic Worker*, XXI (1955), 5–7.

Hentoff, Nat. *Peace Agitator: The Story of A. J. Muste*. New York, Macmillan, 1963.

Hickerson, Frank R. "A History of the University of Toledo." Unpublished D. Ed. dissertation, University of Cincinnati, 1941.

Hicks, Granville. *John Reed: The Making of a Revolutionary*. New York, Macmillan, 1937.

Hillquit, Morris. *History of Socialism in the United States*. New York, Funk and Wagnalls, 1910.

—— *Loose Leaves from a Busy Life*. New York, Rand School Press, 1934.

—— *Socialism Summed Up*. New York, H. K. Fly, 1913.

[Holmes, Oliver Wendell.] *The Mind and Faith of Justice Holmes*. Edited by Max Lerner. New York, Random House, 1943.

Hook, Sidney. *Academic Freedom and Academic Anarchy*. New York, Dell, 1970.

—— *Political Power and Personal Freedom: Critical Studies in Democracy, Communism, and Civil Rights*, New York, Collier, 1962.

Hutchinson, William T. *Lowden of Illinois: The Life of Frank O. Lowden*. Chicago, University of Chicago Press, 1957.

Hutton, Ann Hawkes. *The Pennsylvanian: Joseph R. Grundy*. Philadelphia, Dorrance, 1962.

Ickes, Harold L. *The Autobiography of a Curmudgeon*. New York, Reynal and Hitchcock, 1943.

Iversen, Robert W. *The Communists and the Schools.* New York, Harcourt, Brace, 1959.

Jezer, Martin. "Don't Admire the Turnips," *New Republic,* CLXIII (1970), 26–28.

Johnpoll, Bernard K. *Pacifist's Progress: Norman Thomas and the Decline of American Socialism.* Chicago, Quadrangle, 1970.

Johnson, Donald. *The Challenge to American Freedoms: World War I and the Rise of the American Civil Liberties Union.* Lexington, University of Kentucky Press, 1963.

Johnson, James Weldon. *Along This Way.* New York, Viking, 1933.

[Jones, Mary.] *Autobiography of Mother Jones.* Edited by Mary Field Parton. Chicago, Charles H. Kerr, 1925.

Jordan, David Starr. *Days of a Man.* Yonkers-on-Hudson, N.Y., World Book Company, 1922.

Kazin, Alfred. *On Native Grounds: An Interpretation of Modern American Prose Literature.* Garden City, N.Y., Doubleday, 1956.

Keller, Morton. *In Defense of Yesterday: James M. Beck and the Politics of Conservatism.* New York, Coward-McCann, 1958.

Kellogg, Paul U. "Case of Scott Nearing," *Survey,* XXXIV (1915), 289.

Kennan, George F. *Soviet-American Relations, 1917–1920: The Decision to Intervene.* New York, Atheneum, 1967.

Kennedy, David M. *Birth Control in America: The Career of Margaret Sanger.* New Haven, Yale University Press, 1970.

Kennell, Ruth Epperson. *Theodore Dreiser and the Soviet Union, 1927–1945: A First-Hand Chronicle.* New York, International Publishers, 1969.

Kipnis, Ira. *The American Socialist Movement, 1897–1912.* New York, Columbia University Press, 1952.

Kirkendall, Richard S. *Social Scientists and Farm Politics in the Age of Roosevelt.* Columbia, University of Missouri Press, 1966.

Kolbe, Parke R. *The Colleges in War Time and After.* New York, D. Appleton, 1919.

Konvitz, Milton R. *Expanding Liberties.* New York, Viking, 1967.

Kostelanetz, Richard. *Master Minds: Portraits of Contemporary American Artists and Intellectuals.* New York, Macmillan, 1969.

Kreuter, Kent and Gretchen Kreuter. *An American Dissenter: The Life of Algie Martin Simons, 1870–1950.* Lexington, University of Kentucky Press, 1969.

Lader, Lawrence. *The Margaret Sanger Story and the Fight for Birth Control.* Garden City, N.Y., Doubleday, 1955.

LaFollette, Fola. *Robert M. LaFollette, June 14, 1855–June 18, 1925.* New York, Macmillan, 1953.

LaGuardia, Fiorello H. *The Making of an Insurgent: An Autobiography, 1882–1919.* Philadelphia, Lippincott, 1948.

Lansbury, George. *My Life.* London, Constable, 1928.

Lasch, Christopher. *The Agony of the American Left.* New York, Random House, 1969.

—— *The American Liberals and the Russian Revolution.* New York, McGraw-Hill, 1962.

Lenin, V. I. *Collected Works.* London, Lawrence and Wishart, 1966. Vol. XXXIII.

Leuchtenburg, William E. *Franklin D. Roosevelt and the New Deal, 1932–1940.* New York, Harper and Row, 1963.

Levin, N. Gordon, Jr. *Woodrow Wilson and World Politics: America's Response to War and Revolution.* New York, Oxford University Press, 1968.

"Light on the Nearing Case," *Literary Digest*, LI (1915), 248–49.

Lindley, Ernest K. *The Roosevelt Revolution: First Phase*. New York, Viking, 1933.

Lloyd, Henry Demarest. "The Story of a Great Monopoly," *Atlantic*, XLVII (1881), 317–34.

Lochner, Louis P. *Always the Unexpected: A Book of Reminiscences*. New York, Macmillan, 1956.

Lovejoy, Arthur O. "Academic Freedom in War Time," *Nation*, CVI (1918), 401–402.

—— "The American Association of University Professors," *Nation*, CII (1916), 169–70.

—— "A Communication: To Conscientious Objectors," *New Republic*, XI (1917), 187–89.

Lovett, Robert Morss. *All Our Years*. New York, Viking, 1948.

Lusk Committee. *Revolutionary Radicalism: Its History, Purpose, and Tactics*. Albany, N.Y., J. B. Lyon, 1920.

Lyell, Charles. *Travels in North America*. London, J. Murray, 1845.

Macdonald, Dwight. "The Defense of Everybody," *New Yorker*, XXIX (July 11 and July 18, 1953), 31–55 and 29–59.

McAhren, Robert W. "Making the Nation Safe for Childhood: A History of the Movement for Federal Regulation of Child Labor, 1900–1938." Unpublished Ph.D. dissertation, University of Texas, 1967.

McDonald, Forrest. *Insull*. Chicago, University of Chicago Press, 1962.

McKay, Claude. *A Long Way from Home*. New York, Harcourt, Brace, 1937.

McLoughlin, William G., Jr. *Billy Sunday Was His Real Name*. Chicago, University of Chicago Press, 1955.

Mandel, Bernard. *Samuel Gompers: A Biography*. Yellow Springs, Ohio, Antioch Press, 1963.

Mann, Arthur. *LaGuardia: A Fighter against His Times, 1882–1933*. Philadelphia, Lippincott, 1959.

Marcus, Irwin. "The Scott Nearing Case: Academic Freedom on Trial." Unpublished paper, copy in possession of author.

Marcy, Mary E. "The Reward of Truth Telling," *International Socialist Review*, XVI (1915), 94–96.

Margulies, Sylvia R. *The Pilgrimage to Russia: The Soviet Union and the Treatment of Foreigners, 1924–1937*. Madison, University of Wisconsin Press, 1968.

Marot, Helen. "Progress in Philadelphia," *Charities*, XIV (1905), 834–36.

[Marshall, Louis.] *Louis Marshall, Champion of Liberty: Selected Papers and Addresses*. Edited by Charles Reznikoff. Philadelphia, Jewish Publication Society, 1957.

Maurer, James H. *It Can Be Done*. New York, Rand School Press, 1938.

Mayer, Julius M. *The Law of Free Speech*. New York, National Security League, 1919.

Mead, Margaret. *Blackberry Winter: My Earlier Years*. New York, William Morrow, 1972.

Mendelson, Wallace. "Clear and Present Danger: From Schenck to Dennis," *Columbia Law Review*, LII (1952), 313–33.

Metzger, Walter P. *Academic Freedom in the Age of the University*. New York, Columbia University Press, 1955.

Milner, Lucille B. *Education of an American Liberal*. New York, Horizon, 1954.

Mock, James R. *Censorship, 1917*. Princeton, Princeton University Press, 1941.

"Monopoly," *Fortune,* XII (1935), 40.

Morris, James O. *Conflict within the AFL: A Study of Craft versus Industrial Unionism, 1901–1938.* Ithaca, N.Y., Cornell University Press, 1958.

Murphy, Paul L. *The Meaning of Freedom of Speech: First Amendment Freedoms from Wilson to FDR.* Westport, Conn., Greenwood, 1972.

Murray, Robert K. *Red Scare: A Study of National Hysteria, 1919–1920.* New York, McGraw-Hill, 1964.

Nelles, Walter. *A Liberal in Wartime: The Education of Albert DeSilver.* New York, W. W. Norton, 1940.

"New SCEF Center Has Deep Roots in Struggle," *Southern Patriot,* XXVII (1969), 6.

O'Brian, John Lord. *Civil Liberty in Wartime.* Washington, Government Printing Office, 1919.

O'Neill, William L., ed. *Echoes of Revolt: The Masses, 1911–1917.* Chicago, Quadrangle, 1966.

"On 'World Events' and Israel," *Monthly Review,* XXII (1970), 38–41.

Orwell, George. "Lear, Tolstoy, and the Fool," in *In Front of Your Nose, 1945–1950.* Edited by Sonia Orwell and Ian Angus. New York, Harcourt Brace Jovanovich, 1968.

"The Pacifist Pilgrims," *Literary Digest,* LV (1917), 16–17.

Pearson, Gaynor. "The Decisions of Committee A." Unpublished Ed.D. dissertation, Teachers' College, Columbia University, 1948.

Pennypacker, Samuel W. *The Autobiography of a Pennsylvanian.* Philadelphia, John C. Winston, 1918.

People's Council of America *Bulletin.* 1917–1919.

Pepper, George Wharton. *Philadelphia Lawyer.* Philadelphia, Lippincott, 1944.

Perry, Ralph Barton. "Americanism," *Yale Review,* VII (1918), 663–72.

Peterson, H. C. and Gilbert C. Fite. *Opponents of War, 1917–1918.* Seattle, University of Washington Press, 1957.

Potter, David. *People of Plenty: Economic Abundance and the American Character.* Chicago, University of Chicago Press, 1958.

Powell, Lyman P. "A Clergyman Looks in on Russia," *Review of Reviews,* XC (1934), 62–68.

Preston, William, Jr. *Aliens and Dissenters: Federal Suppression of Radicals, 1903–1933.* New York, Harper and Row, 1966.

"Prophets of the Good Life," *Newsweek,* LXXVI (1970), 100.

Radosh, Ronald. *American Labor and United States Foreign Policy.* New York, Random House, 1969.

Randall, Mercedes M. *Improper Bostonian: Emily Greene Balch.* New York, Twayne, 1964.

"Recent Deaths," *School and Society,* LXIV (1946), 418.

Reed, John. "Back of Billy Sunday," *Metropolitan,* XLII (1915), 9–11.

Rees, Albert. *Real Wages in Manufacturing, 1890–1914.* Princeton, Princeton University Press, 1961.

"Report of the Committee of Inquiry Concerning Clark University," American Association of University Professors *Bulletin,* X (1924), 40–107.

Report of the First American Conference for Democracy and Terms of Peace. New York, 1917.

"Report on the Dismissal of Dr. Scott Nearing from the University of Pennsylvania," American Association of University Professors *Bulletin,* II (1916), 1–57.

Rhoads, James B. "The Campaign of the Socialist Party in the Election of 1920." Unpublished Ph.D. dissertation, American University, 1965.

Rideout, Walter B. *The Radical Novel in the United States, 1900–1954.* New York, Hill and Wang, 1966.

Roche, John P. *The Quest for the Dream: The Development of Civil Rights and Human Relations in Modern America.* Chicago, Quadrangle, 1968.

Rodney, William. *Soldiers of the International: A History of the Communist Party of Canada, 1919–1929.* Toronto, University of Toronto Press, 1968.

Rolnick, Stanley. "Development of the Idea of Academic Freedom and Tenure in the United States, 1870–1920." Unpublished Ph.D. dissertation, University of Wisconsin, 1951.

Roosevelt, Theodore. *The Foes of Our Own Household.* New York, George H. Doran, 1917.

—— *The Great Adventure: Present-Day Studies in American Nationalism.* New York, Scribner's, 1918.

—— *Letters.* Edited by Elting E. Morison. 8 vols. Cambridge, Mass., Harvard University Press, 1954. Vol. VIII.

Rudolph, Frederick. *The American College and University: A History.* New York, Alfred A. Knopf, 1962.

Russell, Bertrand. *Autobiography, 1914–1944.* New York, Bantam, 1969.

—— *The Practice and Theory of Bolshevism.* London, George Allen and Unwin, 1920.

Sanger, Margaret. *An Autobiography.* New York, W. W. Norton, 1938.

Scheiber, Harry. *The Wilson Administration and Civil Liberties, 1917–1921.* Ithaca, N.Y., Cornell University Press, 1960.

Schleimann, Jorgen. "The Life and Work of Willi Muenzenberg," *Survey,* No. 55 (1965), 64–91.

Schlesinger, Arthur M., Jr. *The Coming of the New Deal.* Boston, Houghton Mifflin, 1959.

—— *The Crisis of the Old Order, 1919–1933.* Boston, Houghton Mifflin, 1957.

Schwartz, Abba P. *The Open Society.* New York, William Morrow, 1968.

"Scott Nearing," *Messenger,* II (1919), 23–24.

Sexton, John L., Jr. *An Outline History of Tioga and Bradford Counties in Pennsylvania.* Elmira, N.Y., Gazette Company, 1885.

Shannon, David A. *The Decline of American Communism.* New York, Harcourt, Brace, 1959.

—— *The Socialist Party of America: A History.* Chicago, Quadrangle, 1955.

Sheean, Vincent. *Dorothy and Red.* Boston, Houghton Mifflin, 1963.

Sinclair, Upton. *American Outpost.* Pasadena, Calif., the author, 1932.

—— "Communists in the Making," Institute of Social Studies *Bulletin,* I (1952), 49–57.

—— *The Goose-Step.* Pasadena, Calif., the author, 1923.

—— *Jimmie Higgins: A Story.* Pasadena, Calif., the author, 1919.

—— *My Lifetime in Letters.* Columbia, Mo., University of Missouri Press, 1960.

Slosson, Edwin E. *Great American Universities.* New York, Macmillan, 1910.

Smith, J. Russell. "Dismissing the Professor," *Survey,* XXXV (1915), 131–54.

Steffens, Lincoln. *Autobiography.* New York, Harcourt, Brace, 1931.

—— *Letters*. Edited by Ella Winter and Granville Hicks. New York, Harcourt, Brace, 1938.

Sternsher, Bernard. *Rexford Tugwell and the New Deal*. New Brunswick, N.J., Rutgers University Press, 1965.

Strong, Anna Louise. *I Change Worlds*. New York, Garden City, 1937.

—— *The Soviets Expected It*. New York, Dial, 1941.

Swanberg, W. A. *Dreiser*. New York, Scribner's, 1965.

"Swinging around the Circle against Militarism," *Survey*, XXXVI (1916), 95–96.

Thilly, Frank. "The American Association of University Professors," *American Review*, III (1925), 200–209.

Thomas, Norman. *The Conscientious Objector in America*. New York, B. W. Huebsch, 1923.

Thompson, John. "Away from It All," *Harper's*, CCXLI (1970), 120–23.

Trattner, Walter I. *Crusade for the Children: A History of the National Child Labor Committee and Child Labor Reform in America*. Chicago, Quadrangle, 1970.

The Trial of Scott Nearing and the American Socialist Society. New York, Rand School Press, 1919.

Trotsky, Leon. *My Life: An Attempt at an Autobiography*. New York, Scribner's, 1930.

Tugwell, Rexford G. "Notes on the Life and Work of Simon Nelson Patten," *Journal of Political Economy*, XXXI (1923), 153–208.

Tyler, Alice Felt. *Freedom's Ferment: Phases of American Social History*. New York, Harper and Row, 1962.

Tyler, Henry W. and Edward P. Cheyney. "Academic Freedom," American Academy of Political and Social Science *Annals*, CC (1938), 102–18.

United States Statutes at Large. 65th Congress, XL. Washington, Government Printing Office, 1919.

"The University of Pennsylvania and Academic Freedom," *Outlook*, CXI (1915), 1017.

"The University of Pennsylvania and Professor Nearing," *School and Society*, II (1915), 65–69.

Unterberger, Betty Miller. *America's Siberian Expedition, 1918–1920: A Study of National Policy*. Durham, N.C., Duke University Press, 1956.

Uphaus, Willard. *Commitment*. New York, McGraw-Hill, 1963.

Veysey, Lawrence. *The Emergence of the American University*. Chicago, University of Chicago Press, 1965.

Villard, Oswald Garrison. "Academic Freedom," *Nation*, CI (1915), 745–46.

Voss, Carl Hermann. *Rabbi and Minister: The Friendship of Stephen S. Wise and John Haynes Holmes*. Cleveland, World, 1964.

—— *Stephen S. Wise: Servant of the People*. Philadelphia, Jewish Publication Society, 1969.

"Wages in the United States," *International Socialist Review*, XII (1911), 355.

Wald, Lillian D. *Windows on Henry Street*. Boston, Little, Brown, 1934.

Waldman, Louis. *Labor Lawyer*. New York, E. P. Dutton, 1944.

Ware, Harold and Webster Powell. "Planning for Permanent Poverty," *Harper's*, CLXX (1935), 513–24.

Weinstein, James. *The Corporate Ideal in the Liberal State, 1900–1918*. Boston, Beacon, 1968.

—— *The Decline of Socialism in America, 1912–1925*. New York, Random House, 1969.

White, J. William. "A Letter on the Nearing Case," *Old Penn Weekly Review,* XIV (1915), 5–22.

White, Morton and Lucia White. *The Intellectual versus the City.* Cambridge, Mass., Harvard University Press, 1962.

Whitford, Noble E. *History of the Canal System of the State of New York.* Albany, N.Y., Brandow Printing Company, 1906.

"Who Owns the University?", *New Republic,* III (1915), 269–70.

Wike, J. Roffe. *The Pennsylvania Manufacturers' Association.* Philadelphia, University of Pennsylvania Press, 1960.

Wingo, Patricia Wesson. "Clayton R. Lusk: A Study of Patriotism in New York Politics, 1919–1923." Unpublished Ph.D. dissertation, University of Georgia, 1966.

Witmer, Lightner. *The Nearing Case.* New York, B. W. Huebsch, 1915.

Wittner, Lawrence S. *Rebels against War: The American Peace Movement, 1941–1960.* New York, Columbia University Press, 1969.

The World Congress against War. New York, American Committee for Struggle against War, 1932.

[Young, Art.] *Art Young: His Life and Times.* Edited by John Nicholas Boffel. New York, Sheridan House, 1939.

Zabriskie, George Olin, ed. *The Zabriskie Family.* Salt Lake City, Utah, 1963.

Zieger, Robert H. "Senator George Wharton Pepper and Labor Issues in the 1920's," *Journal of Labor History,* IX (1968), 163–83.

Zinn, Howard. *LaGuardia in Congress.* Ithaca, N.Y., Cornell University Press, 1959.

INDEX